ST.
JOHN
OF THE
CROSS

LÉON CRISTIANI

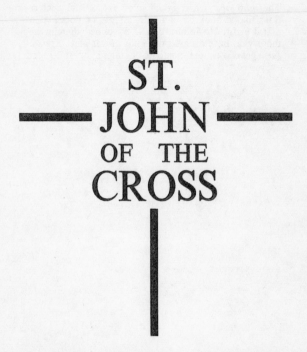

ST. JOHN OF THE CROSS

Prince of Mystical Theology

Translated from the French

DOUBLEDAY & COMPANY, INC., GARDEN CITY, NEW YORK, 1962

Nihil obstat: Edward J. Montano, S.T.D.
                Censor Librorum

Imprimatur: ✠Francis Cardinal Spellman
              Archbishop of New York

The *nihil obstat* and *imprimatur* are official declarations that a book or pamphlet is free of doctrinal or moral error. No implication is contained therein that those who have granted the *nihil obstat* and *imprimatur* agree with the contents, opinions or statements expressed.

This is a translation of *Saint Jean de la Croix, Prince de la Mystique (1542–1591)* by Monsignor Léon Cristiani, Prélat de S. S. (Paris: Editions France-Empire, 68 rue Jean-Jacques Rousseau, Paris, 1960)

Contents

PREFACE

Without doubt, few words are more misapplied than is the word *mysticism*. It is given the most diverse meanings and, indeed, is frequently used in most foolish and contradictory senses.

Charles Péguy was accustomed to contrast mystical theology with politics. According to his view, the mystic is one whose belief, whose love, is such that he will sacrifice himself for it. The politician, on the other hand, resorts to intrigue, to sly shrewdness, and to self-seeking in order that he may make use of his apparent object for his own profit. In the broad sense, it would seem that Péguy desires to equate mysticism with the love of that Good which is sovereign.

But all men do not share the same concepts of the *Sovereign Good*. One man may see it as Science, another as Research; another finds it in Art, and still others in many different things. Thus, there are as many kinds of mysticism as there are concepts of the Sovereign Good. But let us go at once to the root of things: the Sovereign Good is God. By this definition there can be no other good. Thus, true mysticism sets itself apart, in the essential sense, from the many kinds of false mysticisms. Those whom we call *the saints* have understood mysticism as the love of God pushed to that extreme limit which loses sight of the self. Originally, the word *mystical* meant *secret*. Mystical love is the kind of love which can say: *Secretum meum mihi est:* "My secret is my own"; but which, nevertheless, is ever mindful of the words of Christ: *It is God who sees what is secret and hidden.*

The sole aim of this book is to spread knowledge of one of the great historic mystics: Juan de la Cruz, or, as we will call him, John of the Cross. This is a man who, we might say, spoke in two registers: in one, through his life and the example he gave; in the other, through his writings. Rarely does one see such harmonious agreement between word and deed unless it be in that divine and inimitable model who is the prototype of all mystics, that great Lover of Souls, Our Lord Jesus Christ.

NOTE

Quotations

All the quotations from the writings of St. John of the Cross that appear in this book are taken from *The Complete Works of St. John of the Cross,* The Third Revised Edition, translated and edited by E. Allison Peers; Westminster, Md.: The Newman Press, 1953. Quotations from Sacred Scripture are taken from the Confraternity of Christian Doctrine edition of the Holy Bible; the Old Testament section being that of the Douay translation.

Names

As the names of John of the Cross (Juan de la Cruz) and Teresa of Avila, whose name in religion was Teresa of Jesus (Teresa de Jesús), are well known in their anglicized spellings, the English rendering has been used throughout this work. All other spellings of proper names retain the Spanish rendering.

ST.
JOHN
OF THE
CROSS

I

JUAN DE YEPÈS

(1542–1563)

It was a long journey from the small Castilian village of Fontiveros to Toledo, about seventy-five miles to the south. Yet a
poor woman, with two children walking by her side and a third
resting in her arms, courageously set out on that trip. She was
called Catalina Alvarez, and her husband, Gonzalo de Yepès,
had died only a few weeks earlier. Her eldest son, Francisco, was
barely thirteen; the second, Luis, stouter in limb, was only five,
but could stand up to Francisco. The third child, John, was a
mere infant, only a few months old. This is the first sight we have
of the man now venerated by the Church as John of the Cross,
Prince of Mystical Theology.

Many years before, the Holy Virgin Mary, with the sound of
the angel's greeting still ringing in her ears, had set out on an
equally difficult journey as she went on foot from Nazareth to
Ain-Karim to visit her cousin Elizabeth. Catalina Alvarez was a
devout Christian and she no doubt prayed all the length of her
trip, invoking first of all that same Blessed Virgin.

As she prayed, remembrances of things past crowded her mind.

She recalled her married years with Gonzalo de Yepès. Their marriage had been dramatic enough in itself. Gonzalo was of noble birth. Although he had lost his parents, he had uncles who had given him an education and for whom he had become a kind of commercial traveler. They were silk merchants who had clients to satisfy, and Gonzalo went on business trips for them which brought him frequently to Medina del Campo, at that time one of the great centers of Spanish business. Fontiveros was so situated that it was necessary to pass through it on the way to Medina del Campo. Here Gonzalo found a client. We do not know her name, but we do know she was a widow who owned a weaving store. In her workshop she employed a young woman, orphaned and poor, but attractive and intelligent. She was well mannered and dignified, and seems to have been endowed with all the best and most charming qualities. Her name was Catalina Alvarez, and Gonzalo had fallen in love with her. Catalina's employer warned the young man not to become serious with the girl: What would his uncles, so proud of their noble birth and their financial standing, say to an announcement of his desire to marry a girl without a dowry, a girl of humble origin? Gonzalo would not listen to these objections and the marriage seems to have taken place in 1529. All that Catalina's mistress had foreseen came about. Gonzalo's uncles were very displeased, and cut off his income and severed all relations with him completely. This plunged him into poverty; but Gonzalo, full of strength and confidence, set out to work for himself. Feeling he had gained a considerable degree of business ability, he hoped to make a good living in the service of the many clients whom he had come to know. But his hopes proved illusory, and finally he was forced to take up weaving like his wife. The work paid poorly. Then the children came. It was a home marked by bitter poverty. We are told that they rarely had wheat for bread and that even the coarser bread of barley meal was in scant supply at the family board. At length, Gonzalo fell ill, perhaps as a result of all his sufferings. After two years of sickness he died, either in 1542 or at the beginning of 1543. During his long illness his small savings were wiped out. His youngest son John was born in 1542; we do not know the day or the month, although June 24, formerly the feast of the Nativity of St. John the Baptist, seems a likely possibility.

Catalina did not know what to do to keep and educate her three children. Her sympathetic neighbors insisted that Gonzalo's wealthy uncles could not possibly refuse to aid her in her distress. Very likely Catalina had no personal acquaintance with them. She did know, however, that one was Archdeacon of the Collegiate Church at Torrijos, a large city somewhat north of Toledo, and that the other was a physician at Galvez, a lesser town about nine miles from Torrijos.

Then Catalina began her journey, taking a few clothes and some provisions for the road. Her children's futures were at stake.

AT THE HOMES OF THE UNCLES

Finally, Catalina reached Torrijos. One of the uncles, Canon de Yepès was the incumbent of a rich stipend granted by the Cathedral. Would he refuse to help his poor grandnephews, children without a father who were, nevertheless, bearers of his own name? We do not know the conversation which passed between Catalina and the Venerable Archdeacon; but we do know that he very shortly put an end to all the beggings and expostulations of the tearful mother. He, an archdeacon, could not possibly be embarrassed by the presence of children in his house. He therefore firmly shut his door in the face of the unfortunate Catalina. She was thus forced to start traveling again, without rest either for herself or for her children. This was Torrijos, the fine city housing the palace of Dona Teresa, sister of Spain's late and "most Catholic king," Ferdinand V.

The other uncle, the physician at Galvez, was named John de Yepès. He was undoubtedly pleased to see another John de Yepès in the arms of the mother who had brought his grandnephews to him. He had no children of his own, but having a kind and sympathetic heart gave Catalina, whom he had not previously known, a warm welcome, opening up his house to her and the children. John de Yepès listened to her story of the wearisome journey and of the plight of his young grandnephews. At last Catalina felt able to breathe again. How her heart must have rejoiced when she heard the physician of Galvez offer to accept responsibility for the training of her eldest son so that he might follow his granduncle's profession. This boy would be like his own son. He would bring him up, and he would leave him all his fortune. What a relief for this poor mother to be freed of a great part of her heavy burden.

Comforted and happy, Catalina Alvarez left Francisco with the kind doctor, happy that she had made the boy's future secure. After a few days she began the return journey to Fontiveros with Luis and John.

At home again, she resumed her work as a weaver. Her life seemed brighter and she thought she had, at least, gained some of what she was hoping for.

A year passed by. John was now able to walk. Although there was no news from Francisco at Galvez, there was every reason to think that he was happy. But this was not the case at all. The doctor had kindly resolved to adopt his grandnephew and to take care of him as he would his own son, but his wife viewed her husband's plan with a cold eye and a colder heart. Without a word to him, indeed trying to keep him in the dark, she set about making the poor lad's life miserable. Instead of carrying out his granduncle's wish that he be sent to school, she kept him at home, occupying him with the most unpleasant duties, subjecting him to hunger, blows, and ill-treatment. Francisco did not dare say anything. He wept in silence, bitterly regretting leaving his mother's home. Even though he had often been hungry there, there was no substitute for the love his mother gave him—and certainly no compensation for its complete lack. In some strange way, Catalina seemed to be aware that something was amiss. Did

Francisco's unhappiness somehow arouse in her, by a kind of telepathy, some sense of alarm? We do not know what mysterious currents run forth from a mother's heart. At any rate, Catalina set out one day for Galvez and unexpectedly appeared at the home of John de Yepès. Francisco threw himself into his mother's arms when he saw her; he clung to her and would not be separated. Covertly he told her all he had suffered and all that he still suffered. Catalina remonstrated openly with the doctor, who was unable to believe his ears. He vainly tried to reassure her; and vainly, too, promised that all would change, that he personally would take his grandnephew's education into his hands. Francisco begged his mother to take him away, and she granted that wish. Thus the young boy returned to Fontiveros. He was now fifteen, but could neither read nor write. He was immediately sent to school; but he was a poor student, and soon he was helping his mother at her weaving. This was to remain his lifelong work.

His two brothers continued to go to school, but only John completed his education, for Luis died young, perhaps because of the privations which continuously beset this poor household.

A WONDERFUL HAPPENING

John de Yepès was now five years old. In the account of his life which we read in the Second Nocturn lessons of the Breviary a wondrous happening in his childhood is described in these terms: "From his early years, he definitely understood how dear he was to the Virgin Mother of God, for at the age of five, when he had fallen into a well, he was upheld by the hand of God's Mother, and he came forth unharmed."

However, the time of this incident is uncertain. It is true that at the age of five John de Yepès was preserved from death, but his fall into the well belongs to a later period of his life.

John of the Cross himself tells us what happened when he was five. On the outskirts of Fontiveros there was a muddy lagoon

by the banks of which children often came to play. Among
them was the youngest child of the weaver Catalina Alvarez.
Their game consisted in throwing a stick sharply downward into
the water, perpendicularly, so that it would quickly rise to the
surface, permitting them to grasp it again as it rose. Once John,
playing with his companions, lost his balance. He fell into the
water and sank below the surface. For a moment he came up,
but then sank again. This is how the story has been told: "When
he was at the bottom of the water, he saw a very beautiful lady
who stretched out her hand, but he was afraid to grasp it because
his own was so muddy. . . . He was about to drown when suddenly, on the bank, a peasant came forward, bearing a pole in
his hand, and with this pole John was drawn from the water."

This is the account given on two occasions by John of the
Cross himself while he was passing by a lagoon at Andalusía
similar to the lagoon at Fontiveros.

AT AREVALO

The next year, when John was six, Catalina, not finding
enough work at Fontiveros, decided to move. We may imagine
that it was with heartfelt bitterness that she found herself obliged
to leave this town of five thousand inhabitants (today it numbers
only seven hundred) where she had met her beloved and lived
during the years of her girlhood and marriage. It was there, too,
that Gonzalo and Luis lay buried. She had passed twenty years
in Fontiveros—the best part of her life.

But she did not have far to go. On the way to Medina del
Campo there was a lovely town which today has lost its former
splendor although it still retains some of its importance. This is
Arevalo, situated at the highest point of the central plateau of
Castile, between the silver rivers of Adaja and Arevalillo. Here
it was that Queen Isabella the Catholic had passed her childhood.
As at Fontiveros, there were weaving establishments in the town,

and Catalina found employment not only for herself but also for Francisco, now a fine young man of eighteen.

We know nothing of the life of John de Yepès at Arevalo; but we do know some details about Francisco, and we may be sure that what happened to him was not without its effect upon John.

THE CONVERSION OF FRANCISCO

Francisco de Yepès had grown into a fine young man, cheerful, pleasant, fond of good living, of singing, and of dancing. He was generally popular, and had many friends. It was his habit, according to the Spanish custom of those days, to go about the streets dancing the farandole. With his companions, he also liked to make raids upon the gardens and vineyards of the region. More than once, as he was going home, the hour was so late that he would encounter the sacristans on their way to make preparation for the morning Masses in the local churches. Francisco was not wholly at ease that his nocturnal pranks were worthy of a Christian. One evening he and his friends broke into a garden where they found heavily laden almond trees. The band of youths fell to with zeal and then left, carrying the booty which they were anxious to enjoy. But they were disappointed, for the almonds were bitter and scarcely edible.

It had been a useless expedition, and in the mind of Francisco the episode took on a deeper meaning. The harshness of the stolen fruit bit deeper than his tongue and palate: it settled within his heart. Instead of going home to bed, he went to the feet of a confessor and declared his sin to God. Father Carrillo, the incumbent of one of the churches of Arevalo and to whom Francisco made his confession, was a priest of outstanding goodness, given to recollection and prayer, and zealous in the service of souls. He gave valuable advice to Francisco, who felt himself moved by grace to repentance. He so reformed himself that one must regard his as a real conversion. From that time, Francisco broke with his former companions, or at least with those who, by word and example, prevented him from leading a better life. At the end of each day's work, Francisco happily sought out Father Carrillo who gave him good advice and helpful counsel. In good weather he walked through the surrounding gardens and fields, no longer bent on their despoilment, but rather seeking out this solitude in order to meditate and pray for forgiveness. If the weather was bad, he would spend the evening in some church or oratory. Moreover, despite his own poverty, he was generous to those who had less than he. His mother was of one mind with him in this, and she kindly received all the poor whom he brought home. Certainly this great change could not have failed to affect his brother, twelve years his junior, to whom the tall and handsome young man was a constant hero.

It was while the family resided at Arevalo that Francisco de Yepès married. He had made the acquaintance of a virtuous young woman, a native of Muriel, a little village near Arevalo. She was called Ana Izquierdo. They lived, as was a general custom in those days, with Catalina Alvarez, and the young bride also became a weaver. Although they worked industriously, they made only a bare living; but this did not close their hearts to the claims of charity. In winter, which is often very severe in that part of Spain, Franciso de Yepès used to go into the streets and bring home those who had no place to stay so that his wife and mother might help them.

Their sojourn at Arevalo lasted from 1548 until 1551. John grew from six to the age of nine. In the Breviary Lessons we are told that at the age of nine he was already given to secret penitential practices. It seems that the privations which the poverty of the household imposed upon him were not enough. He saw about him such examples of goodness that he turned to voluntary mortification. At this time, he began what he later called, as a teacher of mystical theology, the *nights*. The night of the body, the night of the soul (that is, the gift of himself in renunciation in the fullest sense, the spirit of self-denial demanded by Jesus

Christ of those who wish to follow Him), and love of the Cross were early characteristics of this boy.

AT MEDINA DEL CAMPO

At this time Catalina Alvarez found it necessary to move again, so the family took up residence in Medina del Campo, a city of thirty thousand people about seventeen miles away. Medina del Campo was an active center of life. There were many churches and convents; but it was its commercial importance that made it the central market of all Spain. Men came there even from France, Flanders, and Portugal. Catalina Alvarez had long been familiar with the city and went there to find a means of livelihood for her family and especially a means of education, hitherto scarcely available, for John. Catalina and her children found a home in the northern part of the city on a street named after St. James, and which was not far from the church of that name.

There was also a school nearby for youngsters, especially those who were poor or orphaned. John de Yepès was sent there as a boarder. According to the rule of the institute which governed the school he was not only taught to read and write but was also tested to find the kind of work for which he would be best suited. Perhaps this "vocational testing" program is the reason that John was instructed in the rudiments of drawing, painting, and sculpture. Actually, he had little aptitude for manual tasks, but he learned with marvelous ease. Moreover, he was the most devoted and fervent of Mass servers. The school would furnish altar boys to the Convent of the Magdalene. In the summertime these boys served in the chapel of the sisters between six and ten o'clock, and in the winter, from seven until eleven. Four boys were on duty each day, but the sisters preferred John de Yepès to the others. Before long, he was entrusted with the task of taking up an offering in the city for the benefit of the students of the school. The miracle, which I have already mentioned, suddenly made the boy a popular figure in the town. This occurrence recalls, in certain aspects, the event of some years earlier at Fontiveros, and it seems likely that the two happenings, although really distinct and both true, were later fused into one by those who in later years were to recount the life of St. John of the Cross.

The Story of the "Miracle"

John was playing one day with some other boys in the court of a hospital near the school when one of his comrades pushed him, causing him to fall into the low-lipped well in the yard. As he fell he called for help, and everyone thought he was drowning. However, John, instead of sinking, floated on the surface and called for a rope. He placed it under his shoulders and was drawn up without having suffered so much as a scratch. All at once the boys cried out that it was a miracle. One of those present, a certain Pedro-Fernandez Bustillo, later told the story of this occurrence, which had taken place in broad daylight. Juan Gomez, who was entering his house at the time that the boy was emerging safe and sound from the water, heard it being said that a miracle had been wrought by the Holy Virgin. The boy asserted that it was Our Lady who had personally kept him afloat.

This youngster, who served Mass so well at the Convent of the Magdalene, suddenly became famous. Soon the director of the Hospital of Our Lady's Conception expressed an interest in him and said he wanted to take him into his household. This young and rich personage, Don Alonzo Alvárez de Toledo, had devoted himself to works of charity. His hospital was designed especially for victims of contagious diseases. From the first, John de Yepès attracted the admiration of the patients because of his kindness, eagerness, and zeal. Three things seem to have been among his favorite occupations: the care of the sick, the seeking of alms for the hospital throughout the town, and his own studies. All who knew him at this time tell us that, despite his youth, he was the kindest of nurses, the most willing, and the most patient. The director was delighted, and everyone associated with the hospital admired the boy for his goodness. There were none more successful than he in the begging tours for the hospital conducted through the streets of the town. Yet he did not neglect his studies. John completed what would today be termed his secondary or prep-school education.

JOHN AS A STUDENT

John de Yepès had long ago learned to read and write. As we know, he also had some knowledge of drawing and painting, skills of which he was later to make good use. But who could have predicted that the son of the penniless widow would ever be able to undertake the study of Latin and Greek and other advanced subjects? Although we have no verifying documents, we can be reasonably certain that the future of John's education took shape gradually. Careful planning preceded his going to the Jesuit College at Medina del Campo in 1559. If his second fall into a well and the miracle wrought by Our Lady took place when he was ten, then he must still have been at the orphan school. Seven years, therefore, had passed with the Jesuits. It was a grown boy of seventeen who went, in the free time that his duties at the hospital permitted, to study under the excellent instructors in the humanities who conducted the Jesuit College. It is certain that he had not hitherto been idle; for he had already mastered Greek and Latin grammer before going to grapple with the thoughts of the classical writers.

He had always been an avid reader, devoting himself to every good book that came his way. He would even sacrifice sleep in his desire to read. Sometimes, he could be found in an obscure corner of the hospital, hiding with a candle and bent over his books. At the time he became a student of the Jesuits he was already a scholar who showed a remarkable understanding for what he had read. He was with the Jesuits from 1559 until 1563. The actual courses in classics he took included grammar and rhetoric, according to the nomenclature of the period. Such courses usually lasted four years. The Jesuit College originally had been intended only as a training school for the Society's own novices; but, eventually, secular students, had been admitted as well. The reputation of John de Yepès was already such that he was favorably received in the school, which then had only about forty students. We know the names of the professors—Gaspar Astete, later to be well known as the author of a Catechism, Juan Guerra, Miguel de Anda, and Juan Bonafacio. All were members of the Society of Jesus, but not yet ordained. Under the direction of the superiors, they made up what was called the "Regency of Studies." Classes were held for three hours in the morning and three in the afternoon. The manual of Father Nebriga was used in grammar and rhetoric, and each professor selected readings at his choice from the major classics. After classes, the students devoted themselves to composition in prose and in verse. Of all John's teachers we know best the name of Juan Bonafacio; and we know also the names of the classical authors whom he proposed to his students as models. These were the same as those many of us have studied in our own school days: Caesar, Livy, Cicero, Virgil, Sallust, Horace, Martial, and the rest.

Very soon John became "a good rhetorician and Latinist," according to one of his contemporaries. Francisco reports that John made great progress quite rapidly and with the help of Our Lord, for he dedicated all his free time to study.

The four-year period between 1559 and 1563 was a decisive time in John's life. It was from the Jesuits that he assimilated the most knowledge. They were the true humanists of their time, and their colleges were among the best in Christian lands. When we later see John de Yepès, as Brother John of St. Matthias, at the University of Salamanca, we shall have to bear in mind that this became possible only because of the preparation he had received from the Jesuits of Medina del Campo. The years he spent with them were most fruitful, especially when we consider the work for which Providence had destined him. In the eyes of posterity, he is best known as the author of the *Spiritual Canticle,* one of the great classics of Spanish literature. Although his ventures into the higher ranges of mystical thought are based on the philosophical and theological knowledge so richly endowed on him at the University of Salamanca, the origin of his poetical work is to be sought in the essays, compositions, and exercises undertaken—but chiefly, in the inspiration he received—during his stay at the Jesuit College.

JOHN'S FAMILY

But we must not allow our interest in John's intellectual development to cause us to pass over the affairs of his family, those who so loved him and who now began to admire him as well.

As it turned out, John was the family prodigy. His brother Francisco had made no progress at school. John, on the other hand, learned more easily than others; knowledge came, as it were, naturally to him; you might say it sprang up within him. Yet this did not make him any the less humble, any the less affectionate, any the less devoted to his loved ones. He avoided all those perils of self-centered pride that have ruined the great talents of so many. John de Yepès always remained himself and was devotedly faithful to his family.

His mother, brother, and sister-in-law lived together in a poor dwelling in St. James' parish. When John was free from duty at the hospital, there is no doubt that he saw them frequently and that he kept in touch with all that concerned them. There were many children in the house, for Francisco had seven sons and one daughter. (The girl, called Ana after her mother, was the only child who lived to maturity. She became a Bernardine religious of the Convent of the Holy Spirit at Olmedo.) Life was not easy for this family. They were called *burateros*—that is to say, they were all engaged in the weaving trade. But, above and beyond even the necessity of gaining their own livelihood, they were

devoted to charitable and pious works. John's mother was regarded as being an exemplary Christian. Francisco was far more
than a Sunday Christian, and his spiritual life was of a very high
order. When John of the Cross tells us in one of his masterworks,
Ascent of Mount Carmel, that one cannot attain to anything
significant in the life of devotion without a spiritual guide, he
may have been thinking of the case of his own brother, among
others. Francisco's spiritual director was the Jesuit, Father
Cristobal Caro, who knew him over a long period, encouraged
him and profoundly admired him. When, some years afterwards,
someone spoke in Father Caro's presence of the heroic virtues of
John of the Cross, he unhesitatingly said: "Francisco de Yepès
is as great a saint as his brother."

Nevertheless, our *burateros* were obliged to wage a constant
struggle against poverty. Their work was seasonal; and it was
too ill paid to allow them to attain what we call comfortable
circumstances. Francisco, therefore, looked for settled employment. It had been suggested to him that he take the post of
"equerry" to two honorables ladies of the town, as was then a
prevalent custom. This he did as best he could. He carried his
sword, and he accompanied the two ladies, who were mother
and daughter, to receptions and parties. But this employment did
not last, for, one day, when Francisco tarried at church, he arrived
late at the home of the ladies who dismissed him at once. There-
after he gave himself to works of benevolence. He was particularly devoted to foundlings, and would seek them at night near
the churches. He would have them baptized and stand as their
sponsor. Very often his wife acted as godmother for these abandoned babes. Francisco was not ashamed to beg for the benefit
of these children, whom he gave to the care of the orphanages
and hospitals of the town. John de Yepès kept in touch with all
that concerned his family and, as he was himself associated with
the hospital, it is likely that he was frequently able to use his
influence in the cause of the unfortunates to whom his brother

acted the role of the Good Samaritan. This background to the school days of John could not help but strongly influence him.

But the time was approaching when John de Yepès was to change his calling, and also his name.

II

BROTHER JOHN OF ST. MATTHIAS

(1563–1568)

John de Yepès was now twenty-one years old, and he had finished his four years of classical schooling with the Jesuits. He was a young man of small stature, sallow complexion, and rather pale in color, but with great burning black eyes and a broad and intelligent brow. The time had come for him to choose his life's work. All men on earth must seek an answer to the question: Where shall I go to find happiness, the aim of human life?

Don Alonso Alvárez de Toledo, the great patron of the hospital where John worked, had a simple plan for him. At this time the Council of Trent, which was on the point of bringing to an end the sessions which actually concluded in December 1563, had just initiated its plan for the seminary system of theological training. Prior to that time such institutions had not been known. A man might be ordained to the priesthood after a summary examination, satisfying a bishop who stood in need of his services, providing he possessed the necessary qualifications for the exercise of the ministry. Here was a way of life that seemed appropriate for John. But Don Alonso was not the only one who had an eye on him. In Medina del Campo there were many religious houses which would gladly accept into their ranks so fine a young man. The Jesuits, who knew him to be among the best of their students, would, doubtless, have been delighted if he had sought admission to their Novitiate.

But none of this was to be; for John de Yepès had his own ideas. We do not know where they came from, but we may be sure that he had thought upon the matter in the depths of his heart, as became one who was a client, a protégé, a favored child of the Holy Virgin. Were he to give himself to God, it might well be presumed that he would plan to do this in an Order under the protection of Our Lady; and there was one in the city. One day, without having said a word to anyone, even to his patron, Don Alonso, who would oppose his project, John went southwards across the city and asked to be vested in the habit of the Order of Our Lady of Mount Carmel. The Prior of St. Anne's Convent, Fray Ildefonse Ruíz, at once asked the opinion of his community in regard to the candidate, and without a single dissenting vote the young postulant was joyously welcomed. As a sign of his incorporation into their fellowship, they at once gave him the monastic tonsure, clad him in the brown habit and white cloak of the Whitefriars, and saluted him as Brother John of St. Matthias.

When Don Alonso learned of John's absence from the hospital, he went to the Carmel where he was faced by *fait accompli*. There was nothing for him to do but applaud the sincere purposefulness of the young monk.

AT ST. ANNE'S

In 1563, the Carmelite Fathers at Medina had only a temporary establishment, close by a chapel dedicated to St. Anne on the southeast side of the city, within the walls but very close to one of the city gates. Soon, a magnificent monastery was to rise in this place, but at that time it was just being built.

We do not know how many monks there were at St. Anne's, but inasmuch as John of St. Matthias was only the sixth person professed after the foundation of the house in 1560, the community cannot have been large.

It is interesting to speculate on what young John de Yepès knew of the history of Carmel when he decided to enter it in 1563. At this very date and not far off, in the city of Avila, a religious of true genius, Teresa of Jesus, was setting her hand to the much-needed reformation of her Order.

THE CARMELITE ORDER

According to devout belief within this community, the Order began with the prophet Elijah. This great giant of prayer and of the ascetic life had taken up his abode on Mt. Carmel facing the sea that bordered Palestine. Elisha succeeded Elijah, and their memory was held in reverence by a mystical fellowship called "The Sons of the Prophets." This community is supposed to have continued to exist, in hermitages scattered over Mt. Carmel, until Our Lord's time. The descendents of "The Sons of the Prophets" then became Christians and continued to lead a life of retirement from the world, being now under the patronage of the Virgin Mary, whom they honored under the title of Our Lady of Mt. Carmel.

It was reverence for this tradition which caused the Order to be called, especially in Spain, "the Order of the Virgin." Tradition held that the "Holy Land" hermits led peaceful lives, forming little monastic villages composed of several *retreats,* with separate cells for their members. They suffered dreadfully: first from the Persian invasion; and later, during the conquest of Mt. Carmel by the Mohammedans. But, happily, the followers of Mohammed were themselves devoted to the memory of Elijah, whom they regarded as the Prophet of Fire, and for a while the hermits of Mt. Carmel enjoyed the benefits of this veneration. When the Crusaders came to the East, the number of Carmelite recluses increased considerably, and the future of the Order was thus assured.

So much for the traditional history of the Carmelites; but, as early as 1690, the learned Bollandist, Father Papebroch, thoroughly disproved the legendary account of their origin. However, in the day of Brother John of St. Matthias, the legend was still believed. There is no doubt that his own poetic imagination was fired by the thought of being linked to Elijah. So grandiose an affiliation could not fail to arouse enthusiasm.

In the thirteenth century the factual history of the Order began to take shape. A distinguished prelate, Albert de Verceil, who was the Latin Patriarch of Jerusalem, gave a Rule to the group of ascetics who had sheltered themselves under the impressive name of Mt. Carmel. This fact is established, and is dated at 1208 or 1209. Thus the Carmelites are easily the earliest of what are often called the "mendicant" orders. Among the other representatives of this group are the Franciscans in their various branches (1209), and the Dominicans (1215).

The Rule of Albert de Verceil was formally approved by Pope Honorius III in 1226 with some modifications, especially in regard to the use of food. In his turn, Pope Innocent IV approved the Rule in 1248. The Order rapidly grew throughout the whole region of the Mediterranean and, as long as Christians remained in possession in the East, at Mt. Carmel and in Syria. But the continued attacks of Mohammedans caused them many trying losses. Mt. Carmel was taken by the Saracens, and all the religious were put either to the sword or to flight. Palestine was thus abandoned by the Carmelites, and they spread throughout the various parts of European Christendom. In 1240 the first General Chapter of the Order was held at Aylesford in Great Britain. Alan the Englishman was elected Prior General and in 1245 was succeeded by Simon Stock, who is regarded as a kind of second founder of the Order. The establishment of Carmelite or Whitefriar houses in the great centers of learning at Cambridge, Oxford, Bologna, and Paris are ascribed to him. Carmel thus took its place among the notable bodies of ecclesiastical scholarship. The purely contemplative life, which had been the original

aim of the Order, was enriched by the activities of preaching,
the direction of souls, and advanced theological study, a development similar to that which had taken place among the Order of
Preachers (Dominicans), and that of Friars Minor (Franciscans).

However, within the Order itself there had sprung up a certain
uneasiness not unlike that which was destined, for so long a time,
to divide the sons of St. Francis. Some religious began to lament
what they considered deviations from the spirit of Carmel. The
establishment of town communities put an end to the last traces
of the original hermit-like way of life. The history of the Order
thus paralleled what we shall see in the life of John himself. It
seemed that the contemplative life was invaded by the duties
and urgencies of the active life. All that is nowadays known as
"activism"—excessive confidence in human methods, in human
work, and a gradually increasing abandonment of the interior
life—was already a problem in the Middle Ages. Just as there
were attempts at a *reformation* throughout the Church in general,
so there existed such attempts within the Order itself. At Mantua,
in the fifteenth century, there had been one such effort. Pending
the reform, the monasteries were left much to themselves, and a
great many asked and obtained mitigations of the Rule ascribed
to Albert de Verceil. Popes Eugene IV, Pius II, and Sixtus IV
granted the requests for relaxations presented to them. We will
particularize these requests. The monastic habit was made richer,
warmer, and more comfortable, and the monks began to wear
footwear. After the reform this caused the Carmelites of the old
foundation to be called *Calced* ("the shod"), in order to distinguish them from the *Discalced* ("the unshod"), of whom
John of the Cross was to be the first. Actually, the official
designation of this latter group is the Brethren of the Primitive
Observance.

The details of the reform might well seem long-winded and
dull; it will be better, therefore, to defer them until they show

themselves in the events of the life of John of St. Matthias, who will soon become John of the Cross.

The point of the whole drama lies in the fact that this young man was thirsty for the Sovereign Good; this is because of his own nature and because of grace. John's thirst represents God's call to him. It would seem that before him arose the glorious shade of the prophet Elijah. He lived on God; he needed God; he sought God. This was to be his whole religious life. And this explains why, as the saint will show us himself, he was always to be unsatisfied.

Let us go with him now into the monastery of St. Anne, where he has just been admitted.

JOHN AT ST. ANNE'S MONASTERY

Had Carmel, in those days, been an order governed by uniformity of custom and rule, we would find it easy to picture how our young novice spent his time at St. Anne's in Medina del Campo. But we know that such was not the case. A Carmelite Prior General called Audet had recently tried to establish uniformity by enacting strict laws designed to recall the Order to its original austerity, but he was unsupported. Indeed, in many houses, the brethren raised the standard of revolt against his projects. In Spain the reform was left unfinished. But young John of St. Matthias was to have at least one consolation: although his monastery was one of those which might be termed *lax* in its observance, it possessed, like other monasteries, a chapel in which the Blessed Sacrament was reserved. Accounts which we have of John as a novice tell us of his lengthy prayers before the altar steps. We do not know what he said in these talks with Jesus in the tabernacle; but we are certain that he was to be found there, for we are told that in his humility he prayed as one annihilated. He loved, also, to serve Mass. We are aware, of course, that this had been his delight since boyhood. On the other hand, we know also that courses in "grammar and arts" were given at St. Anne's, and that he took them in company with his brethren, thus bringing to perfection the training which had been initiated by the Jesuits. By these means, his superiors were enabled to form a judgment about John's capabilities. That a little later they would send him to the University of Salamanca is evidence that they had discerned exceptional qualities in him.

During the time of John's novitiate, which lasted one year (1563–64), Giovanni-Battista de Rubeo of Ravenna was elected Prior General of the Carmel by the General Chapter which met in Rome on Sunday, May 21, 1564. The Castilian Provincial Prior, Fray Angel de Salazar, had been present at the Chapter Meeting. When he returned from Rome, it was with the title of Doctor, which had been conferred upon him by the Chapter. He assisted at the ceremony of the profession of John of St. Matthias, who made his vows to the Prior of St. Anne's, Fray Ildefonse Ruíz. As witnesses there were the Provincial Prior, Angel de Salazar, and John's former Patron, Don Alonso Alvárez de Toledo. No doubt, John's mother, his brother, and his sister-in-law were also present. All heard him pronounce the Latin words which signified:

"I, the undersigned, Brother John, promise to show obedience, poverty, and chastity to God and to the Reverend Father, my Brother, Giovanni-Battista de Rubeo, of Ravenna, Prior General of the Order of Carmel . . ."

It is worth remarking that Fray Alonso de Villalba, who was to be an associate of John at the University of Salamanca, tells us that, from the time of his profession, John had obtained from his superior the necessary permission to observe the primitive regulations of the Order, at least to a certain extent.

This is enough to let us know that the Rule, as generally kept, did not fully satisfy the great thirst which welled up within John's heart. A spark had ignited in his soul, a spark never to be extinguished. This he would call later "the living flame of Love."

Some incomplete information which we possess indicates that, probably at some time during the period of his novitiate, John had written "some hymns in heroic couplets in the pastoral style." The theme of these writings (which he put in the third person) was "a thanksgiving to Our Lord for the grace which He had granted him in allowing him to be admitted into an Order of which the patron was God's blessed Mother." Apparently these verses, which probably were like the school exercises he had written for the Jesuits, have not been preserved. None of his known works fits their description, but of them it may be said that we find ourselves face to face with John's first literary ventures.

AT THE UNIVERSITY OF SALAMANCA

At the beginning of the year 1564, on the Feast of the Epiphany, a Carmelite brother presented himself at the University of Salamanca to register ten young students of his Order. Of these, six were entered under the theological faculty and four under the humanistic. We would, today, classify the latter as students in the field of literature and the sciences. Among the new registrants was "Fray John of St. Matthias, native of Medina del Campo, in the diocese of Salamanca." The fact that John is thus described indicates that he did not register in person, but rather that another Carmelite had been charged with the duty of registering as proxy for all the men of the Order who had been appointed to take courses in 1565.

In that year, the number of Carmelites studying at the University of Salamanca was larger than in former years. It is quite possible that, at the General Chapter in Rome (at which Fray Rubeo had been elected Prior General), the Provincial Priors had been told to send for university study all of their subjects who displayed suitable aptitude. In 1548, at the General Chapter meeting in Venice under the chairmanship of the reforming Prior General, Nicolas Audet, such a situation had been foreseen; and the Monastery of St. Andrew at Salamanca had been converted into a college for students from all the Carmelite monasteries of Europe. This decision was a significant one in respect to raising the intellectual level among the Spanish Carmelites. Actually, from this time on, the Prior of St. Andrew's at Salamanca found himself required to receive all subjects who might be sent to him, with dimissory letters, by their superiors, provided they had also the sum of ten *écus* to defray the expenses of one year's study.

The discipline of the monastery and of the college was extremely severe. Faults were treated rigorously, being punished by isolation for eight days, by subsistence on bread and water in cases of relapse, and under the threat of expulsion in the event that improvement did not occur. Expulsion from the college meant, too, that the annual fee of ten *écus* would be forfeited. The young students of the Order were not allowed to leave St. Andrew's except to attend the university classes. Wearing the white cloak of their Order, they walked to their courses, two by two, eyes downcast, minds deep in recollection.

Still in his own convent at Medina del Campo, Fray John of St. Matthias had to demonstrate his understanding of Latin and his general ability not only to qualify for admission as a choir religious, but also to justify being sent to the University at Salamanca.

The organization of a university is more or less unchanging. Then, as now, students lived in colleges which gave them board and lodging, and they went to the university halls only for lectures. Colleges were foundations, set apart for seculars and, generally, in those days, divided among various nationalities so that students found themselves among those of similar origin who spoke their own language, or they were foundations destined to serve members of a specific religious community, that is to say, open only to students attached to a particular religious family. Dominicans, Franciscans, Jesuits, and Augustinians would have their own "colleges," just as did the Carmelites.

At Salamanca, the Monastery of St. Andrew was the college frequented by all Spanish-speaking Carmelites.

SALAMANCA AT ITS HEIGHT

This University was then at its peak. The holders of chairs were called *cathedratics*. Of such lecturers, the more important functioned in the morning. Those who lectured in the afternoon were of lesser rank. The chief chair of theology was called *Cathedra de prima*. In the time of John of St. Matthias, it was a Dominican, Mancio de Corpus Christi, a worthy successor of Vitoria and of Melchior Cano, who held this professorship. But the most remarkable of the professors was Luis Ponce de León, who was a poet as well as a theologian. His poetic work, wholly pregnant with spirituality, is as well known as his prose, the most important item of which is called *De los Nombres de Cristo, Concerning the Names of Christ*. His great distinction did not exempt him from having a bone to pick in 1572 with the Inquisition, which in Spain was especially active and oversuspicious. Luis de León was an Augustinian. We may also refer to others among the professors of theology or Holy Scripture. They were Juan de Guevara, also an Augustinian; Gregorio Gallo, who was acting as *locum tenens* for Domecico Soto, then ill; and Cristobal Vela, who occupied the chair of Scotus. In the faculty of arts, the professors were equally distinguished. There were Enrique Hernández in natural philosophy; Francisco Navarro in ethics; Hernando de Aguilera in astronomy (compounded, in those days, with astrology); Francisco Sánchez in grammar; and Juan de Ubredo in music.

The number of students was enormous. It is estimated that there were about seven thousand of them—a veritable army of learners. The breakdown is as follows: seven hundred fifty students of theology; nineteen hundred of canon law; seven hundred of civil law; two hundred of medicine; nine hundred of arts and philosophy; and two thousand in literary studies. All religious orders were represented. In the largest of the colleges, that of the Dominicans, there were at least two hundred members of that order.

At the time set for lectures, processions of students, walking in pairs, filled all the streets. Although the discipline of even the secular colleges was, in principle, strict, it goes without saying that adventurous elements were not lacking in this great crowd of young men. This would not have been Spain had picaresque elements been lacking in the midst of an atmosphere basically religious. One of the university professors, Pedro Chacón, who wrote a history of his alma mater, tells us that in 1569 the University fostered such great fervor in faith that more than six hundred students, among them some of the most gifted, wished to enter the more austere religious orders.

THE UNIVERSITY CURRICULUM

According to the then-prevalent custom, John of St. Matthias was obliged to follow two sets of courses at Salamanca. First, those courses given in his own college, St. Andrew's; and second, those given in the public lecture halls. Many courses were offered. For example, ten courses were given in canon law, seven in theology, seven in medicine, eleven in logic and philosophy, one in astronomy, one in music, two in Hebrew and Chaldean, four in Greek, and seventeen in grammar and rhetoric. Of these, only a few were selected.

Those among the religious who did not wish to miss the studies given in their own colleges attended only fundamental courses at the University proper, attending the major theological lectures in the morning and afternoon. Or they might choose, in the faculty of arts, courses in physics, ethics, and logic.

When lecture halls were crowded, as was the case when Luis de León spoke, not all the students could be accommodated on the backless wooden benches; but for the great teachers they were satisfied to stand. A *cathedratic,* or full professor, who held title to his chair, was not allowed to read or to dictate his course. A *lector* or reader, who stood below the professorial chair, read the text which was to be commented upon, and the professor would then develop his own thought and explain, in his fashion, the text which had been read. This he did with full liberty, not feeling himself actually bound by the text read, for which he could indeed substitute another if he so chose.

Luis de León was the best liked of all the professors. He was very kind to his students and very considerate of them. He feared not even the wrath of the University's rector, who would fine him for violating regulations whenever he dictated a course of lectures to his students. Finally, in 1570, permission was granted for dictation; and to this we owe the numerous records of lectures actually given at Salamanca. All who are familiar with the history of the study of theology know that among the most authoritative of the collections of Scholastic Theology is that known as the *Salmanticenses* (or the *Theologians of Salamanca*). Generally, a professor would speak very slowly in order that his hearers might take notes, but if he quickened his pace, the students would protest by tapping on the floor.

All lectures were given in Latin, which was obligatory, even though Luis de León was among those who thought that Castilian, or Romanic as it was then called, was fully adequate for all theological teaching, as indeed he proved in his great work *De los Nombres de Cristo*. John of the Cross was not to forget, for his own part, this considered opinion of the most illustrious of his Salamancan masters.

When the lecture was over, the professor was the first to leave the hall, and he went to stand at the door, leaning against a pillar while he waited for the questions which his discourse had suggested to the students.

JOHN AS PREFECT OF STUDENTS

This summarily describes the atmosphere into which John of

St. Matthias was plunged at Salamanca during the four years between 1564 and 1568. Although we cannot specify just which
courses he took at the University, we nevertheless know something of his work there. St. Andrew's College, where he lived,
was a *Studium generale,* that is to say the Carmelite students
were there given courses recognized by the University. The
Carmelites had teachers of their own Order. Chief among these
were Miguel de Bologna and John Baconthorpe. The latter, who
died in 1346, was especially distinguished, had taught at Cambridge, and probably at Oxford as well. He handled theological
matters in a highly individualistic and liberal manner for his
time—he was, for one thing, an early upholder of the belief
that Our Lady was immaculately conceived. He was also known
as the "Prince of Averroists," not, of course, because he had
been a pupil of Averroes, but because in his day he was considered the leading authority on the writings of that philosopher.

John of St. Matthias certainly read and understood Baconthorpe,
and inheriting from those writings a perfect liberty of spirit, it
becomes impossible for us to list St. John either among Thomists
or Scotists—far less among Nominalists. He is forever to be
marked as a profoundly scriptural and patristic theologian. In
St. John's time, this liberality of thought was in high regard at
the University of Salamanca.

But what will appeal to us above all this is that which Fray
Alonso de Villalba, a native of Toledo and a fellow student of
John's, recorded. He tells us that John stood out from all his
fellow students for his sharp and penetrating mind as well as
for his studious habits. We know, in fact, that John was made
magister studentium or, as the Castilian has it, *prefeto de
estudiantes,* prefect of students. This title was sanctioned by the
Carmelite Constitutions. It was given to the most proficient among
the students, and it vested in him responsibility to tutor his fellows and take up with them, subject to the Regent of the College,
their problems and difficulties encountered in study.

We would call John of St. Matthias a brilliant student, the

chief among his comrades. From 1564 until 1567, he was under the Faculty of Arts, which means that he devoted himself especially to philosophy, the sciences, and literature. He was obliged to submit to the examination required of all students under this Faculty before they were admitted to the study of Theology. Something that we learn from Fray José de Jésus-Mariá, who himself learned it from some of John's fellow students, is of great significance for us in this regard. He tells us that while he was at Salamanca John made a special study of the mystical writers; among them he names St. Denys and St. Gregory the Great. This is of such importance for the remainder of our story that it justifies a deeper consideration.

The Middle Ages knew no greater mystic than Gregory the Great. His *Moralia* had been read and reread in the monasteries from the sixth century onward. But other works, less well known and less accessible, were also read, particularly those ascribed to Denys the Areopagite. In John's day, no one doubted that the author of the books so magnificently named—*Caelestia hierarchia; Ecclesiastica hierarchia; De nominibus divinis; De Theologia Mystica,* was truly the disciple of St. Paul, St. Denys the Arepagite. As a matter of fact, the unknown author of these works did profess to be the Areopagite, a device which allowed him to put his own writings under most impressive patronage.

In the French Church, Denys the Areopagite was generally considered to be the same as the first bishop of Paris, St. Denys; but, in our own day, we hold a different view. We think the true Areopagite was the first bishop of Athens, who died in that city during the first century A.D., while St. Denys of Paris lived two centuries later and according to local tradition was put to death on Montmartre. As for the third Denys, the writer of the books alluded to above, we know only that he called himself Denys; and we call him either Denys the Pseudo-Areopagite or Denys the Mystic. His works were written between 480 and 520, that is to say, at about the beginning of the sixth century; this means that they are approximately one hundred years older than the

writings of Gregory the Great who, about 590, refers to them
with noted caution.

In both East and West, Denys the Mystic was a subject of discussion by his early readers who unhesitatingly thought him to
be indeed the Areopagite. This lent to his works such prestige
that few other writers have had as much influence on the evolu-
tion of Mystical Theology.

It is, as I see things, of prime importance that John of St.
Matthias had read, thought about, and penetrated into these
writings. We know, also, through Fray José de Jesús-Mariá, that
what most attracted him to the study of both St. Gregory and
Denys was the desire to find a sound doctrine of contemplation.
We must regard *contemplation* as a keyword in his regard, and
shall often revert to it. Contemplation was to be the central
aspect of the life of St. John of the Cross. During his student days
at Salamanca, there were a great many new doctrines—probably
of the illuminist ilk—being propagated throughout Europe, and,
of course, more especially in university circles. These impressed
him as being dangerous deviations from patristic doctrine. Therefore, he looked into them, weighed them, prayed, and he sought
knowledge from his growing experience of the divine gifts he
indeed possessed. John composed a little treatise to sum up his
conclusions. He knew that a false notion of contemplation was
prevalent, that it was but a travesty of the thought of the Church,
but that it was actively impinging upon and entering into the
fields of the ascetic and the mystical life. Throughout his dissertation, he deplores this; but, unfortunately, we do not possess
the document: like the Hymns to which I have already alluded,
it is among the first fruits of John's literary activity, and like
them, too, it has not been preserved. Fray José de Jesús-Mariá,
who knew this dissertation, thought it to be of "excellent" quality.

Denys the Mystic laid strong stress on God's transcendence,
on the Light which is in Him, and on the blinding force of that
Light, which means that, for man, it is the darkness of night
when God's Light is obscured or absent. John of the Cross owes

much to Denys; for we find that similar ideas are at the base of his own mystical doctrine.

The Saint on His Way

But John's most striking characteristic at that time was that, while he did not neglect in the least the intellectual world and yet avoided all foolish pride in his scholastic successes, he nevertheless held in higher esteem than all his learning the growth of his soul, the upsurging of union with God, the intensity of his prayer-life. The saint within him grew more quickly than the scholar. All that we know of John's life as a student at St. Andrew's in Salamanca confirms this.

His cell was narrow and dark. A little window in it looked out upon the sanctuary of the college chapel. John of St. Matthias did not spend all his time with his books; he passed long hours of the night in prayer before the Holy Sacrament. In the daytime, when his fellow students enjoyed the repose and recreation permitted by the Rule—and even a little more than was actually permitted—John steadfastly remained within his humble cell. Even though they did not emulate him, his companions admired his unremitting spirit. They regarded him with the respect due to someone whose character is out of the ordinary. If there were some students inclined to play fast and loose with the requirements of the Rule, particularly in respect to the keeping of silence within the house, they hastened off when John turned into the corridor. One day, one of these young miscreants cried out: "Let us be off; here comes the devil." More often, they said simply: "Hold on; here comes Brother John." His presence alone was enough to call everyone to order, even though he said nothing; for it was evident that he was vested with the authority proper to a man of serious disposition and ever conscious of God's presence within him. One day, through the small window in his cell, he saw a religious in the chapel who did not appear to him to be behaving in the manner suitable to such a place. Even though he was the other man's junior, he did not hesitate for a moment but spoke so severely to him that the man immediately remedied his behavior.

Although his fellow students could not have known all that passed between John and God, they considered him to be leading a most austere life, and one deeply recollected and mortified. I have already noted that, from the beginning, he had been granted permission to follow the primitive Rule of the Order. This did not imply any difference between the habit he wore and that of his fellows; he was not yet—as he was to be later—a *Discalced* Carmelite. But it was known that he gave himself often and at great length to the prayer that he might make of his studies the basis of his service in God's honor. He practiced all the mortifications the Rule allowed. I have said that his cell was narrow and dark. The only light he had came from a fanlight in the roof and through the small window which looked out on the Sanctuary. A sort of box served John as a bed. It had no mattress and only fagots for a pillow. After he left St. Andrew's, traces of blood were found upon the walls of his cell: They are the marks of John's penitential flagellations. At the time Prior General Giovanni-Battista Rubeo came, during his first trip into Castile, to make his canonical visitation of the House of Studies at Salamanca and of other Carmelite houses, the time for God's plans for John appear to be imminent. This was in February of 1567. He found Fray John of St. Matthias at St. Andrew's and, though we have no record of what passed between the young student of twenty-five and his superior, we know from what came about after that the time was ripe for John's career as a reformer to begin.

THE REFORM OF CARMEL

For a period of at least four years, the reform of Carmel had been under way. It had its origin in the heroic act of Teresa de Ahumada, better known to us as Teresa of Avila. She had established a very small convent, consecrated to St. Joseph, at Avila. She had been subjected to very trying and, at times, most mortifying attacks and criticism by her Sisters of the Convent of the Incarnation at Avila, from her Carmelite brethren, from the clergy, and even from the civil authorities. She almost saw her convent ordered closed as a result of court action. Despite all this, the Convent of St. Joseph of Avila survived. But now it was announced that the Prior General of the Order was coming. What could he have to say?

Teresa had resolved, indeed, that she would obey him; but she was both fearful and prayerful. She tells us in her book *Foundations* that she was fearful for two reasons: She feared the General's disapproval, and she feared he would order her to return to her convent of the Incarnation. Nevertheless, she would tell him all, without embellishment, in simplicity and in truthfulness.

This visitation actually took place on Saturday, April 12, 1567, two months after the Prior General's visit to the *studium generale* at the University of Salamanca.

Fray Rubeo, the Prior General, listened carefully to his daughter Teresa. She told him "practically her life story." He admired Teresa personally and was pleased by what he heard. Moreover, he approved of her course of action and encouraged her to pursue it. Better yet, he gave her the necessary letters making clear that she had permission to establish other "discalced" convents in Castile and to revise the Constitutions of these houses for their use.

When Rubeo left Avila in order to go to Madrid, undeniable links of respect and mutual confidence had been made between himself and Teresa. Nevertheless, Teresa had not dared speak to him of the reform of the Carmelite Fathers as well as that of the nuns. At her suggestion, it was Don Alvárez de Mendoza, Bishop of Avila, who broached the matter to the Prior General.

Rubeo did not say no to the project, but asked for time to think it over and, when he left Avila, it was without having granted the necessary permission. Meanwhile Teresa, who was impatient to make use of the prized authorizations she had received, departed for Medina del Campo, where she planned to establish the second convent of the Carmelite reform. She arrived there on Thursday, August 14, 1567, and founded the convent on the fifteenth, the great Feast of the Assumption.

As was her duty, Teresa went to pay her respects to the Prior of the Monastery of St. Anne in Medina del Campo. It was at this monastery in 1563 that Juan de Yepès had presented himself seeking permission to enter "the Order of the Virgin." It was there that he had changed his name to John of St. Matthias. Teresa, of course, knew nothing of this.

The Prior of St. Anne's was an excellent priest called Antonio de Heredia. He already knew Teresa, and thought very highly of her. It was he who had made the necessary arrangements for the foundation Teresa was about to make. The two had long conversations together. Perhaps it was during one of them that Teresa told him of her great wish to work for the reform of her brethren, just as she had been licensed to do for that of her sisters. However this may be, Fray Antonio de Heredia soon left for Toledo. He had been commissioned by the Provincial Prior to make the Canonical Visitation planned for the time between the end of August and the beginning of September. While Fray de Heredia was at Toledo, a letter patent from the Prior General arrived, authorizing the establishment of *two* reformed convents for the brethren of Mt. Carmel. The letter was addressed to the Procurator General of Castile, Fray Mariano de Léon. The carrying out of its injunctions was entrusted to the Provincial, Fray Antonio Gonzalez, and to the Prior of the Carmel of Avila, Fray Angel de Salazar.

It is very possible that Fray de Heredia may have been charged to bring the good news to Teresa at Medina del Campo. In the same breath in which he told her what he had learned at Toledo he said, enthusiastically, that he wished to be the first of the reformed religious. Teresa was delighted but somewhat upset as well. She knew how excellent a religious Fray de Heredia was; he was fervent, studious, devoted to his cell, and versed in ecclesiastical lore. It was said that he had planned to join the Carthusians and had already made some efforts in this direction.

But within her soul Teresa had a twofold objection to him, although she was careful to say nothing of this. The first concerned his age. He was sixty. It would be too much to put him among the members of a foundation so delicately situated as would be a reformed house. Her second point was that Fray Antonio was overcareful of himself: He had enough little oddities in his personality to make one wonder if he had the firmness and the endurance which would be required in the reformed life, especially in its beginnings. Teresa therefore confined herself to counseling him to pray and wait.

Mother Teresa was still there when another visitor came. This time it was a younger religious, Fray Pedro de Orozco, who found her at Medina del Campo where he had come to celebrate his first Mass. His assignment was ordinarily at Salamanca, where he was occupied with his university studies.

He would, indeed, be the very one to satisfy Teresa's requirements. She really possessed a great respect for theological knowledge. It seemed to her that men whom she called "lettered" were to be preferred to those who were merely devout but lacked instruction. Doubtless, she held some prudent conferences with Fray Pedro without formally inviting him to share in the plan of reform which haunted her heart and mind. Fray Pedro did not understand this and, in any case, he did not offer himself. But he did speak of one of his fellow religious who was in Medina del Campo at this time, a friend from his mother's part of the country. Fray Pedro's friend had also come to Medina to say his first Mass: He was a student at the University of Salamanca, and he was regarded by all who knew him as a person of prodigious gifts. Not only was he the most naturally talented, the most studious, the most learned—being, in fact, Prefect of Studies in his college at Salamanca—but he was also the most humble, the most recollected, the most mortified, and the most penitential of his brethren. His name, Fray John of St. Matthias.

JOHN'S ORDINATION AND HIS FIRST MASS

It is because of Teresa's conversation with Fray Pedro de Orozco that we know an important fact in John's life—the time of his priestly ordination and first Mass. Can we doubt that, in his eyes, this was an event of prime importance? But we are obliged to rely on our own conjectures about this when we seek to penetrate into the deep recesses of his heart. However, it is clear that no history could ever be written without the erection of hypotheses. What do the records tell us? Juan López Osorio was later to declare before the board of enquiry held prior to John's beatification: "Having completed his studies and having received Holy Orders, the Servant of God returned to the Convent of Our Lady at Medina del Campo, where he sang his first Mass." Another piece of evidence which appears credible tells us that on this occasion John asked of God two things: first, that God never allow him to commit mortal sin; second, that he might devote his life to doing penance for the sins he would have committed, failing God's grace. Other evidence confirms this by stating that John, at the time of his ordination and first Mass, had been "confirmed in grace." In the great soul of this servant of God, how great must have been the desire for the Lord, the zeal to expend himself in God's service; what resolutions must he have formed concerning self-renunciation. Although we most readily accept them as true, it is difficult for us to picture the intensity and the perfection of soul which were John's.

A MEMORABLE INTERVIEW

All that Mother Teresa had learned from Fray Pedro de Orozco had aroused in her a lively wish to make the acquaint-

ance of John of St. Matthias. Their meeting, which was to have
such magnificent consequences, actually took place on a date
which we cannot supply with certainty, but it must have been
sometime in September or October of 1567 at Medina del Campo.
There have been few events of greater significance in the history of Mystical Theology. Let us picture this scene in all its
monastic simplicity. It took place in the Carmelite convent where
Mother Teresa, behind a veil which hid her face, awaited her
visitor in the parlor. She was then fifty-two years old. John was
aware of all that she had already done for the reform of the
female branch of the Carmelite Order, but he knew nothing of
her plans for his own brethren.

As he came into the parlor, she saw before her a young
religious of twenty-five, of a little less than middle height, well
built, and of dull but sunburned complexion. His face was at-
tenuated, but rather more rounded than elongated in its shape.
His forehead was broad and thoughtful, and his dark eyes were
filled with goodness and gentleness. Everything about him bespoke candor and innocence: He seemed continually aware of
the divine indwelling, which seemed to flow out from within his
very being, as would an inward light. From the very first moment, Mother Teresa felt certain that Fray Pedro had not misled
her. This man was small in stature but surely great in spirit. All
that he said was full of calmness, prudence, and wisdom; all so
wise, so full of common sense, and of an awareness of the
supernatural that one word sprang up in Teresa's mind, a word
we should not expect her to speak; quietly she called him her
little Seneca—*Su Senequita*.

What can they have talked about? Teresa was not one to delay
upon the unessential.

"I am ready to tell you, Fray John, something which will give
you great joy. There are among your brethren, as among us,
great plans for the reform of Carmel. They were discussed with
the Prior General during the time of his visitation. We have
letters from him authorizing us to go ahead with the reform, and

he has granted permission for the foundation of two houses of men. These will serve as the framework of the reform."

"Mother," replied Fray John, "I am deeply touched that you show such great confidence in me. Like yourself, I have felt that a reform of Carmel is needed. In all sincerity, I must tell you that I have not found in the Order what I came to seek—a life withdrawn from the world, a life of penance and recollection, a life of contemplation. That I might lead such a life I have even thought of withdrawing from Carmel and asking the Carthusians to receive me . . ."

"But, really, my Brother, do you not believe that all you seek can be found in Our Lady's Order? How can you think of leaving the Order on the eve of its reformation? Do you not think it would be a good thing if we were to labor for this reform? Will it not be well to place yourself under Our Lady's protection, in her own Order, just so that you may lead the life which God has inspired you to wish for?"

It is evident that such a reconstruction as we have made of the conversation between Teresa and John is a bit artificial. Nevertheless, it embodies the essence of what was said. Fray John completely gave up his notion of entering the Spanish Charterhouse where he would, most probably, have found it impossible to become that Prince of Mystical Theology whom posterity venerates. He understood what Teresa wanted. He shared her views. He remained within Carmel, but only that he might work for the reform for which she so ardently wished, the kind of reform she had already accomplished among the members of the Carmelite sisterhood.

He gave his word to Mother Teresa, promising to help her. He made but one condition: *that there not be overmuch delay.* Mother Teresa, herself, was not accustomed to let matters lie. The promise made, she set at once about finding a house in order that she might establish the first reformed Carmelite monastery for men.

The meeting was over. Teresa rejoined her nuns and said:

"Help me, my daughters, to give thanks to the Lord our God; for he has given us a brother and a half to begin the reform of our brethren."

A brother and a half. The expression is her own, and it has become famous. One can understand it in two senses: There was a tall brother, Fray Antonio de Heredia, and another so small that he could be taken as being but half a brother. But it seems more correct to think of it in this way: There was a brother small indeed in physical stature but so great in goodness that he constituted a powerful force, and a brother who was tall in stature but less perfect in virtue, so that he was actually but a lesser force to be added to the other.

THE END OF JOHN'S STUDIES AT SALAMANCA

Teresa had indeed promised that there would not be "overmuch delay." Yet, getting under way was not possible all at once. After all, one does not establish a monastery, even if it be only for *a brother and a half,* without first finding premises and furnishing the place. John kept his own counsel after leaving the celebrated foundress. He said nothing to his own superior, just as he had said nothing of his previous plan to become a Carthusian. Some of his biographers think that he now remained at St. Anne's, his home monastery at Medina del Campo, instead of going again to Salamanca to complete his studies at the University. But the register of the University for 1567–68 records on folio 16 that "Fray John of St. Matthias, native of Medina del Campo, priest and theologian," was again a student there. This is to say that from 1564 to 1567 he had spent three years under the Faculty of Arts and that his superiors had sent him again to Salamanca to complete his graduate studies in the School of Theology. It may be that we should look upon this last year of his studies as his second year in Theology; for the theological course was of two years' duration, and when John returned to Medina del Campo it was to become tutor in the courses for the younger men of the house there.

This was not to be for long; on Thursday, July 1, 1568, Mother Teresa came again to Medina del Campo from Malagon, bringing important news for John. Now we can regard the name of John of St. Matthias as outgrown; henceforth, he will be what the future will call him—Fray Juan de la Cruz, John of the Cross.

III

THE REFORM OF CARMEL AND JOHN OF THE CROSS

(1568–1577)

DURUELO

On the way to Avila, during one of the numerous journeys she made in the interest of her many foundations, Mother Teresa met a nobleman named Don Rafael Mejia, who offered her a small house he owned in a remote village at the western end of Castile, called Duruelo, where she might open the first monastery of the discalced. Teresa wished to go to see it, but it was not easy to find. It was in a forgotten spot, little known even to its nearby neighbors. However, she finally did reach Duruelo that Wednesday, June 30. In her book *Foundations* she thus describes the house: "It comprises a good-sized porch, a large room with a garret, and a little kitchen. . . . I believe that the porch could be made into a Chapel, the garret being the choir, and the double room serving as a dormitory." But the whole appearance was so poor and so seedy that Mother Antonia del Spiritu Santo, who was with Teresa, cried out: "Really, Mother, there is no one, no matter how good, who could be satisfied with this place. You must not accept it . . ."

At Medina del Campo, Mother Teresa set forth what she had

seen to Fray de Heredia, first, and later to Fray John. She concealed nothing. Her description did not present the place in any attractive light. Nevertheless, neither de Heredia nor John drew back. "Were the place a pigsty," the former declared, "we would gladly go there." Action followed words. Mother Teresa set about obtaining authority from the provincial superiors of Carmel—the incumbent Prior and his predecessor—who had been deputed to act by the Prior General, so that she might go ahead. Fray Antonio de Heredia, who was Conventual Prior of Medina del Campo, prepared to resign his office. There was nothing to hold John at Medina, and he went with Mother Teresa to Valladolid for the foundation she was establishing there. While waiting, he learned from their actual lives what the spirit was that stimulated Teresa and her sisters in their efforts at a reform of the Order. Teresa became more and more enthusiastic about John. Unhesitatingly she declared him to be "one of the purest and holiest of the souls devoted to God in his Church." And she added: "Our Lord has granted him heaven's best gifts and greatest wisdom." While he was at Medina and before he left for Valladolid, the sisters had prepared a habit for John. One day in the Convent parlor he wore it before them: He had laid aside his robe of fine cloth, as used by the "observants," and had put on the coarse homespun of the Rule. Then he had removed his shoes. Mother Teresa and her sisters were looking upon the penitential figure who was the "first of the Discalced" presented to them.

But this was no more than a "try-on," a kind of fitting. John resumed his usual habit, and on Monday, August 9, the caravan set out for Valladolid by cart. The trip was about twenty miles, enough to need a night's travel.

John spoke to the sisters, telling them of God, of their duties, of the way to pray. He spoke so movingly that the hours sped by and the long journey seemed short to his listeners.

Without going into any details about the new convent at Valladolid where John served as Chaplain, one episode sums up his whole course of action. One day, the Sister Sacristan forgot to put a corporal on the altar before Mass. When she realized it, she sought out Fray John and said: "Father, please do me the favor of taking this corporal, which I forgot to place on the altar, so that Mother Teresa may not see it."

"Sister," said John, "do not fear to be reprimanded. Take the corporal in your hand, and pass right in front of the Mother Foundress. And, if she asks what you are carrying, tell her it is a corporal . . ."

Such was the nature of the saint.

THE OPENING OF THE HOUSE AT DURUELO

Meanwhile, the authorization by the two provincial superiors was granted. Fray Antonio de Heredia therefore went to Medina del Campo to complete his arrangements. As for John, he went to Duruelo to prepare for the opening of the new house. Teresa wished to hurry things lest the permission already given be revoked. John went again from Valladolid to Avila, bearing a letter from the Foundress to Don Francisco de Salcedo. Had he opened this letter, he would have known how highly Mother Teresa regarded him: "He is not tall, but I think he is of great stature in God's eyes. . . . There is none among the brethren who does not speak well of him. He leads a most penitential life, despite his youth . . ."

Shortly afterwards, John set out from Avila for Duruelo, in the company of a lay brother who was to function as mason and plasterer in the conversion of the cottage into a monastery. On their way from Avila they passed by Santo Tome de Zabarcos, Salvadios, Cantaracillo, and Pennaranda. On this autumn journey John and his companion covered the twenty-two miles in good spirits.

They finally came to the house Mother Teresa had described to them: They found the ample porch, the large room, which also had an alcove, the garret, and the little kitchen. John went barefooted and wore working clothes of rough but strong cloth. From the day following their arrival the two men set earnestly to work, John being tireless throughout each day. He worked like a laborer and did not even think of eating. When night came he and the lay brother had not yet breakfasted. John, therefore, sent the lay brother out to get some food from some of the nearby farms where the advent of the religious had aroused much interest. Bread was abundantly given him. The first meal at Duruelo was composed of bread and water and, as John was later to say, "they were as happy as if they were dining on pheasant."

Among the little items which Mother Teresa had given them to furnish the new monastery, or which they themselves had brought from Avila, were ink and packets of paper. John having learned to draw in his youth, made a picture of Our Lord to be placed over the holy water font at the door of the chapel. Here and there he drew crosses and death's heads. Outside the chapel, at the gate of the convent, he set up a great cross also accompanied by another death's head. When the peasants on their way to work passed by the house they knew so well and now saw so changed, they signed themselves and exclaimed: "Why all these crosses and skulls?"

When all was in readiness, John sent word to the Provincial Prior, Fray Alonso González, and to his own Prior, Antonio de Heredia, as well as to Mother Teresa. All was now in order for the opening of the house. However, inasmuch as this had to be done with some solemnity, it had to wait for two months. Meanwhile, either at John's invitation or on his own initiative, Francisco de Yepès came to Medina del Campo to visit his brother. Francisco's heart was joyful when he beheld the life of prayer, penitence, and apostolic work, such as he had always dreamed of. The two brothers were inseparable. After their prayers at the monastery they went, early in the morning, to the nearby hamlets and villages. They were still fasting, and had not even thought about food. When they reached a village John heard confessions, said Mass, and preached a sermon. All were struck with admiration for him. Without accepting a thing from anyone, the two brothers returned quickly to Duruelo. At the halfway point in their journey there was a spring of fresh water. The two brothers sat by the side of the stream and ate some morsels of bread they had carried with them as their sole provision for the day. A peasant came by and invited them to join in his meal. But John, smiling at the man, thanked him warmly while declining his offer. He said to Francisco: "I do not accept even charity, because all that one does for God should be freely given."

THE OPENING OF DURUELO

At last, the first monastery of Discalced Carmelites was opened on November 28, 1568, the First Sunday of Advent. On the eve, there arrived at Duruelo six Carmelite religious, among them the Provincial Prior, Fray Alonso González, and two others of the brethren from Medina del Campo. One of these came to try the reformed life at Duruelo, although he kept his conventual habit. Fray Antonio de Heredia, who was to be made Vicar, was there also, as well as Fray José, still only in deacon's Orders but willing to take part in the movement for reform. All in all, and including John who was, from this day forward, to be John of the Cross, seven were on hand for the ceremonies. Mass was said by the Provincial Prior. Afterwards, three of the reformed religious raised their voices and declared:

"We, Fray Antonio de Jesús, Fray Juan de la Cruz, Fray José Cristo, do begin on this day, November 28, 1568, to live according to the pristine Rule . . ."

And the three first Discalced Carmelites signed their names. Thus, for the first time do we behold the signature of John of the Cross—Juan de la Cruz—which was to become known to posterity.

By this act, these men renounced those mitigations embodied in the Rule of St. Albert of Jerusalem, and the further modifications made under the authority of Eugene IV returning to the primitive Rule, as approved by Innocent IV.

Strictly speaking, we must number the new community at five, the three who then became "Discalced" and Fray Lucas de Celis, who had come to make a trial of the Rule but, as it turned out, was unable to persevere for reasons of health, as well as the lay brother who had come with John and of whom no more was heard. The foundation was still too insignificant to be granted the status of a priory, and Father Antonio de Jesús, who was the Superior, was given the humble title of Vicar.

LIFE AT DURUELO

From this time on, the reform of the Carmelites was under way. It must naturally be recognized as the work of St. Teresa of Avila, operating within the framework of that great spirit which was then stirring throughout the Catholic Church, the spirit which is termed, not with entire exactitude, the Counter Reformation.

It may seem only a small thing that a handful of monks, in an obscure corner of Castile, should give themselves over to penance and to prayer in contrast with a continent torn by frightful wars —wars from which France, for instance, was to be rent asunder for another thirty years. Yet, to those who take account of spiritual strength, it is not a matter of the number of men, but of their quality, their depth, their seriousness, and the work they do in God's sight. There can be no doubt that the little monastery of Duruelo was, from the first, guarded by the angels.

In March 1569 Mother Teresa, going to visit her foundation at Toledo, stopped at Duruelo. Her opinion is expressed with so much delight it should not be passed over in silence:

"I arrived this morning and found Fray Antonio de Jesús sweeping before the chapel door, and smiling as usual. I said to him: 'What is this I see, Father, and what has become of your dignity?' Joyfully replying to me, he said: 'I cannot think without horror of the time when my office impressed me.'

"When I went into the chapel I was struck by the spirit of devotion with which Our Lord had dowered this new house. And I was not alone in so feeling: two merchants from Medina, friends of mine who had come with me, were unable to refrain from tears when they saw themselves surrounded by crosses and skulls.

"All my life will I remember a little cross of wood which was beside the holy water font and on which was pasted an image of Jesus Christ, drawn on paper, and giving a more devotional effect than if it had been of rich workmanship. The curb roof or attic, which was in the center of the house, served as a choir wherein one could say the Office. But one had to bend one's head low in order to enter to hear Mass. In two corners of the chapel, one found little hermitages so low that one could enter only by crawling into them. It was so cold there that they had to pile the place with straw. The ceiling was so low that it scraped one's head; and the two little windows gave upon the altar. These good brethren had only stones as bolsters, above which were set crosses and skulls. From Matins until Prime they devoted themselves to private prayer, and God gave them such grace that they did not even notice, as they began Prime, that their robes were covered with snow . . ."

And the saint continues with interesting details about the apostolic work of the Duruelo brethren and the happy influence which they exercised upon the surrounding countryside.

"They went about, preaching," she writes, "in all the nearby villages. This was one of the reasons which made me wish to establish this house, for I had been told that in this region there were no monasteries, and that the peasantry were entirely deprived of religious ministrations—a deplorable condition of affairs . . .

"Within a short time, the Fathers were held in high esteem, something which filled me with joy. They went as far as a league and a half or two leagues [about four or five miles] away in order to preach the Gospel, walking unshod through the snow or ice; for it was not until afterwards that they were required to wear sandals. And, after having preached and heard confessions, they went back into their monastery still fasting. In all this good work, they were really happy, and it seemed to them that they were doing very little . . .

"People from places round about brought them more provisions than they needed. Some gentlemen who came to confess offered them more comfortable and larger quarters . . ."

We shall presently see that these offers were soon to be accepted because of the smallness of the monastery at Duruelo.

But Teresa's account must be cited further because it vividly recalls just what life was like among the first Discalced Carmelites, among whom John of the Cross was outstanding.

"After having made note of the devotional spirit of this barely habitable house," she says, "I was greatly edified by their manner of life, by their spirit of mortification, and of prayer, and by the good example that they gave. A nobleman and his wife, who are well known to me, and who came there to see me, were unable to stop praising the goodness of the Fathers and the benefits they were conferring on the whole region. Therefore, being convinced that all this betokened great things for the service of God and for our Order, I ceaselessly gave thanks to Our Lord. . . . The merchants of whom I have already spoken told me that they would not have missed seeing these things for anything in the world; and one may judge the power of virtue in that they declared that they esteemed the poverty of the brethren more highly than they did their own wealth.

"After I had discussed certain matters with the Fathers, my own weakness and imperfection prompted me to ask that they moderate somewhat the strictness of their penitential observance because (after having so fervently prayed that God grant me some helpers capable of undertaking this great work, and now having seen its beginnings) I feared very greatly lest Satan, desirous of bringing to ruin what had been begun, entice the

brethren to excessive austerities which would completely under-
mine their health. . . . But, inasmuch as our good brothers had
virtues which I lack, they paid little heed to what I said."

And the saint concludes her account in this fashion:

"I bade them farewell and I went off in a state of contentment.
Nevertheless, despite what thanksgiving I offered to God for so
unusual a favor, it was not all that I owed Him or what the
situation itself warranted. Actually, I knew very well that this
favor was greater even than that which had enabled me to
establish convents of women. With all my heart do I pray
God that He may give me grace to discharge at least some of
what I owe Him. Amen."

AN INCIDENT AT DURUELO

There is an interesting though slight incident which shows the
animating spirit of humility which motivated the lives of the
Duruelo brethren.

During that first winter, it snowed a great deal. St. Teresa
speaks of this fact. It snowed even in the choir of the monastery,
that is to say, in the attic which served as the choir. On a day
on which Fray Antonio de Jesús, the Superior, was scheduled
to speak, snow had fallen in abundance. All the surrounding
hilltops were snowcapped and some of the roads obstructed by
snowdrifts. John of the Cross thought that the good Superior,
being no longer young, would be unable to walk to his assignment, and looked for a donkey on which Fray Antonio might
ride. In addition he made boots of straw to protect him from the
intense cold, and fastened the homespun with a large pin to
better keep his robes together. However, in doing this, he
pricked Antonio's leg, and the good Father complained of his
clumsiness. "Don't complain," said John mirthfully, "it will now
hold your robe together all the better."

Evening fell, and Fray Antonio returned. With the brethren,
he partook of the frugal common repast. Then, according to

custom, and in his capacity as Vicar, he began to question the others:

"Speak, Fray John of the Cross, and say what faults have been committed here today."

"Your Reverence," said John as he rose from his place, "complained this morning when I stuck him with a pin . . ."

And Fray Antonio confessed his sin of impatience.

The reputation of the Duruelo brethren for monastic austerity was so great that earnest recruits began to arrive.

This led to two important consequences. The first, which was necessary in order that postulants might be received, was the conversion of their house into a priory licensed to train novices. The Provincial Prior, Don Alonso Ganzález, who had opened the monastery and who had promised to visit it again, actually came at the beginning—probably in the spring—of 1569. He was quite satisfied with what he saw and, in order to foster the growth of the community, named Fray Antonio de Jesús, until then Vicar, Prior of Duruelo, with Fray John of the Cross as his sub-Prior. A few months later, two novices arrived: Fray Juan-Baptist and Fray Pedro de los Angeles. With them, John of the Cross was able to begin to function, according to his providential calling, as spirtual master of the Carmelite Reform.

THE TRANSFER TO MANCERA

The second result of the arrival of new recruits was that it became necessary to remove the priory from Duruelo. Despite the fervor which characterized the house, it was impossible to close one's eyes to the limitations of the locality itself.

God made provision for the needs of the case.

We have learned from St. Teresa that some neighboring noblemen had offered larger and more suitable houses to the Fathers. "One of them," she writes, "who was called Don Luis, and who was Lord of Cinque-Vallos, had caused a chapel to be built in order that he might set up within it an image of Our Lady, most

worthy of reverence. His father had had it sent to him from
Flanders . . . and he revered it so that he wished to keep it until
he died: 'It is so beautiful that I have never seen one so lovely.
Nor am I alone in this thought.' Now, when Fray Antonio came to
visit this gentleman and when he saw the altarpiece of Our
Lady, it inspired him with so much devotion that he agreed to
transfer his monastery to this place. The name of the village was
Mancera. He believed that they could establish themselves there
despite the fact that there was no well, nor the likelihood of
digging one. Don Luis had a little house built for the brethren,
suitable for the kind of life they led, and he gave them suitable
furnishings.

"I do not wish to pass over in silence the way in which Our
Lord provided water for them, for it seems that it was by a
miracle. After supper, one day, Father Antonio, the Prior, was
in the cloister with his brethren, speaking to them of their need of
a water supply, when he rose up and, with his staff, traced a
cross in a corner of the cloister. Then he said simply: 'Bore a
well here.' They obeyed him, and when they had dug but a little
way there gushed forth so great a quantity of excellent drinking
water that they were hard put to moderate its flowing . . ."

We should say, today, that good Father Antonio was a fine
dowser; be that as it may, he was not aware of it.

The transfer from Duruelo to Mancera took place on Monday,
June 11, 1570, some eighteen months after the inauguration of
the first monastery. Duruelo, with its leaky roof, narrow little
rooms, and walls adorned with crosses and death's heads, was
now to be abandoned.

In compliance with the wish of the Provincial Prior, the transfer was carried out with due solemnity. He himself came to
preside, and was attended by many priests from neighboring
Carmelite houses, such as those at Salamanca and San Paolo de
los Perdones, together with members of the diocesan clergy,
neighboring landowners, and many of the devout populace.
All walked with the Discalced Carmelites, emaciated in appearance,

as they went forward processionally, barefooted and clad in their penitential habits. The long procession started at Duruelo and wound over the plains where wheat and barley waved under Castile's splendid sun. Mancera lay about two and a half miles to the northeast. Overlooking the village was the castle of Don Luis, a relative of the Duke of Alba.

Nearby stood the new monastery, which had been erected in only three months. The Rector of the parish and his people awaited the procession at the village limits and brought the Carmelites and their escorts to the church. Fray Alonso González sang the Mass. The original idea had been that Fray Alonso de Villalba, a fellow student of John of the Cross at Salamanca, would preach; but, no doubt at the desire of the donor, it was Father Antonio de Jesús, a most gifted preacher, who actually delivered the sermon.

The opening of the house in Mancera was thus accomplished in style. Four months later, on Sunday, October 8, 1570, the Feast of the Maternity of the Blessed Mother, the two novices who had come from Duruelo made their profession into the hands of John of the Cross, the sub-Prior, acting in the absence of the Prior. Now there were six discalced religious at Mancera. The community developed rapidly.

AT THE CONVENT OF PASTRANA

At this time, another foundation was in preparation, one which St. Teresa speaks of with affection in her book *Foundations*. In connection with this house, Teresa, in her writing, demonstrates the ardent spirit which animated her work as a foundress. She had a very real understanding of what we call the great movement of the Catholic Counter Reformation.

Teresa thus expresses herself in writing:

". . . I admit that for me it is a great joy to increase the number of churches and, when I ponder on the immense number of them destroyed by heretics, it seems to me that there can be nothing one should not be willing to do in order to achieve great good and to receive the great consolation that flows from having insured that Jesus Christ, true God and true man, will come in many places, upon our altars, in the Blessed Sacrament. This is something to which many people give too little thought . . ."

In our own time, Charles de Foucauld reflected this feeling. Every time that one sets up a focus of adoration and love one works for the world's greater spiritual balance.

But to return to the story of the foundation of Pastrana. In this place there lived a hermit called Ambrogio Mariano Azaro. He was a Neopolitan, a man of ardent and enterprising spirit, a former soldier who had fought in 1557 at the Battle of St. Quentin. He was a capable engineer and lived a solitary life in the heart of the Sierra Morena where Prince Ruy Gómez had given him a hermitage. He knew, however, that the Council of Trent had advised hermits to enter some religious Order.

Having learned of the work of the Foundress of the reformed Carmel, he offered her his hermitage that it might be made into a convent for the Discalced. Without loss of time, the saint had discussed with him the principles of the reform and had then vested him and a fellow Neopolitan, Juan Narduch, in the habit of the discalced brethren. Azaro immediately assumed the name of Fray Ambrosio-Mariano de San Benito, while Juan Narduch took that of Fray Juan de Miseria.

Thus, on Wednesday, July 13, 1569, after the necessary authorization was secured, life began in the hermitage community of San Pedro de Pastrana. At once novices flocked to the place. The contemplative life which existed there became known at Alcala, and students of the University hastened to join in it. Pastrana was on the way to becoming the major novitiate of the reformed Carmel.

But Teresa was well aware that after her departure from Pastrana, it was necessary for someone to assume authority, a man who would be so steeped in the Carmelite tradition advocated by the reform that the influences of the eremitical life

—which had formerly been led by the first two discalced brethren of Pastrana—might not go to extremes. It was without hesitation or delay that her mind turned to John of the Cross for this
responsibility. He was always the very model of a discalced
brother, the perfect Carmelite of the reform. She spoke, accordingly, to Fray Antonio de Jesús, Prior of Mancera, and the
decision was made very quickly, probably about the middle of
October 1570, shortly after the professions at Mancera.

JOHN OF THE CROSS AT PASTRANA

John left for Pastrana at once. From Mancera he took with
him the lay brother who had just been professed, Fray Pedro
de los Angeles. They went on their way, barefooted and without
provisions, depending instead on what charity they might encounter. They never accepted food in the homes of the rich, nor
would they take any rest there even after the fatigues of a long
day's journey. Long afterwards—perhaps fifty years—Fray
Pedro recalled the windings of their travels over rough roads and
still remembered the noble words of John of the Cross who eased
the difficulties and made the length of their journeying an en-
richment.

The poetic nature of John of the Cross opened his eyes to
God's presence in all of nature. When they came to Pastrana, he
was delighted. The monastery to which they were called was well
situated in a place set apart and graced by a mountain view as
well as by a prospect of valleys sown with hidden grottos. Everything promised silence and recollection. In the monastery itself
were four professed religious and ten novices; among the latter
were several very promising students.

John of the Cross had a mission to discharge, and he lost no
time in undertaking his duties, marked, of course, by his enthusiasm. We now see John as the spiritual master of the Carmelite
reform. He organized the novitiate at Pastrana according to the
principles used at Duruelo and Mancera. There are characteristics

of Carmel which express themselves in ways of carrying out the
duties of daily life, in the hours at which things are to be done,
in the Rule, and in the basic truths of the spiritual life; and he
brought all these characteristics to bear on the present situation.
He was obeyed, despite his twenty-eight years, as though he had
been a veteran of the Order. He gave special attention to the
training or "formation" (as they say in religious houses) of Fray
Gabriel de la Asunción, whom he planned to make acting Novice
Master until he could, with full authority, be appointed accordingly.

All this preliminary work took about a month. Afterwards,
his tasks accomplished, John, still accompanied by Fray Pedro de
los Angeles, returned to his own monastery at Mancera, blessing God on his homeward journey. Once more he gazed upon
the beauteous scenery, and in all he beheld God. He could then
have sung, as in his famous *Spiritual Canticle:*

> "My Beloved, the mountains,
> The solitary wooded valleys,
> The strange islands, the sonorous rivers,
> The whisper of amorous breezes, . . ."

So we find our two travelers again at Mancera, about the mid-
dle of November 1570. This is established by the fact that John
was there, at that time, to greet Mother Teresa who had come
from Avila on her way to the house she had recently founded at
Salamanca. With her were several sisters and also a young novice,
Sister Ana de Jesús, who then for the first time met John of the
Cross. Fourteen years later he was to dedicate the complete
Spiritual Canticle to her, of which the lines just cited form a part.

Shortly afterwards, Mother Teresa, having regulated things at
Salamanca, traveled to Alba de Tormes, where she was to set up
another convent for her sisters. John was present at the opening
of this foundation and, as always, gave of himself, either working
with his hands to give the finishing touches to the new house or

responding to requests for conferences in which he raised the souls of the sisters to the heights of Carmelite spirituality.

JOHN OF THE CROSS AT ALCALA

In April 1571, John of the Cross again set out on a journey. Once more, he was selected when someone was required to function in a special office.

On the first of November in the preceding year, the Order of Carmel had established a house of study for its best students at the College of Alcala. Among the students there was one sent from the Monastery of Pastrana. The College of Alcala was of prime importance to the Order just as was the University at Salamanca, which we learned about from John's own student days.

A rector was needed for their College at Alcala, and every Carmelite knew that the choice of this rector was a matter of considerable importance. Advice was sought from the Apostolic Commissioner, a Dominican named Father Pedro Fernández, who was stationed at Naples and who discussed this matter with Fray Antonio de Jesús, the immediate superior of John of the Cross. In the eyes of Antonio there was no need to seek further, for he saw in John of the Cross the very man they needed. The Apostolic Commissioner readily agreed, and the appointment was made at a public session. John of the Cross was directed to proceed to Alcala immediately and to assume the duties of Rector of the college which had been established there as the Carmelite House of Studies. He left at once, accompanied by Fray Pedro de los Angeles. The latter, after having accompanied his master to Alcala, then returned to Mancera. John never again returned to the birthplaces of the Carmelite reform; Duruelo and Mancera were to know him in person no more.

We go with him now to Alcala, the ancient Complutum, where stood the illustrious university founded by Cardinal Cisneros.

Here John was in his true element. It was not very long since his own student days at Salamanca, and the two universities were rather alike, being rivals in the best sense of the word.

We are well aware of the way things were arranged: the Carmelite students did most of their work at their own college where they were tutored and made their own preparations. And then, each day, they went forth in ranks of two to the university halls to listen to the lectures of the major professors.

The chief duty of the rectors of the colleges lay in the realm of spiritual government. John counseled the students that they might preserve recollectedness, that is to say, that they might "keep alive in their hearts an abiding sense, loving and calm, of God's presence." We should bear these words in mind constantly, for they serve accurately to sum up the whole teaching of John of the Cross; indeed, they are a compendium of his view of mystical theology. It is certain that, although the major works of St. John were to be written somewhat later in his life, he had already been living his doctrine and had already set its seed in others. His students were regarded as being truly models in Alcala. As they went forth through the city streets, they showed themselves in silence and dignity, their eyes being turned, as it were, inwards, so that they saw only the place on which they would next step. They avoided all the more or less childish distractions of ordinary students. They were unshod and poorly clad, wearing their Order's white cloak over coarse habits of dark homespun. Men stopped to allow them to pass by, while others followed them on their way to the university to gaze longer on such exemplars of decorum. Whenever the Rector was encountered outside his convent, which was only on rare occasions, he gave a striking impression of holiness: His face bespoke gentleness and peace, his words were loving and kind. Students who saw him were won over by his grace and charm. One such was the future Fray Inocente de San Andrea, who came to John to confess and then spoke of his wish to enter Carmel. The young man was welcomed and sent to Pastrana to gain knowledge of the Order.

There he received the habit and became one of the more enthusiastic and more faithful disciples of John of the Cross.

Nevertheless, John's way did not please everyone, for there
were some who found them excessive. He laid great emphasis on
penance: the words "renunciation" and "mortification" were constantly on his lips; and is not this a bit inhumane, or—what
amounts to the same thing—superhuman? Some complaints of
this nature came to the ears of the Apostolic Commissioner, the
Dominican Father Pedro Fernández, who has already been mentioned.

This official wished to see things for himself, and therefore
went to Alcala to visit the college of the Discalced Carmelites
and question the students. Each one was given the opportunity
to speak to the visitor in confidence. Then when the visitation
was over, Father Fernández said to the students:

"Go on as you are: The world is full of learned men; it has
need of those who do penance! . . ."—"*Está lleno de letras y
falto de vida penitente!* . . ." He ended by expressing the hope
that they would remain faithful to their observance of monastic
life until their days were over.

Such was his official approval of John's doctrine. All is summed
up in the words: "*Devout and learned, but first of all, devout.*"

A TELLING CHARACTERISTIC

For the benefit of those who may believe that John was given
to stressing unduly certain maxims found in the book called *The
Imitation of Christ* and that he thus held pure knowledge without
esteem and even with loathing, it will be enough to cite a small
fact which pertains to this period of John's life.

The patrons of the church of Alcala were two rather obscure
personages, named St. Justus and St. Pastor. Some people, who
thought highly of the learning and the piety which marked John
of the Cross, requested that he write the lives of the two saints
whom local tradition held were child-martyrs. But he would

never agree to this proposal, and with delicacy and gentleness constantly avoided giving his consent to it. Finally, when he was pressed for a reason for refusing, he replied in words worth remembering:

"It is because when I write a book of devotion it must also be a book historically accurate."

Thus did he express a very conscientious and strict view of history. When one writes history, it must be with history that one deals: One must never invent "facts" on the pretext of edifying one's readers.

John of the Cross was indeed correct. We must confess that even in his greatest poetic flights he remains scrupulously faithful to sound principles of mystical theology, the most strict and authentic of the sciences.

I should like also to refer to another characteristic which balances that which has just been noted.

While at Alcala, John was called back to Pastrana that he might settle a serious misunderstanding which had divided the novices and the Novice Master.

That official was Fray Angel de San Gabriel, a former novice of John of the Cross when he had spent a month at Pastrana. Fray Angel, a native of Madrid, was a man of impetuous and volatile temperament who had embarked on bringing his novices to the highest pinnacle of perfection in very short order. To this end he bade them do penance, and a most unhealthy spirit of competitiveness began to show itself in the community. Some of the details of this affair, which can be gathered from available sources, reveal deplorable exaggerations. Complaints soon abounded. As we have seen, John of the Cross had once been referred to the Apostolic Commissioner on the ground that his disciplinary rule was too severe. However, the Apostolic Commissioner had fully approved of John and his methods. In his turn, John was now called upon to judge complaints against his own disciple, Angel de San Gabriel. Among the protesting novices was Fray Jerónimo Gracián, later to be Prior Provincial of the Discalced Carmelites. He had come to Pastrana to lead the contemplative life but had not found what he sought. The practices of external penance which were pressed upon him seemed alien to his true vocation. John of the Cross did not sustain the imprudent novice master. Fray Jerónimo wished, above all, to take counsel with Mother Teresa, and she, on her part, decided to consult the noted theologian, Domingo Bannez, a Dominican. We have the report of his findings in the case. Although he does not condemn the intentions of the young Novice Master of Pastrana, he finds him basically in the wrong, and is thus in agreement with John's own judgment. Actually, it is among the most definite principles of John's teaching that, although penance is a means, it is not the end of the spiritual life which must, at all costs, remain something subordinated to higher things.

As the letter written by Father Bannez is dated from Salamanca on Wednesday, April 23, 1572, we can fix the date of the difficulties at Pastrana.

John of the Cross himself went to Pastrana to curb the overzealous Novice Master and pacify the troubled novices. Then he returned to Alcala where he resumed the duties of his rectorate. The novitiate at Pastrana, thus restored to order by John's efforts, became the most important and the most certain focus of training in the principles of the Carmelite reform.

But looming on the horizon was another change of assignment for John.

Happenings at Avila

During John's rectorship at Alcala, an unexpected change occurred in Mother Teresa's life. By direction of the Apostolic Commissioner, Fray Pedro Fernández, whom we have already mentioned, she was appointed the task of re-establishing her Order in the great Convent of the Incarnation at Avila. This was a place she knew well, for it was the same convent from which she had gone forth to initiate the reform in the smaller house which she had dedicated to St. Joseph. Things had not been going well in the large convent, which housed about 130 religious, more indeed than could be taken care of in view of the revenues of the establishment. Those were days of general economic distress throughout Spain, and there were some people literally starving to death. The Rule followed by the Carmelites of the Old Foundation had been greatly mitigated and relaxed, and each nun was then permitted to receive visits from her parents and friends. The visitors brought gifts of provisions for individuals rather than for the entire community. There was, accordingly, more than one mode of life led in that convent; and although some of the sisters were abundantly supplied with provisions, others were plainly undernourished. The visitor's room was usually filled with guests who furnished supplies only for their friends. Needless to say, such a situation was not conducive to the general good of the community.

To set things to rights in such a place would be no easy task. The mere fact that the mandate by which Teresa became invested with the authority of Prioress depended not on her election by the community but rather on her designation to office by the Apostolic Commissioner insofar as concerned the assumption of her new duties was concerned, produced serious difficulties. What, after all, could be expected by the residents of the Convent of the Incarnation at the hands of a Superior who had been sent there to "reform" the place? Would she not impose her own views upon the community? Would she not especially wish to revise the Rules which regulated the whole matter of the reception of visitors? Would she not take into account the fact that it was by means of the visitors' room alone that gifts and provisions might be provided for those of the sisters who were underfed?

In a prudent act at the start of this assignment, Teresa had asked for assistance from the Provincial Prior of Carmel, Fray Angel de Salazar. But when the new Prioress of the Convent of the Incarnation presented herself before the gates of the convent in the company of the Provincial Prior, she found them closed to her. She was refused entrance; and cries of revolt against her authority could be heard coming from within. It was thought that entry might be made at one of the other doors. But the rebellious sisters quickly became aware of such an attempt, and the clamor was redoubled in violence. The discouraged Provincial Prior then called out: "Is it that you do not wish to receive as your Prioress Mother Teresa de Jesus . . . ?" thus indicating his intention of going away and giving up the effort to install her there. At this, however, a protesting voice was raised within. Sister Catalina de Castro shouted out: "We not only wish to have her here, we love her as well!" Then she intoned the *Te Deum,* which was taken up by other nuns. Finally, while pandemonium reigned throughout the community, a side entrance to the convent was opened, and Mother Teresa was able to enter into the cloister.

Mother Teresa greatly loved this convent in which she had passed the first twenty-five years of her religious life, and in which she had many friends and admirers. It was not her wish to govern it with an iron hand. Her purpose in coming was to smooth out affairs and bring peace to souls; that is, to ensure for the needy a truly religious means of sustenance, thus giving them bodily assistance while caring for their souls.

Since Teresa was highly esteemed throughout the city and had many generous friends, means were quickly found for supplying the most pressing needs of the community. Actually, all these sisters were, basically, good religious, even though they were not all adherents of the principles of the Carmelite reform movement. All that was needed was to make them understand, and Teresa was successful from the beginning.

It was fortunate that they were on the threshold of Lent, a time of penance, for this enabled Teresa to regulate the question of the visitors' parlor which was the cause of so much of the trouble which beset everyone in the convent. Mother Teresa was able to write to her friend, Doña María de Mendoza: "We are able now to give thanks to the Lord for the changes that have taken place here. The leaders of the opposition are now entirely satisfied and are giving me their strong support. During this Lent, no visitors whatever are being received in the parlor, neither women nor men, not even the fathers of the sisters, and this is a great innovation in this place. All is now at peace. Truly, there are good servants of God here, and almost all of them are making decided progress."

Nevertheless, Mother Teresa felt her own need of someone to help her in her work, for her health was not good. She thought, at once, of John of the Cross, and planned to have him made Spiritual Director of her community. With John, she could be sure that spiritual affairs would be in good hands. But how could she arrange it?

Clearly, only one man could exercise authority in this matter —the Apostolic Commissioner, Fray Pedro Fernández, who was in Salamanca at this time. Teresa therefore sent the chaplain of her own little convent of St. Joseph at Avila, Fray Gulian de Avila, to the Commissioner to plead for John's appointment.

The whole question was a delicate one, and the Apostolic Commissioner at once raised an objection: How could he appoint a Carmelite Father of the reform to be Spiritual Director of a Convent of non-reformed religious? They all knew the difficulties which had attended the arrival of Mother Teresa. Would he not be provoking a new revolt if he sent John of the Cross there? Would not the Fathers of the Observance themselves (as those of the Old Foundation were called) be greatly disturbed if they saw taken away from them the spiritual direction of one of their own convents and placed in the hands of one of their brethren known for his monastic severity?

But Fray Gulian de Avila pressed for the appointment. He presented the matter as envisioned by Mother Teresa. John of the Cross was the embodiment of goodness, kindness, and spiritual knowledge. And what was more needed at a convent as important as that of the Incarnation at Avila if not direction

which would be at once strong and kind? This argument convinced the Apostolic Commissioner, and he agreed to Mother
Teresa's request. Perhaps he thought it worth a try, and one can
always try: He would see what the result would be, and could
always take further action if the need arose. Therefore he sent
Fray Gulian de Avila back to Mother Teresa with the appointment she had asked. She was so happy about it that she immediately made announcement of the appointment to the sisters by
saying: "I am giving you a saint to be your confessor."

We do not know the exact date of the arrival of John of the
Cross at the Convent of the Incarnation; but, in the month of
September 1572, the happy results of the appointment were al-
ready evident, for Teresa was able to write to her own sister,
Juana de Ahumada: "Great things are being done here by the
Discalced Father who is our Confessor; he is Fray John of the
Cross."

JOHN OF THE CROSS AT AVILA

It was indeed a saint whom Mother Teresa had given her
community as their confessor. He never did anything to belie her
praise of him. "We do not always agree," she said, one day; "but
I have been unable to discover any imperfection in him." John
very quickly acquired over the sisters that extraordinary ascend-
ency which caused his first biographer, Alonso de la Madre de
Dios, to write, as long ago as 1618:

"The brethren and the sisters who had him as their Spiritual
Director stated that they loved him more than their own fathers
and mothers, and that by his heavenly influence this man of
God so impressed them that they found it easy to do all that he
required of them."

Father Lucien-Marie, the distinguished editor of the French
edition of John's writings, comments on Alonso de la Madre de
Dios' remark by saying:

"They loved him more than their own fathers and mothers—

an eloquent pleonasm which expresses very well the kind of relationship, in the spiritual realm, which the fatherly spirit of the saint aroused in the souls of those who followed him along the paths of divine love."

It was at this time, during five years (1572–77) of quiet and peaceful activity, that John of the Cross put into practice principles dear to his heart, treating each soul as if it were a world greater than the world we see about us, a world apart in which God must reign, a world full of problems which it was his duty to understand and to solve. His was no vague and abstract doctrine; he aimed to say to each man and to each woman words which were best adapted to him and to her, so that he might enlighten, guide, and perfect them. This ability is exemplified in certain of John's maxims gathered from the notebooks of religious. There are thousands of these maxims, and every one of them is oriented toward some particular case, but in such a way that, marvelous to relate, they nevertheless retain a timeless and priceless value.

These maxims were given in the confessional, or in allocutions to groups of religious; sometimes they were written by the saint himself in his personal correspondence, in letters which offered spiritual nourishment to their recipients for periods of weeks or even months, should their Spiritual Director have to be away.

Nevertheless some of the sisters delayed in accepting John. An incident at the beginning of his stay at Avila reveals this. Teresa avoided imposing upon all the other sisters her own chosen confessor. Priests who followed the relaxed or mitigated form of the Rule were also available as confessors, and the sisters were free to choose whomever they wished. One day a nun came to confess. John of the Cross was in the confessional, unmoving and unseen. The nun, who was an adherent of the Fathers of the Old Foundation, asked in a low voice: "Calced or discalced?" Fray John at once understood the meaning of the query and covered his feet with his robe as he replied: "Let it be calced, my daughter." Then he heard her confession. All her reserves quickly melted away, for he had a wonderful gift of discernment which enabled him to pierce the mysterious recesses of the soul. One word was enough to make him understand everything.

His influence as a confessor, joined with that of the holy Prioress—who must not, indeed, be deprived of her share of the credit—finally ended the abuses which had formerly abounded in the convent. The most serious of these abuses—slight enough though it appear in our eyes—was the love the nuns had of gossiping in the parlor. John of the Cross, agreeing with Teresa, did not declare open war upon this fault. He began rather by making the sisters love to pray, for prayer is, after all, "a talking with God." As soon as the sisters had formed the habit of this kind of conversation, the talking with others in the parlor became unbearable to them, and they gave it up of their own accord; for they had learned to love what endures and to prefer it to what is futile and fleeting.

THE DWELLING PLACE OF JOHN

On his arrival at Avila, John was at first housed at the local Carmel with the Fathers of the community resident in the city. He was not the only discalced member for, by direction of the Apostolic Commissioner who had his own plans for that monastery, there were a number of reformed Fathers mingled with the others who still followed the mitigated observance. The Prior, the Sacristan, the Procurator, and the Porter were among the former group. This made matters easier for John than would otherwise have been the case; but Mother Teresa desired that the principal confessor of her nuns should be housed closer to her own convent, and had this done. It seems likely that she did this after the Prior of the Carmel, the discalced Fray Baltásar de Jesús, had been replaced by a follower of the mitigated observance.

John's new lodgings were poor and bare. Here he was free to practice mortification fully. The nuns prepared his frugal meals and, if it happened that he was offered some delicacy, he would send it back to the convent to be given to the sick.

Within these poor lodgings an incident of a most delicate nature occurred. Fray John was alone, quickly eating his modest collation; the door had been left open for the sisters who served him. When he raised his eyes, he saw that a young laywoman had entered. He recognized her as a beauty of a noble house. She was enamored of John, and had been seeking an opportunity to find him alone to offer herself to him. John was to declare, later, that he had never been in such a predicament. However, he did not reveal his disturbance, nor did he seize a whip to cast out the woman. With his usual gentleness, which never condescended to weakness, he spoke to her; he made her ashamed of her sinful intentions; and he so thoroughly brought her to her senses that she acknowledged her fault and went off as quietly as she had come. When she returned home, she wept bitter penitential tears.

On this occasion the demon was vanquished. But this was not to be Satan's last effort. In one convent—most likely that of the Incarnation—there was a nun who was the object of frequent visits which caused gossip, for the visitor was a wealthy gentleman who openly showed his feelings for the sister by the costly gifts he gave her. Fray John saw the danger. He spoke to the sister and made her conscious of the scandal she was arousing, and prevailed upon her to resolve that she would never see this person again. The gentleman was so angered by this that he plotted a terrible revenge. He waited outside the convent one evening until the confessor emerged on his way to his own lodgings. Then he threw himself upon John and beat him with a stick so violently that he fell to the ground. John knew very well who the man was, but he voiced no complaint. In his happiness at having freed the sister's soul, he said merely that "the blows of the stick seemed as sweet to him as the stones had been to St. Stephen."

But John was to have to fight an even more dramatic battle with Satan.

AN EXORCISM BY ST. JOHN OF THE CROSS

In the Augustinian Convent in Avila, Nuestra Señora de Gracia—where Teresa had been educated as a child—one of the religious there was looked upon as a prodigy. The whole city regarded her with admiration. She was still young and had entered the Convent as a pupil at the age of five and then remained there as a nun. She possessed a wonderful knowledge of Holy Scripture which she could explain to all, although she had never had a teacher of Scripture nor had she ever studied it. Her knowledge amazed everyone, and people came from all over the town to listen to her. Soon the Superiors became uneasy, and they wondered how she had acquired this knowledge. They brought to the Convent a procession of the most noted theologians, not only of Avila—which might not be too impressive—but of Salamanca, the nearby university. Many of the men whom we have met in John's student days were among these judges: Mancio de Corpus Christi, Bartolomeo de Medina, Juan de Guevara, and even the greatest master, Luis de León. We do not know exactly what judgment they pronounced, but it seems likely that all inclined to think the knowledge of the young nun to be worthy, holding it to be a kind of infused knowledge due, as they said, to "goodness of spirit."

Nevertheless, the Superiors were still doubtful. They turned to John of the Cross for his advice. He refused to give it, stating that it was not for him to judge something which had been handled by distinguished experts. However, the Superior General of the Augustinians, then sojourning at Avila, insisted on looking into this very unusual circumstance. Mother Teresa added her own urgings, and the young Father Confessor to the nuns of the Convent of the Incarnation went to the Convent of Nuestra Señora de Gracia, after having, most prudently, obtained all necessary permission from the representatives of the Inquisition at Avila. It was only after this permission had been granted that he set his hand to the affair. Nor did he go by himself to the Augustinian Convent; on every visit he was accompanied by one or another of his brethren. Sometimes it was Fray Francisco de los Apóstolos, the Porter at the Carmel of Avila; sometimes it was Fray Gabriel-Batista or Fray Pedro de la Purificación. The journey was a wearisome one, for the two convents were at opposite ends of the city.

John entered the confessional to hear the young nun. An hour went by, while the Superior General of the Augustinians and the religious of the house waited. And then came the confessor's opinion:

"Ladies and gentlemen, the nun is possessed."

The Superior General then publicly called upon John to undertake the exorcism of the evil spirit, and he, thus confirmed in authority, accepted the difficult task. We possess full and precise details about the actual exorcisms. For the space of two months they were held regularly once or twice a week and resulted in the most horrendous scenes. One witness tells us of "seven legions of devils" in the young nun. From the very first exorcism, the possessed acknowledged herself to have been under the domination of Satan, shortly after her entry into the convent, when she was barely six years old. Her contract with the demon had been drawn up and carried out according to all the rules of sorcery: The child had once drawn enough blood from her arm to enable her to write a pact with Satan, making him the gift of herself. The exorcisms aroused the unfortunate religious to an astonishing extent, sending her into convulsions and manifestations of demonic fury. She insulted John, rolled upon the ground in foaming rage, or hurled herself upon the exorcist and his assistants who desired only to help her. One day, while John was being assisted by Fray Gabriel-Batista, the possessed nun became so ferocious that all the other sisters took flight and Fray Gabriel-Batista bolted to go off with them. But John grasped his hand and cried:

"Have no fear; are you not a priest?" All this time, Satan foamed from the mouth of the unhappy nun:

"As for *me,* I am a nobody! I have none to help me."

Unmoved, John held a crucifix above her and went on with the prayers of the exorcism. The possessed sister dashed the Cross to earth, but John forced her to pick it up and to kiss it, despite her protesting cries.

On another occasion, John commanded the nun to translate the words: *Verbum caro factum est et habitavit in nobis.* She obeyed by quickly saying: "The Son of God was made man and dwelt amongst you." "You lie," cried the exorcist, "it is not 'amongst you' but rather 'amongst us.'" "Indeed," replied the nun, "it is rather as I have said; for He was not made man that He might dwell *'amongst us,'* but that He might dwell *'amongst you.'"* Thus did Satan make himself heard through the mouth of the possessed religious.

While conducting these sessions as an exorcist, John also gave spiritual instruction to the possessed sister and succeeded in bringing her to tears and to believing that men love God. But the demon tried a ruse as a last resort. Two Discalced Carmelites appeared one day at the gates of Nuestra Señora de Gracia. In every detail they resembled John of the Cross and his usual companion. They had come, they said, to visit the possessed sister. The sister who received them showed them where the confessional was. When the possessed sister came out of the confessional, she seemed desperately upset. The Mother Superior asked her what had happened, and she replied: "Today, Father John of the Cross has told me to do everything that he has hitherto advised against." The Mother Superior at once realized what had happened and wrote to Fray John. He aroused Fray Francisco de los Apóstolos, who was then his companion, and said: "We must be off to the convent." When the nuns saw him again, they breathed freely and it was easy for John to unveil the artifices of the demon who had presented himself in John's guise in order to deceive his victim.

At length, after months marked by the continuance of the exorcisms and by many heroic incidents, the devil gave back the compact signed by the young nun, who was thus delivered from a prolonged and dreadful nightmare.

A whole chapter could be devoted to the demonic haunting to which John of the Cross was subjected, just as was the Curé of Ars. One day, Fray Francisco de los Apóstolos remarked to the saint, while he was in the little garden which surrounded the latter's home near the Convent of the Incarnation, that he seemed paler than usual, and asked why.

"The devils have so mistreated me," John answered, "that I wonder how I manage to keep alive at all."

There were times when the devil snatched John from his bed, just as he was later to do to the Curé of Ars, and left him trembling upon the floor in the dead cold of the Avila night. Yet this did not prevent him from battling with courage and depriving the demon of the prey of which he had felt assured.

GRACES OF ELECTION

But just as devilry in the life of the Curé of Ars was not the principal feature of the Curé's life, so battles against the demon were important but certainly did not occupy the chief place in the life of John of the Cross.

Among the glories of this period of his life which tradition has preserved for us is an event which took place on the Feast of the Blessed Trinity in 1573. There was no mystery of religion for which the young confessor had a more ardent degree of devotion. Later on, when someone asked him why this was so, he smilingly replied that, as far as he was concerned, the Trinity "is the greatest Saint in Heaven."

On this particular celebration of the annual feast, the only ones in the convent parlor, so far as is known, were John and Mother Teresa; she was behind the grille and he before it. He spoke of the great mystery being commemorated on that day, not as a learned theologian using technical and set phrases, but as an ardent contemplative pouring out his soul. When he finished, he rose from the ground in levitation. At this moment, Sister Beatrix de Cepada y Ocampo entered the parlor and witnessed the scene. Mother Teresa asked John if this manifestation were the result of his prayer, and he answered simply, "I believe so."

Another happening took place which was regarded as a miracle by the nuns. One of the sisters, Doña María de Yera, fell ill. She was given every known remedy, but to no avail. Then it was decided to carry her to a larger room. As they were bearing her forth on a mattress, she lost consciousness. John was called as he was entering the enclosure with a companion. When he arrived at the side of the sick sister they said to him: "Father, look what has happened. She has died without the sacraments . . ." John said nothing, but fell on his knees and prayed. After a few moments, the nuns told him that the dead woman had returned to life. John went back to her side and smilingly said to the Infirmarian: "Well, my daughter, are you satisfied?" Then he heard Sister María's confession, gave her the sacraments, and helped her to pray and meet death.

María de Yera seemed like an angel, and after she had died, the other religious were convinced that they had witnessed a miracle.

IV

THE PRISON AT TOLEDO

(*1577–1578*)

There is much that could be said concerning the five years John spent at Avila, but these good days were numbered. A dread trial was now to strike the Reform and the person of its chief protagonist, Fray John of the Cross. For an understanding of the strange events which took place we must look into certain human —all too human—preliminaries.

During the Middle Ages, shocking disagreements between white monks and black monks—for so the Cistercians and the Cluniacs were styled because of their robes—turned into bitter quarrels; a classic example is the case of Bernard of Cluny arrayed against Peter the Venerable.

What took place with the Reform was of the same stripe. It would be folly to place the blame summarily on any one person; suffice to note that it is not surprising to find pettiness and disagreement among men.

The Fathers of the older observance who for the sake of convenience, we will call the followers of the mitigated Rule, were at first well disposed to the Reform which Teresa of Avila had initiated among the Carmelite nuns. Nor had they expressed any objection among themselves to the opening of monasteries for the Discalced. It may be recalled that Rubeo, the Prior General, had authorized only two monasteries in Spain to follow the Rule.

These two houses were Duruelo (now transferred to Mancera) and Pastrana. At the suggestion of the Prince of Eboli, Ruy Gómez, the Prior General had also agreed to the foundation of the College of Alcala at that University where, as we have seen, John of the Cross did magnificent work with the students.

The Prince of Eboli continued his efforts. In 1571 he had obtained permission for a Discalced foundation at Altomira, and in 1572, for one at La Roda. Diego de León was empowered to found another monastery in Andalucía; this was done in 1574 at Almodovar del Campo.

But, during this period, contradictory reports were being made to the Holy See, and in 1567 King Philip II secured a Brief vesting in Apostolic Visitors unlimited power in respect to the Observants and the Reformed alike. This was a power independent of even the major Superiors of Carmel. In the year following, 1568, the Prior General petitioned Rome to cancel the provisions of this Brief.

Conflicting influences were at work here. We have seen that the Apostolic Commissioners had highhandedly regulated Carmelite houses since 1569. There were two Commissioners, both of them Dominicans: one for Castile, the other for Andalucía. In Castile, we have seen how Father Pedro Fernández worked. He had acted prudently, doing nothing without first securing the cooperation of the Carmelite Provincial Prior, and we have suggested that he had his own ideas about the reform of Carmel. He had established men of the Reform in high positions in some monasteries of the Observants so that the Reform might slowly make itself felt. It is certain that he had kept the Order at peace, and it was against this peaceful background that Teresa and John of the Cross had been able to exert so healthy an influence upon the great Convent of the Incarnation at Avila.

But in Andalucía things took a different turn. There the Apostolic Commissioner was the Dominican, Francisco de Vargas, who, when faced with Carmelite opposition, acted with unprecedented authority and provoked hostilities which showed themselves very sharply indeed.

Little by little, feeling against the Reform mounted among the Observants. The less restrained of the latter hoped for the complete destruction of the Reform on the grounds that it threatened the very life of the Order. In 1547 the Spanish provinces of Castile, Aragon, Catalonia, and Andalucía united in deliberation on the whole matter with the Portuguese province. They decided that the Prior General should be advised to approach the Pope with the object of ensuring that only Carmelite priests would be appointed as Apostolic Commissioners. This, they declared, would "free the provinces of Spain from visitation by externs"; and a delegate from the meeting, Jerónimo Tostado, a man of Portuguese origin who was a Doctor of the Sorbonne, was sent to Rome to give the Prior General a personal report on the situation. On Thursday, August 3, 1570, the result of this mission became evident, for Rubeo then secured from the Pope the desired assurance of "freedom" as desired by the Spanish Carmelites. They were, henceforth, to be visited only by the Fathers of the Order. Rubeo, however, began to have new doubts inasmuch as he did not wish to come into open conflict with the Spanish Court. He did not make the Papal Brief public until May 1575 when the General Chapter was held in Piacenza.

But during the interval the Holy See informed the Nuncio to Spain, Ormaneto (a man well disposed to the Reform), that the brief had been granted, and that it would result in the nullification of the menace represented by the Dominican Commissioner Fernández de Vargas. Evidently acting in concert with the King, Ormaneto then nominated no more Visitors, but appointed the same two men as reformers and added a third, father Jerónimo Gracián, for the Province of Andalucía. It should not be forgotten that Father Gracián was one of the pillars of the Carmelite

Reform, a great friend of Teresa of Avila, and a disciple of John of the Cross.

Thus, all the plans of the Observants were brought to naught, and their anger increased. The result was an open conflict between the two jurisdictions, and it became a question as to whether the victory in Rome would lie with Rubeo as representative of the Observants or with the Nuncio, Ormaneto, who sympathized with the Reformers. Feelings were warm on both sides. Protests and denunciations rained in upon the King. Rubeo hesitated to strike at Teresa but did send her two letters asking for further details. These letters were late in arriving and by the time she was able to reply, the fat was already in the fire. Had her answers reached Rubeo earlier it is likely that matters might have taken another course. But in May of 1575 a General Chapter of the Carmelites was held at Piacenza, Italy. None of the Discalced took part in it, nor did the more understanding and less hostile among the Observant Priors, like Angel de Salazar. The silence of Teresa, which we have just explained, was taken as being indicative of rebellion. At Piacenza everything went against the Discalced. The Chapter began with the reading and promulgation of the Brief "liberating the Order from visitations by externs," of which we have already spoken. Then the Chapter proceeded to five fundamental decisions: (1) There was to be but one Visitor for Observants and Discalced alike. (2) All the Discalced Convents established under license of the Prior General were suppressed. (3) The establishment of any new convents for the Discalced, whether of men or women, was forbidden. (4) Mother Teresa was summarily ordered to select from any of her convents one to which she might retire and from which she was not to stir. (5) The secular arm was invoked that these provisions might be put into effect.

Thus the war was on. Teresa could do no more than obey. Toward the middle of 1576, Father Jerónimo Tostado arrived in Spain as Visitor of the Order.

In the normal course of events, he had to present the King and the Nuncio with his credentials, and it was then that the conflict of jurisdiction became evident. Neither King nor Nuncio would acknowledge the authority of Tostado. The Nuncio actually confirmed Jerónimo Gracián as special Prior Provincial for the Discalced; and Tostado, being driven out of Spain, proceeded to Portugal to begin his visitation there. Teresa could write to the Priory at Seville: "God has delivered us from Tostado."

THE STORM BREAKS

What were the Discalced Carmelites to do in the face of all these contradictions? Out of obedience they would tend to submit to the Piacenza decrees. They held a Chapter at the Convent of San Pablo de la Moralija and respectfully scrutinized the decrees. But then Jerónimo Gracián was told by the Nuncio to carry out his duties as Visitor—among Observants as well as among the Discalced—and this order was given under threat of excommunication. Much disturbed, on Friday, August 3, 1576 he convoked a meeting of the Discalced at Almodovar, one of the monasteries in Andalucía which Piacenza had marked for suppression. This meeting opened in September. Here were assembled the nine Superiors of the reformed houses: Mancera, Pastrama, Alcala, Altomira, Granada, La Penuela, La Roda, Sevilla, and Almodovar. Out of deference to the first of the Discalced Carmelites, John of the Cross was also invited, although he was merely the Chaplain of the Convent of the Incarnation at Avila. The Chair at the meeting was taken by Jerónimo Gracián in his appointed capacity by the Nuncio as Provincial Superior. They began by discussing the *Reformed Constitutions,* as drawn up by Gracián—which was in accord with the practice established by John of the Cross at Duruelo. The main point at issue bore upon the relative places of the *active* life and the *contemplative* life. In the assembly there were two parties. One favored developing the active life, termed by them "the apostolic life." Among such may be named Jerónimo Gracián himself, and also Fray Antonio de Jesús, who always thought the title of "the first Discalced Carmelite" pertained to him rather than to John of the Cross. The other party maintained that the whole point of the reform lay in emphasizing the contemplative life and in reducing the active life to the bare minimum.

Naturally, John of the Cross agreed with the latter party. He was instrumental in bringing about the following decisions: (1) Only preaching and absolutely necessary ministerial work would justify leaving the monasteries. (2) Any such external ministration and conduct of public worship should be within limits which would not infringe upon the contemplative life in any way.

But the Discalced were not able to confine themselves to the settlement of their own affairs. In order to meet the danger from the Observants, they determined to send two of their number to Rome in order to arrange for the separation of the Discalced from the Observants as being the only means of preserving the Reform which they had begun. On the other hand it was decided that Fray John of the Cross should cease to officiate at the Convent of the Incarnation at Avila to prevent any further offense to the Observants, for regrettable incidents had already taken place there. Actually, in the beginning of 1576, Father Valdemoro, Prior of the Carmel of Avila, had not scrupled to seize John of the Cross and his companions by force, and to take them from their residence and send them as prisoners to Medina del Campo. But this did not last long. The civic authorities of Avila complained to the Nuncio, and Ormaneto immediately commanded the Observants, under penalty of excommunication, to restore John of the Cross and his companion to their own place. At the same time he forbade any Observant Father so much as to enter the Incarnation Convent, even for the purpose of saying Mass. Such an incident shows how things stood at Avila: The city was split into two camps, the majority of the citizens favoring the Discalced, while a vociferous minority took the part of the Observants. All of this helps one to understand the drama which is about to unfold.

John of the Cross was not responsible for any of this. He did not hesitate to give up his chaplaincy at the Convent of the Incarnation, and it is indeed likely that it was he who requested the Chapter of Almodovar to send him elsewhere. As a matter of fact, he was named to be Prior of Mancera; but, unfortunatly, the nomination came too late.

THE CATASTROPHE

Before accepting the position of Prior, John had to inform the Nuncio (by whose order he had been released from prison in January 1576). It seems that the Nuncio would not agree to his relinquishing the office he had filled to the spiritual comfort of so many of the sisters at Avila. Perhaps, too, some of them may have taken steps to keep him there. In any case John returned to Avila and continued to occupy his chaplain's house near the convent, where a fellow Discalced Carmelite, Fray Germán de San Mathias, lived with him. The Observants chafed at their own powerlessness, but the meeting of the Discalced at Almodovar appeared to them to have been an act of defiance; and, in any event, the continued presence of John of the Cross at the Convent of the Incarnation as well as the admiration which the nuns there manifested toward him became more and more unendurable in their eyes.

Matters might have remained in a state of check to both sides save for an unforeseen happening. Tuesday, June 18, 1577, the Nuncio, Ormaneto, died. He had been the great friend of the Reform and had energetically defended the Discalced against their opponents. When the Observants learned of his death they sensed victory and exerted influence at Rome in order that the new Nuncio might be one well disposed to themselves. As a matter of fact, the successor of Ormaneto to Madrid was destined to be Monsignor Sega. His policy was the reverse of everything that his predecessor had done.

John of the Cross had a clear presentiment of what was to

happen in his own regard: He told a distinguished member of the community at the Convent of the Incarnation Sister Ana María, that the storm was about to burst upon his head. This was indeed so apparent in the city that it was common talk, and some gentlemen favorably disposed to John took turns, for several nights, standing guard over his house.

THE ARREST

Some documents state that the beginning of the tragedy took place on December 4, but inasmuch as Teresa had already written to the King on the fourth in order to beg his aid, it seems clear that the date of John's arrest must be set some days earlier. On the night of Monday, December 2, then, Fray John and his companion were asleep in their house. Suddenly there arose a frightful tumult which could be heard even in the sisters' convent. No one knew what was going on. Some of the Observants, accompanied by lay people and armed men, broke in the door of the Chaplain's house, noisily entered and, seizing Fray John of the Cross and Fray Germán de San Mathias, fastened manacles on their hands and hastily dragged them past the city wall in the direction of the Carmel. They said they were acting in the name of Father Tostado, Vicar General of the Order. One of them was the Prior of the Observants of the Carmel of Toledo, Father Maldonado—a name to bear in mind. He came, he said, to give absolution, on behalf of Father Tostado, to the sisters of the Convent of the Incarnation who had committed the "crime" of electing Mother Teresa as Prioress. Actually, it seems that he was really there to effect the arrest of the two Discalced Carmelites who had acted as confessors to the nuns.

John of the Cross offered no resistance. Witnesses tell us that he behaved "like a lamb." When he was told that all was being done on the orders of Father Tostado, he answered merely: "Very good; let us go!"

The most deplorable thing about the whole affair is the manner in which the prisoners were treated at the Carmel. Maldonado had them whipped on two occasions. It seems that every effort was made to induce John of the Cross to give up the Reform. But here his persecutors were up against a stone wall. Fray John knew his rights. Nothing could move him, least of all harsh treatment. He took the whole affair as a magnificent occasion to offer thanks to God for having sent him into the "night" of which he was to speak at length in future writings. It was this "night" which would most surely lead to the dawn and the divine sunlight.

On the second day of their captivity, John of the Cross took advantage of the carelessness of his captors to return, secretly, to the Chaplain's residence where he destroyed any papers he thought might prove compromising to the adherents of the Reform. No doubt these included letters from Mother Teresa and similar documents. When the Observants noted his absence, they hurried to the Chaplain's quarters and pounded on the door. From within John called out: "Yes, yes; I will be there at once!" And, having finished destroying the papers, he opened the door to them.

The Observants were outraged by this occurrence and it was undoubtedly then that they decided to retain the two captives in custody. Fray Germán de San Mathias was sent under a strong escort to the Monastery of San Pablo of Moralija, from which he was soon to escape. But Fray John was treated more severely. The redoubtable Prior Maldonado took him to Toledo to confront him with Tostado.

THE JOURNEY

It seems that John's enemies were concerned about possible efforts to help him; nor they had not forgotten what had happened at his first arrest. Surely, Mother Teresa would move heaven and earth to obtain his liberty. And every one knew that, as the saying goes, "she had a long arm." Actually, as we mentioned earlier, she had written to the King, on December 4, these terrible words: "I would rather know that he had been taken by the Moors." She knew how frail his health was, and knew that ill-treatment might kill him.

It was, no doubt, in fear of her intervention that Maldonado ordered that his prisoner be taken to Toledo by back roads and many detours. While the Convent of the Incarnation lamented, Mother Teresa, in her Convent of St. Joseph at Avila, was on the alert for the latest news she could get of Fray John of the Cross. The captive who had been blindfolded and put on a mule was being led through the night over unfrequented roads. Even now it is not known exactly what route was followed. It is believed, however, that the whole journey was made over solitary byways, avoiding even villages. The weather was typical of the season, being marked by snow and ice. On his arrival at Toledo, about the middle of December 1577, the prisoner was led still blindfolded down narrow back streets to the Carmel there.

According to the older biographers, John of the Cross had, it seems, one chance to escape. He was ill-treated all during the journey, probably more often by harsh words than overt acts, but he never answered back. The gentleness and goodness so characteristic of John had an effect on the young man who led the mule. During a stop at an inn, the youth told the innkeeper what he knew of the situation. The two took pity on the unknown prisoner and decided to help him. Secretly, they suggested to John that they take him to the mountains and hide him in a place from which he could easily reach some refuge of his own selection. Fray John refused, but thanked them for their kindness. He was unwilling to endanger others and was determined to entrust himself to God's hands, to be led by Him.

THE TRIAL

The poor friar, already thin and enfeebled by mortification, was almost worn out by the wearisome journey undertaken during the worst season of the year. The bruises from the double whipping he had suffered at Avila were still painful. His own habit had been forcibly taken from him and he was clad in the fine cloth of the Observants. He must have made a sorry sight when he appeared before the Visitor General of his Order, Fray Jerónimo Tostado. Besides this presiding officer the tribunal included Father Maldonado (who had accomplished his mission of bringing Fray John to trial) and several other leading figures in the Community.

First of all, the accused heard the reading of the decisions which had been taken during the General Chapter at Piacenza. We know their over-all import, but in the summary already given there is no indication of how hostile in tone they were to the Reform. As the text puts it: "Inasmuch as certain disobedient, rebellious, and contumacious members, commonly called the Discalced, have, in violation of letters and statues of the Prior General, lived and are living without the Province of Old Castile, at Granada, at Seville, and near the village called La Penuela, and since they have refused due acceptance to the orders and letters of the Prior General, alleging in their excuse lies, fabrications, and subterfuges, punishment is to be meted out to these said Discalced Carmelites, under penalty of Apostolic censure; and the aid, should it be necessary, of the secular arm is invoked . . ."

The delinquents were allowed only three days to submit. The Apostolic Visitor who presided over the tribunal insisted on this point. Here he was not manifesting his own arbitrary will, for he himself was bound to obey the General Chapter.

What was Fray John to say? Could he admit the charge of being a "rebel"? There was only one answer: What had just been said had no application to him. It concerned only the Discalced of Andalucía. They were formally described as being outside of Old Castile. Were he accused of having lived away from the authorized monasteries of the Reformed Fathers, he could reply that it was only obedience that had brought him to the chaplaincy at the Convent of the Incarnation. He had, after all, been appointed there by the Nuncio, Ormaneto, and the Apostolic Visitor, Fray Pedro Fernández. Moreover, the King's Council had refused to recognize the authority of Tostado. Had the death of Ormaneto in any way altered this refusal?

We do not know exactly what Fray John replied to this tribunal. What is certain is that he did not yield an inch in defense of his rights, and that he was steadfast in his resolution to support the work of the reform of Carmel. It was in vain that they sought to force him to change; neither threats nor promises did any good. Nevertheless, the attempt was not abandoned. If we may trust our sources, there were further efforts made to influence and mislead him, even after the fruitless appearance befor the tribunal. The most childish offers were made to him. One brother, among the most outstanding in the house, came to whisper in his ear that John would be given a comfortable cell and a library; another told him of a fine golden cross which might be his; and a third announced that he would be raised to the rank of Prior. We who know Fray John realize how mean and unworthy all this would seem to him. As far as the threats were concerned, he simply said that they would be ineffective, even were his life at stake; to those who tempted him with gold he replied, according to Ana de San Alberto: "He who seeks Christ stripped of all things has no need of gold or jewels!"

CONFIRMED IN HIS ERROR!

The court was now ready to pronounce sentence. This had been delayed as long as possible, but the time had now come. Fray John of the Cross was declared to be "rebellious and contumacious," in other words, confirmed in his error. The Constitutions provided that such an offense was punishable by commitment to the monastic prison at the pleasure of the Prior General. In this particular case, however, no reference had to be made to that Official, for the Visitor, Tostado, had been delegated plenipotentiary power.

Fray John was accordingly sentenced to monastic imprisonment, a sentence relatively bearable. But when it was learned
that at the end of two months his companion, Fray Germán de
San Mathias, had escaped from the convent where he had been
confined, a special sort of prison was prepared for John at
Toledo. It was within the monastery in a narrow, unlighted room,
airless and foul, like a tomb. It was about six and a half feet
wide and about ten feet long. A transom of approximately nine
inches opened on a corridor and admitted a meager amount of
light. The place had served as a storeroom attached to a nearby
chamber used by transient guests. A plank was laid on the floor,
with two worn blankets. This was the prisoner's bed. Despite the
wintry cold, Fray John was deprived of his scapular and cape.
Nothing was left to him but his Breviary.

The winter season was hard to bear at Toledo. A few years
earlier, Mother Teresa had experienced it. Fray John was sorely
afflicted by the cold. The flesh of his toes became frostbitten and
the cold penetrated to his very bones.

When summer came he was still there; and then his punishment was of another sort, but not less dreadful—stifling heat,
infectious smells—breathing became all but impossible, and the
closeness was overwhelming. Fray John was destined to spend
nine months in this prison. Yet it was to be the most fruitful
period of his life; he came face to face with God during this
superhuman trial. How his heart sang, even though his body
suffered excruciatingly!

Fray John suffered from hunger. They gave him only some
bread and one sardine. His jailer, who was, of course, a Carmelite lay brother, sometimes took pity on him and brought scraps
from the meals of the Community. But there were days when
the smell of the food offered could only be described as flavored
with death.

Bodily ill-treatment was not John's sole affliction. Everything
possible was done to harass him. Voices in an adjoining room
were raised in insults and rumors against the Discalced Fathers—

they were pigheaded; they were in open revolt; Monsignor Sega, the new Nuncio, knew of this and had decided to repress the so-called Reform; the Visitor, Tostado, had already closed down the Discalced monasteries.

Sometimes the harassment hit even closer to home: "Why do we guard this man?" someone would cry. "Let him disappear; no one will ever know the difference!—Even if he ever leaves here at all, it will only be to go to the cemetery . . ."

No wonder when his food smelled strange, Fray John wondered if he were being poisoned.

Mother Teresa had good reason indeed to exclaim: "I would rather know that he had been taken by the Moors."

Three times each week, on Mondays, Wednesdays, and Fridays, he was made to fast, being given only bread and water. These were also the only days on which he was taken from his prison. He was led to the Community Refectory. While the brethren sat eating their meal, he knelt and picked at his dry bread. At the end of the repast the Prior would launch into an indictment of the rebel, who listened in silence and without losing his interior peace, while he heard the serious charge of obstinacy being brought against him. Of what was he accused? Of being a hypocrite; of having wished to go barefoot and clad in coarse homespun so that he might be venerated as a saint; of having sown revolt in the Order.

And the Prior would conclude: "Who is to blame for all this? It is none other than a wretched little friar who has plunged all of us into trouble and disunity!"

Each Wednesday, at the end of this denunciation, the "contumacious" monk was made to bare his shoulders and all the brethren addressed themselves to the administration of what was known as "the circulating discipline." The Community formed a circle around him while he remained on his knees, with his body bent forward. Then, as each of the religious went by him, he was dealt a stroke of the discipline. The brethren were supposed to strike hard so that the blows might be heard. This punishment lasted the time it took to recite the Vulgate Psalm 50, *Miserere mei, Deus*. John's shoulders would redden with blood. Many years afterwards, Fray John still suffered from the blows he had received there.

Certainly, not all the religious of this monastery had the hearts of tyrants. Although the Prior, Father Maldonado, was responsible for carrying out the sentence against the "contumacious" culprit, there were others, especially among the younger monks, who were moved at the sight of so much suffering borne always with gentleness and courage. Some of them even whispered to each other: "He is a saint, say what they will about him."

Moreover, among the religious living at the Toledo monastery, there were some who had known Fray John when he was still called John of St. Matthias.

This acquaintance with him stemmed from his days at Salamanca. Many of the brethren had been among his fellow students. They recalled his scholarly successes and the title he had been given as *magister studentium*—prefect of students. The Superiors might bring accusations against him and say horrible things about him, but these men could neither forget his gifts nor his goodness. A mere nine years had gone by since his days at Salamanca, and they saw in him the selfsame brother he had ever been, lowly, simple, and courageous. They would not have been Spaniards if this unconquered strength had not stirred their hearts.

But the Carmelite *Constitutions* regarded with great severity any favor shown to a prisoner. The least indulgence in this regard was enough to deprive the sympathizer of his place in the Community; he would be reduced to the lowest status and would lose his vote at Chapter meetings.

This is why none dared raise the slightest objection to the treatment being meted out to Fray John. He himself would not have asked it of anyone. As I have said, his heart sang in the midst of his terrible suffering. This was his night, the night he did not ask for; the night God had chosen to give him. He had resolved to draw all the profit he could from this night for so long a time as God would allow it to endure.

He had no knowledge, of course, of the many attempts being made on his behalf, by Mother Teresa. In any event, they were quite fruitless. All the other Discalced Religious who, like John, had been imprisoned for a while had, on the other hand, been speedily set free—Fray Antonio de Jesús, Fray Gracián, Fray Ambrosio, and many others. Fray John alone was forgotten. He had been so well hidden that, even if it had been suspected that he was at Toledo, no definite knowledge could have been had of it. The Discalced nuns of Toledo sought to find his whereabouts through their own chaplain, an Observant who was devoted to them. He tried, but the silence was absolute and no one would break it. John had truly been consigned to oblivion.

A SLIGHT CHANGE

After six months, however, there came about a change in the regimen of John's life which was rather favorable to him. Another jailer had arrived from Valladolid. A young man who entertained no prejudgement of John, he inclined to mercy rather than to strictness. He deserves to be remembered—his name was Fray Juan de Santa María. One Wednesday he even dared fail to take John to the refectory to receive the "circulating discipline." We do not know what reason he gave for this failure. Perhaps it was because of John's state of health, or it may have been due only to forgetfulness on his own part. In any case, he was much surprised when John reproached him in friendly fashion by saying: "Father, why have you deprived me of what I deserve?" The jailer was disturbed and astonished, and began to understand the saintliness of his prisoner.

Shortly afterwards, he brought him a clean tunic to replace the garment hanging in shreds on John's poor body. Perhaps he asked, too, if he wanted any small thing. Or, better still, he inspired, perhaps, such confidence in John that he felt free to request some paper and ink to write down his thoughts and thereby nourish his devotion. However it happened, the young jailer must have consented because Fray John was able to put to good use those fleeting moments when light crept through the cell's narrow transom. Thus he was able to write down the poetic words that never ceased to well up within his heart, even in the midst of bitter trials.

How great is the contrast between this outward wretchedness and this inner joy, between the unbearable "night" and the glorious light. How can we look at the writings which have come down to us and which we can take up to read and reread, to meditate upon wonderingly, to absorb within our very lives, without giving thought to when and where they were written? Do they not represent the triumph of spirit over matter, of faith over mere feeling, even over reason itself? What can be of importance among God's creatures in the eyes of the man who envisions so personally the One Whom he styles his "Beloved?"

We know that John, kneeling in his fetid cell, wrote the major part of his wonderful poem the *Spiritual Canticle,* the commentary upon which was to be dedicated, six years later, to Sister Ana de Jesús. Here, too, we find what are often called John's "romantic verses," his short poems about the Creation and the Incarnation, of the Word, the poem *Super flumina Babylonis,* and the stanzas which are to be gathered from the *Dark Night.*

Certainly there are traces of distress in these verses; but they are chiefly hymns to the beauty of creation, a beauty which is, in John's eyes, a reflection of the beauty of the Word.

"Whither hast vanished,
  Beloved, and hast left me full of woe,
  And like the hart hast sped,
  Wounding, ere thou didst go,
  Thy love, who follow'd, crying, high and low? . . .

"I'll seek my love straightway

Over yon hills, down where yon streamlets flow.
To pluck no flowers I'll stay;
No fear of beasts I'll know;
Past mighty men, o'er frontier-grounds I'll go.

"You forest, thicket, dene,
Which my beloved set in close array;
You meadow-land so green,
Spangled with blossoms gay,
Tell me, oh, tell me, has he pass'd your way?"

And in his ecstasy, Fray John hears Creation's answer. His prison walls do not impede its voice. How lovely are all things seen through loving eyes!

"Rare gifts he scattered
As through these woods and groves he pass'd apace,
Turning, as on he sped,
And clothing every place
With loveliest reflection of his face."

John's verse ranks with the most brilliant written throughout all ages. And, let it be recalled, what we have just read was written in a dark cell, in the midst of insults, bodily wretchedness, threats, privations, and incertitude.

Father Tostado made no secret of his desire to destroy the Reform completely. And, in any event, he had no intention of releasing the man who, even while in his clutches, seemed able to resist his authority.

Everything looked bad for the Reform of Carmel. And things were even worse for the first Discalced Fathers. Perhaps John did not know what had been happening in Spain in respect to the Reform; but there was talk loud enough for him to hear of the triumph of the Observants.

Almost nine months had passed since John had been taken from Avila by force.

Now a new idea came to him, an idea which seemed, at first, unbelievable and impossible of realization; it was the thought of escaping. Two kinds of preparation were to precede the attempt.

JOHN'S PREPARATIONS

First of all, there was a spiritual preparation to be made; for Fray John wished only one thing: that God's will be done.

We might almost think that we are able to hear him cry out in prayer: "My God, as You will; all that You will; only what You will!

"If I am destined to die here, then *Thy will be done;* but, if you wish that I try to escape, then inspire me!"

This prayer was answered. It was sometimes later said that from this time on John enjoyed revelations, visions, and apparitions that led him to flee from his cell. But we must be distrustful of such unfounded allegations. We will later show how much John of the Cross, as a mystical theologian, remained ever hostile to a too-ready willingness to look for supernatural manifestations and to trust to them. In speaking of his escape he never made allusion to anything more than "inner impulses" sent him from God during the days prior to his departure from prison.

Besides this spiritual preparation, however, preparation of a material nature also had to be made. Fray John had previously never so much as stirred from his dungeon, except for the excursions under compulsion to the refectory. He did not know the dungeon's exact location or whether escape from it might be possible at all. He had been brought to it during the night. The only way to and from it that he knew anything about was the path he took when he was conducted to the refectory to undergo the "circulating discipline."

Fortunately his guardian was, as has been noted, quite approachable, and could be engaged in conversation. Fray John offered to help him with his tasks and suggested that he would help him clean up if only he would allow him out of his cell while the brethren were taking the siesta. The unsuspecting jailer agreed. This is how Fray John was able to explore the places surrounding his prison cell. He went as far as the great windows which looked out on the court, and to the walls of the convent beyond, which was situated near the Tajo River. During the warm season these windows were left open throughout the night. Fray John was also able to obtain a needle and some thread from his jailer, ostensibly to make some needed repairs to his habit. One day, while he was cleaning his cell, he went to the arched windows of the courtyard. Fastening a small stone to the end of a thread, he dropped the thread out the window; when the stone touched bottom, he drew the thread in again. When he returned to his dungeon, he carefully measured the length of the thread with that of his two worn blankets. End to end, the two coverlets were not quite as long as would be necessary. But, by looking out the window, Fray John had ascertained the remaining distance about five feet, which could be safely covered by letting himself drop. This made the project quite feasible. He then sewed the two blankets firmly together to make the ladder for his escape. However, greater difficulties were ahead. It was evident that he could leave only at night. And, each evening, his jailer fastened the padlock on his cell door. Fray John examined this padlock, which was held together by screws. He successfully loosened these, working at them often to enlarge the holes more and more. He did this so well that, by shaking the door strongly from within, it was possible to dislodge the padlock.

From then on all was in readiness. It was only a matter of choosing a good night—a night when the moon was as full and the sky as clear as possible. After John had made his decision to flee, he began to think of his jailer and of all the retribution the prisoner's escape might subject him. Under the pretext of thanking him for his kindnesses, John gave him a cherished treasure, a beautiful crucifix fashioned of rare wood with the Corpus and the Instruments of the Passion in bronze. He had received it from someone whom he greatly respected—perhaps it was from Mother Teresa herself—and always wore it under his scapular on the side nearest his heart. In his own mind, John was bidding him farewell; but the good young friar knew nothing of this and did not have the slightest suspicion of the truth. We know that he kept this precious remembrance of his wonderful prisoner by him all his life.

The fourteenth day of August 1578 had now come. Fray John had all but made up his mind that this would be the night of his escape. He was at prayer within his cell, his back to the door, when it swung open. John did not move. The visitor was Father Maldonado, the harsh Conventual Prior of the Carmel of Toledo, who had come to see him. The Prior kicked John as he demanded:

"Why do you not arise when I come in to see you?"

The prisoner humbly replied: "Excuse me; I thought it was the guard; and, moreover, it is with great difficulty that I rise quickly now; for I am very weak."

"Well enough; but what are you thinking of just now?"

"I am thinking that tomorrow is Our Lady's feast, and I would be very happy if I might say Mass."

"Impossible," remarked the Prior as he went out.

John had to get away. God Himself seemed to be urging his escape. Surely this life could be tolerated no longer. John resolved that, on the first occasion, he would make an attempt to escape.

John's Escape

We are now about to go with John on a path marked by trials rarely encountered except in novels. But, in this case, history is more thrilling than the most unusual fiction.

It was the Octave of the Assumption, as the time was then called, perhaps on the night of August sixteenth, although the exact date is not known to us. Fray John was ready; his two blankets were well stitched together and the lock on the cell loosened for escape. His jailer brought him supper but, since he had forgotten water, went off for it while John took advantage of his absence to tamper further with the lock while he would be

unobserved. Soon his meal was over and the door was closed. The
night was so warm that all other doors had been left open for the
sake of fresh air—it was a lovely night, lit by moon and stars.
Two visiting monks were asleep in the passage leading to John's
dungeon. For a long while they chatted quietly in the dark before
falling asleep. Fray John listened to them and held his breath,
praying earnestly and continuously. Soon all was silent. The
prisoner struck sharply at the door and the padlock fell with a
slight clatter. One of the sleepers cried out: *"Deo gratias!* What
is that? . . ."

There was no reply, and the priest went back to sleep. John,
the blankets in his hands, passed between the visitors' beds.
With him he had a heavy pipe from a candlestick to use as a
clamp to fasten the blankets to the window ledge when he let
himself down on them to the ground. At first all went well.
Through the great window, which was open, the waters of the
river could be seen glistening in the moonlight. Fray John attached the first of the blankets to the window. Then he took off
his tunic and threw it below. After this, he wrapped his legs
around the blankets and, clutching with hands and knees, he
slid down the length of cloth. When he had reached the end of
the second blanket, he jumped. Fortunately he landed on the
cloister wall, which was quite stout at this point and surrounded
by stones which were being used for current repairs. A few
steps further and he might have fallen on the rough bank of the
Tajo. The fugitive put on his robe again. He followed the wall to
a corner which opened upon a little courtyard. Before him was
the Convent of the Sisters of Our Lady's Conception. Fray John
searched the courtyard, seeking a way out. There seemed to be
none. The walls, moreover, were very high and seemed beyond
scaling. There was a door, but that led to the convent of nuns.

It was a frightening moment. He would be unable to get out
of the cloistered courtyard, and this would cause a great scandal
should he be found there the next morning! Greater, however,
would be the reprisals were he to find himself once again with his

jailers at the Carmel. What was he to do? For a moment, he was again resigned; if this was God's will, the only thing to do was to accept it courageously! He would go back, then, and, after confessing his fault, deliver himself anew to his captors. But he made one last effort. In an angle of the small court he found several holes in the wall and, supporting himself against the other side of the angle, climbed up slowly, stone by stone. Almost before he knew it, he was at the top. Fray John drew a breath of relief. He followed the run of the wall, dragging himself along, until he came to an alleyway. Then he jumped off, carefully checking that there was no one nearby to see him.

IN TOLEDO

Now he could thank God and Our Lady. So far, all was well. Yet he was not out of danger. He knew nothing about Toledo. He did not know how he might find the Convent of the Discalced Carmelites where he hoped to find a refuge for the present.

Actually, it was quite nearby; but he did not know this. He went down the alley to the street. A door opened and a light streamed out as a woman called to him: "Father, come here, and you may sleep until the morning; for they will never let you in to your monastery at this hour!" He replied only with a hasty word of thanks and continued on his way. Thus he came to the Zocodover Plaza which he found filled with merchandise in preparation for the market. The market gardeners who were sleeping alongside their stalls saw him go by and raucously insulted him in gutter terminology for as long as he was within hearing. We cannot say just where he went, but he thought he had left the Carmel far behind, and was fearful that he would be unable to enter the Convent of the Carmelite Sisters before daybreak. Just then he encountered a nobleman who was proceeding with drawn sword and attended by a servant with a lamp. Fray

John went up to him and said: "I beg of your kindness that in charity that you will allow me to pass the rest of the night on a bench in your courtyard, for I cannot gain entrance to my monastery at this time. In the morning I shall go . . ."

The nobleman grudgingly agreed and, after allowing John to enter, shut first the street door and then the door which led within the house. John was left alone in the corridor where a stone bench stood against the wall. There he stayed until daybreak. He prayed continuously; sleep would not come to him, and he was watching for the first streaks of dawn.

Finally the morning light came, but no one came to open the door for him. Soon it was eight o'clock, and he longed to be on his way. A servant, at last hearing him knocking at the door, let him out to the street. People were going by and Fray John asked someone to direct him to the Convent of the Carmelite Sisters. He was shown the way and very soon found himself before the outer gate of the nuns' Carmel. It was closed, but John called out and asked to be admitted. The sister who was stationed at the small gate, Leonora de Jesús, questioned him from behind the turning-box: "Who is it?"

"*Hija, fray Juan de la Cruz soy, que me he salido esta noche de la carcel . . .*" ("*My daughter, I am Fray John of the Cross and have this night escaped from prison. Tell this to the Mother Prioress . . .*")

Sister Leonora rushed off, and soon the Mother Prioress, Sister Ana de los Angeles, hurried out. Fray John begged her for help for, if the Fathers of the Carmel should recapture him, he would be in grave peril. Mother Ana could scarcely believe her eyes or ears; but she did not lose her self-control. It was, above all things, necessary that Fray John enter the cloister—a matter that is sternly governed by Canon Law—but the Mother Prioress recalled that a resident of the house was ill: A confessor for the sick person would have a right to enter the cloister. Mother Ana had the door opened by the sisters who kept the keys to the three locks provided by the Rule. Fray John went within, and the three locks were closed again. He was there as confessor to a dying nun, Sister Ana de la Madre de Dios.

The whole Community was astir as the nuns saw the fugitive. He was emaciated, unshaven, and clad in rags. He was scarcely able to stand upright, scarcely able to speak; he was clearly at the end of his endurance. All the evidence which we have of this circumstance indicates that he was close to death. He succeeded, nevertheless, in warning the Prioress that the Fathers of the Toledo Carmel would certainly seek him in her convent.

She understood the danger. Quickly, she assigned another nun to the turning-box in the place of the young and inexperienced sister who had received John. If anyone had come questioning her, she might have allowed fear to betray her. The Prioress put Sister Isabela de San Jerónimo in her place, an adroit and resourceful woman in her speech.

This precaution was a good one for two brethren from the Carmel did appear and discreetly enquired if Fray John of the Cross might not, by chance, be there. With a good show of astonishment, the sister answered: "It will be wonderful if you will find a priest here!" She had not lied to them. She gave them the keys of the parlor and those of the Chapel. They went to search and, although they rummaged into everything, found no one. Then they went off, silently. The police, however, had been alerted. Some prowled about St. Joseph's Monastery, which was the house of the Discalced; others went over the roads leading out of Toledo. They searched everywhere, going as far as Avila, and even to Medina del Campo.

All this while Fray Juan de Santa María, the compassionate jailer, was being punished according to the regulations of the Carmelite Constitutions. He had been given the lowest place in the community and was deprived of the right to speak or vote in Chapter meetings. Nonetheless, this did not prevent him—and some of the other brethren—from rejoicing at Fray John's escape.

SUCCESS

But all was not over. Fray John could not remain within the cloister of the nuns. He had comforted the sick sister and heard her confession. The other nuns had tried to help him regain some of his strength but, because he had been much weakened by privation, they had found it difficult to know what he would be able to eat. The Sister Infirmarian, Sister Teresa de la Concepción, had an idea: She brought him some cinnamon-flavored baked pears. He was also given somewhat better clothing, from the wardrobe of the convent chaplain. His own garment was repaired. Now it was midday, Masses were over, and the convent Church had been closed. Fray John passed through a small inner door and spent the evening in the Chapel. Some of the sisters gathered round him. Slowly and softly he recited for the sisters in the Choir on the other side of the screen some stanzas he had written in his cell. The nuns were overcome with delight. One of them took down the verses while Fray John recited them. "It was like being in Heaven to hear him," the sister said later.

> "Far away in the beginning
> Dwelt the Word in God Most High
> And in God His bliss eternal
> Had He everlastingly.
>
> That same Word was God Almighty,
> And Beginning was His name,
> For He dwelt in the beginning,
> Out of no beginning came. . . ."

The hours were speeding by on this first day of freedom, and the night would soon come. It was necessary to find a shelter for John. Fortunately, Mother Ana was resourceful and full of ideas. She secretly sent a message to Don Pedro Gonzáles de Mendoza, Canon of the Cathedral and Administrator of Holy Cross Hospital. He was a great benefactor of the house, and hurried to answer the Prioress's mysterious summons. Mother Ana told him all that had happened. The Canon unhesitatingly offered his own apartments to Fray John. He covered the Discalced Carmelite's habit with one of his own robes, called a carriage, and took John to the hospital. It was near the Alcazar, only a short way from the Convent of the Observants, on the one side, and from that of the Discalced, on the other. That very morning, Fray John had passed the hospital in his flight. From its windows he could see the arched window from which he had climbed down the night before; he could even see the little court where he had found himself so fearfully trapped. The Carmelite Fathers seeking him were far from aware that he was so close at hand. However, he was now safe from all searchers. The good Canon had his own private quarters at the hospital. He was willing to take care of John for as long as he thought his safety required. Moreover, he had enough leisure at his disposal to surround the poor prisoner with every care so that some day soon he might be sufficiently strengthened to return to a house of his own Order.

V

IN ANDALUCÍA

(*1578–1586*)

THE CHAPTER MEETING AT ALMODOVAR

At the beginning of October 1578, we find John of the Cross at the Chapter Meeting at Almodovar. What had occurred? Had he been summoned to this meeting? More than one of his modern biographers think so. Father Crisogono, whom I consider to be the best and the soundest among them, is not certain of this. It is possible that he went of his own accord.

Shut up in the quarters of Canon González de Mendoza, John would have tried to learn all that had taken place during the nine months of his imprisonment. Little by little, and probably by bribing his informants, he must have received news of the Reform that meant so much to him. He would have learned that the chief exponents of the movement had been called to meet at Almodovar to consider how to defend their cause—a cause which now appeared badly compromised. Naturally, he would want to be present at this meeting.

When he revealed his plans to Canon de Mendoza, he very likely had to override objections to his departure. No doubt the Canon greatly feared for his safety. But John, who had personally suffered so intensely on behalf of the Reform, was resolved to participate in the meeting; the Canon, seeing his resolve and knowing the reasons that formed it, agreed to his going. It is worth noting, and indicative of the Canon's nature, that two servants of the household were put in attendance to John, not only as far as Almodovar, but to his final destination. They were instructed to guard and assist him in all his needs. His stay with the Canon had been, as well as we can tell, a period of about six or seven weeks.

After his acute suffering this was certainly too brief a period to effect a complete recovery. As a matter of fact, we shall see that John of the Cross was still so weak that he was barely able to speak.

He set out for Almodovar in great secrecy. There was a monastery of the Discalced there, and two chapter meetings of the Reformed Carmelites had already been held. Chief among those assembled was Father Antonio de Jesús. Actually, the Discalced Fathers were far from being certain of what to do; they did not even know if they had the right to meet or make any decisions. Might not such actions be considered in high places as acts of rebellion? They had been deprived of their provincial Prior, Fray Jerónimo Gracián (whose powers had stemmed from the deceased Nuncio, Ormaneto), and believed they should elect a successor. It is said they sought advice from four canonists and had been told that this meeting would be legitimate. As for Mother Teresa, she was in great fear at the thought of the dangers to which they might expose themselves. She had expressed these to Father Antonio de Jesús who was, however, firm in his resolution, and who told her he would consider it sinful if he did not act as planned. Teresa abstained, but was far from reassured. She had learned of Fray John's escape and of the sorry condition in which he had come out of prison, was greatly concerned about the state of his health, and in her letters urged that he be given every care. At Almodovar John was received with great respect and the honor due one who had suffered so heroically for the cause. Fray Pedro was later to declare how deeply he had been impressed by John's goodness and gentleness and by the appreciation he showed for the smallest attention given him. Father Antonio de Jesús, who presided at the Chapter meeting, began by justifying its convocation. He pointed out to the assembly that the canonists whom he had consulted had not been unanimous but, from the very beginning, all the members of the Chapter were convinced of the legality of the proceedings. Three important decisions were reached: first, the Chapter elected a Provincial, Father Antonio de Jesús, himself; second, the decision previously arrived at, during the former meeting at Almodovar in September 1576, by which delegates were to be sent to Rome to seek the separation of Discalced Fathers from the Fathers of the Observance as the only way of guaranteeing the permanency of reform in the Order, was confirmed; and third, provision was made for Fray John of the Cross, who was designated Conventual Prior of the Discalced Monastery at Calvario in Andalucía, in the place of one of the delegates being sent to Rome.

Of these decisions, the second was a matter of the greatest delicacy, and for that reason Fray John suggested that it should be signed by all who were in attendance at the Chapter. They agreed with him; but very shortly, more than one of the signers were to regret this.

TURMOIL

The Chapter was still in session when Father Juan de Jesús Roca arrived from Madrid. The Nuncio had ordered him to go back to his own monastery at Mancera, where he was Conventual Prior. But he learned of the meeting at Almodovar and knew, too, the ill will of the Nuncio; so he thought it his duty to proceed quickly to Almodovar to warn his brethren. From the beginning, he infected them with all his own fears. He thought the Chapter meeting illegal. It was being held without the permission of the

Nuncio. Jurisdictional powers had been assumed and exercised by the election of a Provincial Prior, by the naming of delegates to Rome, and by the conferral of the office of Conventual Prior on Fray John of the Cross. What would the Nuncio say to all this? He would surely seize the opportunity to strike out with renewed vigor against the Reform movement, and they could all look forward to the most violent retaliation.

This was not the mind of Father Antonio de Jesús. He defended what he asserted to be the legitimacy of the Reform and, moreover, said he was ready to go to Madrid to appear before the Nuncio and lay before him the justification of the Chapter which had just been held; and that he would seek his approval—even his blessing—for the decisions that had been reached. The better to put an end to any more objections from Fray Roca, he directed that friar to remain at Almodovar for a month—the time it would take Father Antonio to go to Madrid to finish matters and to return, it was hoped, victorious.

When Mother Teresa was told of all this, she became more and more disturbed. She knew very well that the Nuncio could not easily be won over, that the frontiers of the kingdom were well guarded, and that it would not be possible to send delegates to Rome without Sega's knowledge and, thus, without invalidating their mission. The enemies of the Discalced had shown themselves more than capable of behaving disgracefully by the treatment meted out to John of the Cross. How, she thought, how could anyone fail to realize what a renewal of the conflict might mean?

On this matter, although not acting in concert with her, Fray John of the Cross agreed. He did not think much of the delegation to Rome. There had been hesitation in choosing the delegates and finally Father Pedro de los Angeles was named. Fray John, as though he could foresee the future, said to him: "You will go to Italy barefooted, but you will come back shod!" The facts proved this: Fray Pedro, who had been so attached to the penetential life of the Reform, did everything wrong at Rome and, in the end, made a complete reversal of his position to such an extent that he ended up by joining the Observants.

However, the officials of the Chapter of Almodovar, under the guidance of Father Antonio de Jesús whom they had elected Provincial Prior, boldly went to Madrid and sought an audience with Monsignor Sega, the Nuncio. This turned out to be a mistake: The Nuncio flew into a rage at their very first words. He would not even allow them to set forth their position, and rained upon them unrestrained abuse, not only in their own regard, but also in respect to Mother Teresa herself and all the Discalced. He branded all that had been done at Almodovar as open defiance of his own authority and jurisdiction. He delivered everyone of the Discalced into the hands of the Observants, and sentenced to monastic imprisonment the leaders of the Reform who had dared to approach him. Father Antonio de Jesús and Father Gabriel de la Asunción were shut up in the monastery of St. Bernardino at Madrid, Fray Mariano was confined in that of the Dominicans at Atocha, Fray Gregorio de Nazianzo in one at Seville; and, finally, everyone—including, undoubtedly, Fray John of the Cross—who had had any part in the Chapter of Almodovar, was excommunicated.

ON THE WAY TO ANDALUCÍA

Did Fray John know of the censure which now rested upon him? It seemed that he did. He had not actually remained at Almodovar to await the outcome of the expedition to Madrid. Having been designated as Prior of Calvario in Andalucía, he had gone off at great speed to take possession of his new post. Moreover, he could not indefinitely detain the servants of Canon de Mendoza who accompanied him. But, in the last analysis, it seemed that the farther he got from Toledo, the safer he would be.

He resumed his journey in the company of Father Francisco de la Concepción, Prior of the Discalced Monastery at La Penuela, and of the Canon's servants, who were both impressed by the goodness John manifested along the way of the journey.

They traveled through the remaining part of La Mancha, along rough roads that took them over mountains and through valleys and woods. It was a region abounding in rosemary and arbutus, and where the scenery and terrain resembled the brushwood of Provence or Corsica.

Their first stop was at La Penuela; here they left Father Francisco. Then, after a long and tedious journey through mountainous country, they arrived at Beas in Segura.

AT BEAS

Here John of the Cross came to the convent which was to be so dear to him. It was a house of Reformed Carmelite nuns having as its Prioress one of Mother Teresa's most dedicated daughters, Ana de Jesús. Later, at the beginning of the next century, she was to be responsible for the introduction of the Carmelite Reform into France and Flanders. Ana de Jesús already knew Fray John of the Cross; she had met him at the Convent of the Incarnation at Avila where he had been the Confessor. However, it had been several years since she had seen him. He was greatly changed—pale and emaciated, he was hardly more than skin and bones. She could scarcely hear the words he spoke with such effort.

As a true Carmelite, Ana de Jesús wanted to give him some joy and solace, and arranged to have two of the younger sisters sing a hymn for him while he was in the convent parlor.

As he came in and took a place before the grille, the two fresh and pleasant voices began to sing for him, to the tune of some then popular air, these verses by an unknown author:

"Who ne'er had met with pain,
  Within this vale of tears,
  Knows naught of higher joy,

Knows naught, indeed, of love;
For on Pain's path are form'd the hearts of lovers!"

These words caused John to react very emotionally. He was still quite weak, and the feeling that gripped him was too much for his shattered nerves. He clutched the grille and made a sign that the singing should stop. Tears glistened in his eyes. It seemed as if he would speak and all waited to hear what he would say. But no words could pass his quivering lips as he hung by both hands to the grille. The sisters gazed silently at him. This charged atmosphere lasted for an hour, an hour of high prayer during which the saint was unable to say a word. Finally, and gradually, he came to himself. When he spoke, it was of the worth of suffering, of all that it teaches the soul willing to learn from it. He told them of how Our Lord had made him understand how much He values it and how slight is all we can do for Him in thanksgiving for all His goodness in comparison to suffering resignedly for His sake. The sisters were full of wonder and enthusiasm.

They kept an unforgettable recollection of this conference: Here was a man who had undergone so much, who showed so obviously the marks of the cruelest kind of suffering, and who, nevertheless, spoke to them always of the Cross, who extolled the Cross to them, and who went so far as to regret that he had not suffered more.

It may be assumed that at the urgings of the Prioress of Beas John agreed to spend some days at the convent. This meant that there would be further conferences in the parlor and that John would hear the confessions of those sisters who might wish to come to him.

We have a curious little detail about those conferences in the parlor. It was always difficult for John to speak, and his words came forth but rarely, and then only with effort. Mother Ana de Jesús observing him to be so gaunt and weak, could not understand how he could speak of her Superior, Mother Teresa, as "his very own daughter"—*Muy su hija*. She was even somewhat scandalized, and spoke of his sermon to her nuns in this manner: "Fray John is a very good man, indeed; but he is far too young to be speaking of our Mother Foundress as 'his daughter.'" She wrote of all this to Mother Teresa, bewailing, in the same letter, that her daughters at Beas lacked a good spiritual director to whom they might speak of their souls' needs.

Mother Teresa replied at once, and read her a lesson in these words:

"I was glad to receive your letter, my daughter, in which you foolishly bewail the fact that my father, John of the Cross, is with you. He is a man of heaven, a true Man of God, and I must tell you, my daughter, that since he left here I have not been able to find his like in all Castile: there is none other who walks the heavenly way in comparable fervor. You cannot know how much his absence costs me. Realize that you have a great treasure in this holy man, and that everyone in your convent ought to open her heart to him. Then will each one see how much progress she will make, how much she will grow in the Spirit and in perfection, because of the special grace to this end given him by Our Lord.

"I declare to you that I would be glad were my father, Fray John of the Cross, here; for he is verily the father of my soul and is marked by the greatest skill in spiritual dealings. Let all my daughters approach him in singleness of heart, for I can assure you they will be in his hands as they would be in mine, and that they will receive great comfort. He is highly spiritual, and is great in experience and in doctrine. . . . Be thankful to God who has willed that you have him with you . . ."

Could Teresa have spoken with more conviction or with greater respect and confidence?

Mother Ana de Jesús took her at her word, and never had reason to regret it. Far be it from her to have done otherwise.

However, one of her nuns was ahead of her, as we know, in enjoying the happiness of learning how rich was the mystical doctrine of which John of the Cross served as the channel. The first religious who came to his confessional at Beas was called Magdalena del Espíritu Santo.

Many years afterwards, thinking back on this first meeting of souls in the confessional at Beas, she said: "It filled my soul with a great light which brought me comfort and peace."

Father Crisogono, whose account I am following carefully, notes that "We do not know how many of the nuns thus came to him for confession; but, inasmuch as Mother Magdalena says that she was the first, it seems that we may take it that she was not the only one."

Actually, this first stay of John at Beas should be thought of as no more than a foretaste of what was to be. No other monastery proved dearer to him.

AT CALVARIO

Fray John had not forgotten that his destination was the Monastery at Calvario, of which he had been named Conventual Prior. No doubt, he thought he could now release Canon de Mendoza's servants, who stood in such admiration of him; we do not know, therefore, who went with him over the winding and difficult paths which lead from Beas to Calvario. At each turning, the countryside presented a new aspect; to the north, all seemed bare and arid, while southward it was verdant with leafy trees heavy with fruit. There were many climbs and descents to be negotiated on the way, but this journey was the first of many he would make from Beas to Calvario during the years he acted as spiritual director to the nuns at the convent in Beas. About fifteen hundred yards from the Guadalquivir River was the monastery of Calvario. This had formerly been a farmhouse, but now a chapel was attached to it. Behind the house there was a small garden, some plots of land under cultivation, and a modest vineyard. Here and there bloomed figs, oranges, plums, and cherry trees. It was also reputed to be an area rich in game and fish. Small brooks wended their way to the source of the Guadalquivir. In the nearby mountains there were pine trees, cork oaks (the *Quercus suber,* which abounds in Spain and Portugal), roburs, and rosemary shrubs, which remained flowering until December. All was bright, glowing, and fragrant in this delightful countryside.

What, we might ask, did the theologian of "the night of the senses" and the "night of the soul" think when he saw all this? What would this convinced teacher of the *Nada*—nothingness—say?

His first reactions must have elicited feelings of real joy. Here, hard on the heels of the horrors of the Toledo prison cell, he found himself surrounded by the beauty of God's creation. Yet as Prior he would have to practice and exemplify to his religious subordinates that renunciation and penance which the human flesh so greatly fears—and which is so easily tempted. Actually, the monastery was attractive to those devoted to solitude, and long hours were passed at prayer. The Community had about thirty members, all wanting to lead lives of penance. They were aware of the difficulties which had marked the opening of their monastery which was now but five years old. They knew, too, the meaning of actual privation and poverty. More than once, they had been on the verge of starvation.

No, John of the Cross had little need to preach mortification to these friars; on the contrary, he had to curb their penitential excesses. But, as always, he gave an example of total scorn for material things to his brethren, whether in the matter of meals or in that of living accommodations.

The usual meal of the monks at Calvario consisted of bits of bread dipped, in the Andalusian fashion, into cooked herbs. The cook followed an original means of determining which herbs to feed to the brethren—everything that the monastery ass would eat could be given safely to human beings, he said, for it was then certain to be not poisonous. However, the herbs he selected were often so bitter that after the first cooking they had to be mashed on a board and recooked before being served.

They did not always have enough food, and the Community was, on more than one occasion, to be highly edified by some unusual happenings. One day there was no bread and, when the bell summoned the brethren to the Refectory, they found the tables bare. Fray John quietly ordered a further search to be made. A dry crust was found and placed before him. John then pronounced the usual grace before meals and told the brethren to thank the Lord for their penury, which allowed them to share Christ's own poverty. When he had finished, the monks arose from the table without having eaten and returned to their work in their cells. Somewhat later, the porter, Fray Brocardo de San Pedro, came to the Prior with a letter which had just been delivered. Fray John read it and began to weep. The porter thought that it contained bad news of either John's family or of some one of the other houses of their Order. He asked the Prior the reason for his distress. "My brother," replied John of the Cross, "I weep because the Lord takes us for such cowards that he thinks we can no longer bear to fast: this letter informs me of a shipment of baked bread and another of flour which are coming to us."

Actually, the promised gifts arrived shortly; but this was not all. That same evening, the servant of Doña Felipa and Don Andres Ortega, parents of one of the future members of the Community, came to the monastery. Although this family had known nothing at all of the penury which gripped the monastery, they had sent to Calvario two carts filled with food.

Ten days afterwards Cristobal de la Higuera, a great admirer of John and a benefactor of the Community, came, as he often did, to consult the Prior. It was already quite late and John of the Cross ordered that supper be served the guest. While the latter was at the table, the lay brother who was waiting upon him cried out: "Eat, my Lord, of what remains of the miracle wrought by our Father, John of the Cross." He then related the recent events, expressing the reverent feelings of the whole house, which was grateful for these timely gifts of Providence.

Spiritual Life at Calvario

All this concerns only the material aspects of life at Calvario. What progress was being made in spiritual matters? I have already noted that life existed there within a munificent setting. Would John of the Cross close his friars up in their cells and order them to shut their eyes to the splendors surrounding them? In his writings, one might be tempted to think that such would be his course; but on the contrary, he was an enthusiastic and appreciative viewer. It was his wish that none of this be lost by either his religious or himself. He freely encouraged his Community to share in the beauties of creation and, more than once, expressed the wish that the time of their prayer be passed in its midst. At other times he would put everyone to work in the gardens or on the monastery lands, as the season might require.

"When they went out to prayer," writes Father Crisogono "Fray John, instead of reading the points for meditation from some book, would sit among his brethren on a hilltop and speak to them of the wonders of God's creation upon which they were feasting their eyes. He would tell them of nature's beauties as being a reflection of the divine Beauty making itself thus felt in flowers and in the crystal waters which flowed around their feet, in the birds' chirping among the trees, and in the sunlight in which everything was bathed. . . . Soon they spread themselves over the mountainside so that, hidden among the masses of stone, sitting near a stream or on a pile of rocks, they might give themselves up to meditation . . ."

These details are not mere fancies; they are based on authentic manuscript evidence.

All their work was sanctified in the same way as their prayer, which, indeed, it prolonged. Their sole rule was to see God in all things and to do His will. Any deviation from obedience was severely punished, as an example will show.

One day a friar who was gathering plums said to his partner: "Would you like to eat one of these?"

"Oh no, my brother; for the devil is now lurking within that plum."

On yet another occasion, a friar, Father Luis de San Jerónimo, yielded to temptation while plucking cherries and ate one. He soon felt bowed with remorse. The cherry seemed to have stuck in his throat. When evening came the friar could hold himself back no longer. After the Community's frugal supper he rose from the table in the Refectory and in the hearing of all accused himself of his fault as though it were a major crime. The Prior agreed with this view of it:

"This," he said, "is an unheard of thing. It causes great scandal in our Community. Never have we known acts of gluttony and disobedience! . . ."

And he ordered the culprit punished, though we are not told how.

Nevertheless, the Father Prior did not look with full disfavor on concession to the natural desire of his friars for some comfort and distraction. During the time allotted to work, everyone was expected to do his best, whether it was in sowing, harvesting, gathering fruit, or marketing. But there were days of relaxation. Fray John allowed lay friends of their monastery to visit with the friars on feast days and to bring them sweetmeats for the occasion. John, however, was an abstainer from such things, but would encourage the others to partake of them. The most frequent visitors were Cristobal de la Higuera, Juan de Cuellar, and Diego Navarro. They have left us their recollections of this chapter in John's life. Cristobal de la Higuera often saw John doing the dishes in an earthenware basin. He states that John was always the first in his Community to take upon himself the lowest and meanest tasks.

The three friends loved talking with him, although they sometimes found themselves greatly surprised.

During the conversation, a time would come when Fray John

of the Cross would show evidence of inattention and preoccupation by seeming, as it were, to turn inward. His friends were understanding: Conversation would be suspended, they would step back a bit, and, after respectfully removing their hats, would leave the saint to pursue his own conversation with God. At other times, John would smilingly tell them of his sufferings in prison at Toledo. He would never blame anyone nor bewail what had happened to him. On the contrary, he would declare that he had wished to suffer even more to atone for his faults against God's will.

This was John of the Cross the Prior of Calvario, surrounded by his friends. There was nothing repelling in his austerity; he was never constrained. Penitence is worthy only to the extent that it is an expression of love. Faith and love alone matter; external things are valuable only because of the faith and love in which they are rooted.

We will see this also in John's work with the nuns at the convent in Beas.

SATURDAYS AT BEAS

We will recall the early complaints voiced by Sister Ana de Jesús Prioress of the Carmelite convent at Beas, and the reply made by Mother Teresa. Fray John was now requested to assume charge of the spiritual affairs of this convent. He accepted at once and, every Saturday, either alone or with one of his brethren, made the long journey from Calvario to Beas. Half the way was a descent; the other half, a climb; and there were, naturally, numerous detours around the mountain. At the convent of Beas John undertook his duties in a way which distinguished him from his predecessor. That man had confined himself to hearing confessions. Within half an hour he had scampered, so to speak, through all he had had to do. There had been no attempt to offer spiritual direction; he had merely listened to the recitation of faults, no doubt always of the same trifling nature. But John

of the Cross knew what the true Carmelite spirit demands: No
one was there for anything less than the achievement of perfection, that is to say, that the soul might become one with God.
This requires a well-grounded spirituality, and John of the Cross
was already a master in the science of Mystical Theology. He had
complete command of it, having attained even a deepened mastery, based on his own personal experience as well as that of the
sublime mysticism of Teresa of Avila, of whom he justly did not
fear to style himself the "father."

Teresa's letter to Sister Ana de Jesús made this quite clear
when she urged the nuns of Beas to open their souls freely to
such a master as John. They were to do this in all earnestness
and directness. And he would supply just what was most needed
in every case. He would never be hurried. He would show no
preference for one religious over another: Each one might feel
that he had come there to direct her personally. He did not
spend merely Saturdays at Beas but remained there on Sundays,
as well, not returning to Calvario before Monday morning. This
allowed for the full celebration of the liturgy. To the advice
John gave to individuals in the confessional, he added conferences
for all the nuns and, something which they appreciated even
more, short letters of spiritual advice which matched the capacity
of each of them.

It was almost as it had been at Avila at the Convent of the
Incarnation. But at Beas he was a man of a yet deeper and more
certain experience. The nuns wrote down his most telling remarks. Some fragments of the result of this note-taking remain
and are precious indeed.

In order that they might be instructed by John, the religious of
Beas put their other duties aside, sometimes curtailing the final
moments of their frugal meals. When they listened to John
they felt that they were listening to one who spoke with the
tongue of an angel. They knew of no one better equipped than
he to do what Mother Teresa—borrowing a phrase from St.
Gregory the Great—had called "putting wood on the fire."

One day the cook, a simple soul called Sister Catalina de la Cruz, put this question to John:

"Father, why is it that the bullfrogs, which are in the garden near the water, throw themselves into the stream whenever I come near? . . ."

"Because," he said, "it is in its depths that they feel safe. There they are secure and protected; and it is in this manner," he went on, "that we too should behave: We must turn away from created things and plunge into the depths, into the center of all things—God—hiding ourselves in Him . . ."

Later, in a letter written to his spiritual daughters at Beas, he remembered to add a word for the cook: "Tell our Sister Catalina that she must hide herself and seek the depths."

Sometimes John would question the sisters and comment on their replies, either developing their thought further or, whenever it was needed, placing it accurately for their benefit.

Once he asked them what prayer is.

Sister Francisca de la Madre de Dios, whom he was questioning, replied:

"It means considering God's beauty and being glad in it."

Fray John was delighted with this answer. He went on to speak of the beauty of God and made this theme the subject of his remarks for days.

Then he added to the *Spiritual Canticle,* which he had composed in his prison cell at Toledo, these final stanzas:

> "Let us rejoice, Beloved,
>   And let us go to see ourselves in thy beauty,
>   To the mountain and the hill
>   Where flows the pure water;
>   Let us enter farther into the thicket.

> "And then we shall go forth
>   To the lofty caverns of the rock
>   Which are well hidden

> And there shall we enter
> And taste the new wine of the pomegranates.
>
> "There wouldst thou show me
> That which my soul desiréd,
> And there at once, my life, wouldst thou give me
> That which thou gavest me the other day.
>
> "The breathing of the air,
> The song of the sweet philomel,
> The grave and its beauty in the serene night,
> With a flame that consumes and gives no pain."

How could the nuns who heard these verses coming with overflowing love from their Father's lips have feared the austere rules of "renunciation" which he always taught them by word and example?

This must have been the time that John of the Cross began to put his wonderful writings into final form, taking care to wed the poetry of holy love with the strictness of that law which is the basis of perfect purity.

MT. CARMEL

There is evidence that John had fully developed his characteristic doctrine before he left Calvario and Beas to go to establish the university college at Baeza. We know that he drew his own conception of Mt. Carmel for the nuns, and that they in turn copied it into their Breviaries.

The actual drawing which he made for Sister Magdalena del Espíritu Santo exists, as she was always most careful to preserve the notes and instructions her spiritual father gave her.

We see, first of all, a mountain drawn simply, as if by a child. At its summit is enthroned Divine Wisdom awaiting the soul in order to enrich it with His gifts and His union. The path to the right side fails to attain the summit; it is the way of imperfect souls who are overly attached to the material things of this world. Instead of arriving at its goal, the path sheers off among the precipices. The path to the left also fails to reach the top of the mountain: This is the way of those imperfect souls who stop at the mere acquirement of supernatural good, lingering over it in what John of the Cross termed, in words which have become famous, "the proprietary spirit." The summit of the mountain cannot be attained by those who take either of these paths. The middle road has written upon it thirteen times: Nada!—Nothingness! For it is in the surrender to being nothing that one attains union with Him Who is All.

All of this will be further explained when we come to study the mystical doctrine of John of the Cross, and we will see the justification for his title: Doctor of Nothingness.

Before we follow him to Baeza where a great task awaited him, another incident of this period should be told. He had not been Prior of Calvario for more than six or seven months at the time and, excepting for his weekly visits to Beas, rarely left his monastery. One day he was called to the village of Iznaforte, about seven miles away, to perform the rite of exorcism for a possessed man who lived there.

John could not leave this poor soul in Satan's slavery, and went, accordingly, in the company of some other friars whose account of the affair has been reported by Fray Juan de Santa Eufemia.

When John had come to the top of a hill from which the village could be seen, and was in the sight of the possessed person, the demon cried out:

"Here comes another Basil upon this earth to persecute us!"

But John did not allow this to intimidate him. He went through the Office of Exorcism and very soon the poor man was delivered of his affliction and restored to spiritual health.

It was during the course of a journey such as this that a wanton woman went up to Fray John and invited him to stop with her, saying that he would find it pleasant to spend the night in her company! But John brushed her off sharply with the words: "I would rather have a devil from hell for my bedfellow than someone such as you! . . ."

And, paying her no more notice, he went on his way.

AT BAEZA

In the spring of 1579 an important mission called John to Baeza, a large city in Juan Province.

Baeza is about fifteen miles from Calvario. Here Blessed John of Avila, a remarkable preacher known as the Apostle of Andalucía, is held in great veneration. In 1579 he had been dead only ten years and was widely remembered. He had founded a flourishing university at Baeza in 1540, and John of the Cross was now being sent to this institution. A number of the professors of the university, attracted by the reputation of the Discalced Carmelites of the monasteries at Penuela and Calvario, had expressed the wish that a college for the Discalced be established. In conjunction with what we already know, a fact of this kind helps us to understand the religious atmosphere in Spain at this time. Ever since John of Avila had preached there, a spirit of devotion had governed Baeza. It was, moreover, the prevailing thought there that the more learning is added to devotion, the more it offers to God the service which pleases Him best. St. Teresa showed a distinct preference for learned priests, *letrados*—those well instructed and trained—to those who may be pious but uneducated. It was common for men and women at this time, upon entering the confessional, to ask if they were dealing with a *letrado*. It frequently happened that John of the Cross, reading the mind of a questioner in advance of his query, would say: "Ah yes, my daughter; I am a *letrado* in spite of all my sins."

John of the Cross fully sympathized with the opinion that priests should be better educated; naturally, he desired the best possible instruction for the Discalced Fathers. Therefore, when he was informed that the Faculty of the University of Baeza wished to set up a college for the Carmelite students, he went there to find a place suitable for the suggested foundation. John of the Cross soon made up his mind—great mystics go into action quickly and efficiently—and before very long all the preliminaries were under way. It was costly to set up the college, but a benefactor, Diego del Moral, who told of it later, immediately subscribed a large sum for John's use. The interior of the building John selected was quickly adapted to its new use: There would be a chapel, lecture halls, and rooms for students. When John returned to Calvario he made enrollment preparations within his community, selecting from the younger members those who were to be sent to the college at Baeza. He went to La Penuela for the same purpose. The nuns of Beas, who had been informed of his plans, came to his assistance by preparing whatever was necessary for the adornment of the chapel and the house of study.

Finally all was in readiness, and on Saturday June 13, 1579, John of the Cross and three of his brethren, filled with the joy of those who are in the service of the Lord, set out by foot for Baeza.

They arrived in the city that evening but found that no one had expected them or was even aware of their arrival. They quickly put the Chapel in order and adorned the altar. After putting a bell in one of the windows they made final preparations for the Feast of the Most Holy Trinity, which was to be celebrated the following day. This was a feast day that John particularly loved. On June 14, 1579—Trinity Sunday—the first Mass was said in the new college.

The neighborhood was greatly astonished when, at an early hour that Sunday morning, the bell of the Discalced Carmelites was heard ringing for Mass. People came to investigate at once. The first to arrive was a young man called Agustín who, six months later, was to put on the Carmelite habit. A young girl, Juana de Arjona, told (long afterwards) how she, too, had come running at the sound of the bell and, seeing Fray John sweeping the chapel, offered to help him. Before long she was to become one of the spiritual daughters of John of the Cross.

Shortly after the first Mass, students who had come from La Peñuela arrived and now it was possible to begin college sessions for the community of six religious under John of the Cross as Rector of the house and Fray Gaspardo de San Pedro as Vice-Rector. The Bishop of Jaen, Don Francisco de Grado, and the Visitor of the Carmelites, Fray Angel de Salazar, gave authorization in good time to the entire program.

The Doctors of the University, who desired the establishment of the foundation, were delighted. All of them were disciples and admirers of John of Avila, and their names are known to us: Father Nuñez Marcelo, and Doctors Carlebal, Diego Perez, and Ojeda. They came on the first day to greet the new arrivals, as they wished to be on hand when they got settled. Nothing escaped their attention and they noted in particular that neither the Carmelite students nor their Rector had any bedding. Saying nothing, they went off, but at nightfall a knock came on the door of what was now called the College of Our Lady of Mount Carmel (but which was later to be known as St. Basil's College), and the scholastic who answered it went to Fray John and told him that Father Nuñez Marcelo had brought bedding for them. Although Fray John was quick to thank the charitable donor, he would not accept the gift; they had, he explained, all that they needed. It was Fray John's conviction that, in order to absorb the cost of establishing their foundation, they should take on the mantle of poverty in all its rigor. No, the members of this house would sleep on the ground.

Well, at least that their sleep, it might be assumed following the fatiguing work of getting installed in their new home, would come easily. But that was not the case. Fray John was in a narrow room, separated from the cell of Fray Juan de Santa-Ana by one that, at the moment, was vacant. They had scarcely fallen asleep when a mysterious crash was heard. Fray John wondered whether his nearest brethren was upset by this, and getting a light, went to see. Fray Juan de Santa-Ana was terrified. John, wanting to soothe the troubled friar, told him simply that the noises were made by "spirits." As a matter of fact, the noises were of the same origin that were to resound almost three hundred years later in the Presbytery at Ars. John of the Cross did not have the slightest doubt on this point, and the next day when he went into the unoccupied room where the loud crashes had come found no traces whatsoever of any disturbance and his certainty of their origin declared itself.

Fray de Santa-Ana, a witness of all this, tells us that the same noises persisted for a whole week, and that the demon was seeking a way to trip John of the Cross when he would come out of his cell in the morning. But order was restored shortly, and these disturbances ceased entirely.

THE RECTOR OF BAEZA

John of the Cross soon became well known in Baeza. Everyone recognized his knowledge and elevation of spirit, and respected his authority. It was during his residence in this university town that he began to arrange those beautiful writings which were to earn him—in 1926—the official title of Doctor of the Church. We know, moreover, that he was fully aware of the importance of higher study as it was conceived in his day. He had been, for four years, a student at Salamanca where his talents had placed him at the head of his fellow students. He had also been, as will be recalled, Rector of the Students' College at Alcala. He now spared no pains to organize his new college and set it on a level with the other colleges in the university.

Baeza now has a population of twenty thousand inhabitants, but in those days it had fifty-five thousand. The city was marked by an intense awareness of both intellectual and industrial activity. The Carmelite students attracted the attention of all by their seriousness, dedication to work, and love of silence and of study. They were known as "the holy ones." Everyone who came in contact with John pledged his trust, and he was constantly sought out for advice. The Faculty of the University were awed by his knowledge of Sacred Scripture, and if they were unaware —as we may suppose—of the work he was then doing upon his book, *Ascent of Mount Carmel,* they had, at least, frequent opportunities to attend the scholarly contests he established among his students after the model of Salamanca and Alcala, and to which all the professors were invited. Fray John took the chair at these gatherings and all present marveled at the assured manner in which he led theological and Scriptural discussions, and by the way he did the summation.

On the other hand it was the same John who distinguished himself in academic discussions who could be observed occupying himself with the meanest household chores, who set for himself the task of keeping the Chapel in the state of spotless perfection, and who strove to decorate it in a way he considered truly artistic and devotional. It was this same man who was to be encountered among his younger brethren at recreation time taking part in their parleys, injecting into them his characteristic spirituality and poetry of expression, and delighting them to the point where they hated to miss a single word. And it was he who ministered to any who might be ill, who soothed them, cheered them, coaxed them to eat when they had lost their appetites, and to whom no medicine was too costly when it could restore them to health. One day when John was speaking with a sick patient who had no desire to eat, he named all the delectable dishes one could wish for—*which of these will please you?*— and went through the list of all the good things which might be appealing until he was able to arouse the interest of the sick friar. When he was successful, he sent out for the dish the sick man designated.

This exemplifies the great tenderness John showed for all who were in his charge—the most brilliant students or the least educated of the lay brothers.

Among the original members of the college was Fray Gerardo,

an outstanding intellectual and a pious man, who was unable to complete his studies. He had been attacked by purpura and was frequently in a state of delirium. The friars took turns watching over him. One morning about three o'clock Father Inocente de San Andrés was at the sick man's bedside. He was exhausted and fell asleep. In his delirium, the sick friar got up, dressed, and knelt in prayer by his bed. At that very moment Fray John, who was aware of everything that went on, came into the cell. He was saddened at the sight of the gravely sick friar upon his knees while his nurse slept. Kindly, but firmly, he gave the nursing-brother the necessary admonishment and set all in order in the sick room.

THE PLAGUE OF 1580

One of the most severe trials the new college had to face was that of an epidemic which ravaged all Spain called the *catarro universal*. (In 1919 we called this same illness *Spanish influenza*.) It was as contagious as the Plague.

John of the Cross was on a visit to the nuns at the Convent at Beas when he learned that the epidemic had struck his college. He returned at once, passing through Calvario without stopping. When he got to Baeza, he found that all eighteen friars had been afflicted. His first thought was to buy food, prepare it, and serve it. He spent long hours trying to cheer and encourage his sick brethren.

But now, from Calvario, nine other brethren arrived, all of them sick. There were not enough bedclothes nor was there enough food. The Brother who was Procurator came to the Rector and asked permission to go begging to the benefactors of the house. But John of the Cross calmly replied: "God will provide." As a matter of fact, and without anyone having been importuned by requests, the following day supplies of bed linen —twenty-four or twenty-five mattresses, bolsters, sheets, and nightshirts—arrived at the house. They also received food.

Teresa de Ibros, one of Fray John's penitents, was aware of the poverty of his Community and the trouble which lay upon it, and she had taken it upon herself to go begging for the friars.

Nevertheless, the epidemic continued. One day, John accompanied the College Infirmarian, Fray Martín de la Asunción, on a visit to his family, where they encountered sixteen stricken members, eleven of whom had been given the Last Sacraments. John gave words of comfort and encouragement to all. When they returned to the college he saw that Fray Martín was very sad, but assured him that not one of his relatives would die.

"Who has told you that?" Fray Martín naïvely asked.

The Rector made the simple reply: "He Who can do all things."

And that was the truth; none of Fray Martín's family died.

But during the course of this epidemic, the mother of John of the Cross died. She had been living all these years at Medina del Campo with her son Francisco and her daughter-in-law. John of the Cross was not able to be with her during her last hours, but Francisco was with her. Catalina's death was that of a good Christian, and the Carmelites of Medina del Campo, near whose convent she had lived and to whom St. Teresa had recommended her, buried her in their own chapel.

A SPIRITUAL DIRECTOR

The three years John spent in Baeza were marked, which was usual with him, as a time devoted to much spiritual direction. Baeza was a city that made enormous demands on John's ability in this regard.

It is difficult to imagine the atmosphere into which he was cast. Baeza was a devout city. John of Avila had not only converted the people, he had aroused in them a desire for the interior life. To accommodate its fifty-five thousand inhabitants were nineteen parishes. The churches were crowded. There were many families who lived holy lives. The Discalced Fathers, surrounded by people of this intent, found themselves impelled to the most moving of all apostolates. Their small chapel was always full of worshipers. People came there to confess, to assist at the services, and, above all, to seek counsel and spiritual direction. Very soon John of the Cross was known, valued, and sought after as spiritual director. Certain of the University's Doctors—Becerra (the Rector in 1580), Sepulveda, Carlebal, Diego Pérez, and, particularly, Father Nuñez Marcelo—sought John's advice. In him they found the holiness, knowledge, penetration, and sense of spiritual reality which are the most important aspects for a truly fine spiritual director. The leading students followed the example set by their instructors. And also, the most devout women of the city naturally wished to take advantage of his counsel. Although he was not yet forty years old, his experience was considerable, for, in addition to his own spiritual achievement, he had grown in depth and penetration by his contact with some of the greatest souls that Spain ever offered in the cause of religion.

But all evidence unites in declaring that there was something unique in John. St. Teresa had no doubt of what this was, and she frequently mentions that the Holy Spirit spoke from the mouth of John of the Cross. One of Teresa's spiritual daughters, Ana de San Alberto, Prioress of the monastery of Caravaca in Andalucía, spoke to her on behalf of her nuns who required special direction for their spiritual development, and Teresa replied: "My daughter, I shall have Fray John of the Cross come to you. Think of him as if he were myself. Open your hearts fully to him. Accept what he tells us, for *he is a soul with whom God shares His own spirit.*" Then she wrote to Fray John to suggest this ministry to him and, when he had agreed to accept it, she wrote again to the Prioress of Caravaca:

"My daughter, Fray John of the Cross will come to you. Put your souls in his hands in your convent as though he were myself; for *he has Our Lord's own spirit.*"

So we see that John, aside from his duties as the Rector of

Baeza, was also called upon to undertake long journeys to minister as a spiritual director. And in doing this he did not abandon his work among the nuns at Beas. Nevertheless, he was now far away from them. A whole day's walk separated him from their convent; but he did come to them at regular intervals. Undoubtedly he could no longer visit them every week, as he had done when he lived at Calvario. Now he could not go to them more often than once a month. But he remained with them for a longer time—eight days at each visit. One of the brethren journeyed with him. They went on foot, staves in hand; and when they did have an ass at their disposal, it was almost always the Rector's companion who was mounted.

Among all that we know of these visits to Beas, one thing should be remarked. During the intervals between the hearing of confessions and the holding of conferences, Fray John and his companion would walk about in the convent garden or its immediate neighborhood. John would talk about things of the spirit. Then he would suggest that they separate for each to privately meditate and praise the Lord in the midst of His creation. It will not be surprising to learn that the younger religious, in obeying his Rector, nonetheless managed a backward glance at him. And he himself later testified that he would often see Fray John either by the side of some flowing stream, or bent over a flower, in an attitude of expectant attention, the picture of one who was seeking God through the agency of His created beauty.

All that we know of John leads to the same conclusion: The "nights" of which he will speak imply no rejection of the beauteous day manifested by created things. In the next chapter we will attempt to explain the "maxims" and spiritual poetry of St. John of the Cross, regarded as revelatory of his mystical doctrine. The apparent austerity of that doctrine should not blind us to John's deep enthusiasm and love when he was faced with Beauty incarnate.

VI

JOHN'S EARLY WRITINGS:
THE MAXIMS AND THE POEMS

JOHN'S REASONS FOR WRITING

John's writings formed at least as important a part of his life as did his overt actions. He was not, at any time, what we would call an "author," in the sense of being a writer who could become objective and find outside himself the constituent parts of a book to be given to the public. John of the Cross never published anything. It was not until twenty-seven years after his death that his works were brought to public light. They had all been composed to satisfy the needs of souls he had directed, and they embody his most intimate and heartfelt thoughts. He said to others only what he believed God Himself had said to him. Before he wrote the works which I shall list and analyze, he had written bits of advice, counsels of direction, and themes for meditation to serve the needs of the nuns in his spiritual charge. I have already pointed out that all this had started during the days when he had been at Avila as the confessor of the nuns at the Convent of the Incarnation. He composed short letters which the sisters preserved as though they were priceless jewels. At other times, they noted down one of his thoughts or something he had taught them, and added this to their piously inspired collection. We are far from having all the private collections of his thoughts which may have been written down from what he said, either at Avila before his imprisonment at Toledo, at Beas while he was Prior at Calvario, or while he was Rector at Baeza. The collection of counsels or maxims which is found in his complete works is actually, therefore, far from being complete. Nevertheless, it must be considered as the basic expression of his mystical teaching. It is obvious that this collection must be taken up with discretion and prudence because the maxims very often, if not always, are keyed to the needs of some particular nun. They have, therefore, a personal value, and are on a scale which prohibits pure and simple generalization. When he set these maxims down, in the course of writing to the sisters, it was in response to some need of one of their souls to some confidence he had received in the confessional, or to some special end to be kept in view and achieved by an individual. Yet even this should not cause us to go too far in limiting the meaning of these shafts of light. There are two reasons against so doing: The needs of one soul are, very often, the needs of a great many other souls as well, if not, indeed, of all souls. Then, too, the advice given to individuals by John of the Cross in his writing ordinarily takes on that breadth which is characteristic of the highest mystical doctrine.

In any event, even a summary study of these maxims offers the best introduction to John's great works in the field of mystical theology, for they were his first work. In them he synthesized his experience as a spiritual director. And it is in them that his teaching is rooted. The ideas we find in them are radical notions in his whole theology. It is by means of his maxims that we are able to grasp the "tone color" of his spiritual direction.

It is impossible in a book of this length to enter into a deep discussion of the maxims. We shall, therefore, take up only those which I believe are the most striking and the most spiritually suggestive. Before a man as inspired as John of the Cross, one feels inclined to put aside all merely human curiosity. One wishes only to learn from him. How good would it be to be able to say, with one of those who benefited most from his spiritual correspondence, sister Francisca de la Madre de Dios:

"In all things, the Saint allowed his great love of God to show itself; his words and even his writings set aflame with the warmth of divine love the souls of all who hear them, and the present witness [that is to say, Sister Francisca] has of herself felt this —so much so that, even when she might be in a state of spiritual coolness, the reading of some one of his letters would suffice to work a change."[1]

Such are the maxims which, when once grasped, are remembered; such are those which remain a part of the soul's life forever. If one can ever speak of a dominant idea, it is in such a case as this.

AN OBJECTION

However, an objection can be raised to these transcripts of inspired words and writings: May not St. John have been tempted to look upon himself as an oracle? Surrounded by the veneration in which we know he was held, may he not have thought himself above humility?

It is a simple matter to reply to this. Saints have the capacity of remaining humble despite the heavenly glory. The Curé of Ars could not have felt vain pride in that gift of leading souls which had so patently been granted to him. John of the Cross was not unaware that the maxims which he composed could be called *Dichos de Luz y Amor,* "Sayings of Light and Love." Actually, this is the title which he gives them in the Prologue which precedes a set of his maxims, those which were destined for Sister Francisca de la Madre de Dios.

[1] Cited in *Oeuvres spirituelles* (Desclée, 1949), p. 1292.

But one would have to read the whole of this Prologue to appreciate the spirit in which these "jottings" were written and sent out:

> "Moreover, O my God and my delight, my soul has desired, for love of Thee, to employ itself in these sayings of light and love for Thee, for, although I have the tongue wherewith to utter them, I have neither the deeds nor the virtue which pertain to them, and it is with these, my Lord, that Thou are pleased rather than with the language and the wisdom of them. Let other persons, who may be so impelled by them, perchance make progress in Thy love and service, wherein I am lacking, and let my soul find an occasion of comfort in having been the cause for which Thou findest in others that which is lacking in itself.

> "Thou, Lord, lovest discretion, lovest light, lovest love above the other operations of the soul. Wherefore these sayings will be of discretion for the journeyer, of light for the journey and of love for the journeying. Far hence be worldly rhetoric; far hence the loquacity and arid eloquence of weak and ingenious human wisdom, wherein Thou hast no pleasure; and let us speak words to the heart, bathed in sweetness and love, wherein Thou hast great pleasure, removing perchance causes of stumbling and offences from many souls that stumble unwittingly, and unwittingly do err, thinking that they are successfully following Thy dearest Son, Our Lord Jesus Christ, and becoming like to Him in their life, character and virtues, and in the form of detachment and purity of their spirit. But do Thou grant it, Father of mercies, for without Thee, Lord, naught will be accomplished."

This is scarcely the tone of a man who considers himself an oracle. He was not, and he never wished to be, anything but the docile instrument of his God, the God who had granted him, together with His grace, both "light and love."

A BASIC MAXIM

Let us now turn to the maxims themselves and choose among them as a bee selects those flowers from which it will make its honey.

The one which appears to me to be the most characteristic, the most meaningful, the most Evangelical, the one which is, to my thinking, most imbued with divinity, is No. 57:

"At eventide they will examine thee in love. Learn to love as God desires to be loved and lay aside thine own temperament."

One almost hesitates to attempt a commentary for fear it will weaken the impact of the original. But perhaps a few words will serve to deepen our understanding of this maxim.

At eventide—This is evidently at life's end. You are then to be judged as you have loved. It is your love which will be your eternal vestment. The whole edifice of mystical theology has its foundation in this truth. Whoever has loved passing things will be forever linked to them. Whoever has loved God will be forever one with Him. Yet there are degrees in love. The perfection of love is none other than love itself. We must then learn to love God, not in the way we would like to, but as He would have us. To this end, all that matters is that we serve Christ; that we put on Jesus Christ.

Whoever has grasped this *maxim of light and of love,* whoever has spent his whole life in putting it into practice, is certain of attaining just that degree of holiness to which God, in His infinite love, has ordained for him from all eternity.

When Jesus Christ was asked which was the first of His commandments, He replied: "Thou shalt love the Lord thy God with thy whole heart, and thy whole soul, and with thy whole strength, and thy whole mind. This is the first and the greatest commandment. And the second is like to this: "Thou shalt love thy neighbor as thyself."

Hence, it is evident that we shall be judged by our love. What is more important?

When looked at closely, the majority of the other maxims turn back to this one or flow from it. For it is always to the great love of love that John of the Cross leads us, whether in his maxims his other writings.

SPOUSE AND FRIEND

Let us look at another maxim which is as meaningful as the one cited above. This is No. 65:

"Take God for thy Spouse and for a Friend with Whom thou walkest continually, and thou shalt not sin, and shalt learn to love, and the things that are needful shall be wrought prosperously for thee."

If there was ever a universal maxim, surely this is it. Such a counsel is given not only to the sisters of the Carmelite Order, not only to other Orders in the Church: It applies to every Christian. All who are baptised in Christ can aspire to the high plane to which it points. And every soul who fulfills it can be certain of attaining the height to which God calls it. "Star differeth from star in glory," we are told by St. Paul; and not everyone is called to the same degree of perfection, for grace acts in close conjunction with nature. God's gifts are diverse, just as each flower is distinct one from the other although all have their charm and their value. What is certain is that we can do nothing without God: It is He who raises us to beauty. Union with God, the ideal of the mystical life, is the *sine qua non* of self-fulfillment. We must remember this and not imagine that the mystical life is a field reserved for a small elite group. Every soul is called to it. As a matter of fact, the very highest places are not to be attained by all, any more than the greatest peaks in the Alps are to be scaled by the ordinary mountaineer.

But by right, all are called; and all, at least in their willingness, can achieve the summits.

However, let us refer again to St. John of the Cross:

"Take God for thy Spouse and for a Friend . . ."

One would wish to cry out with St. Leo the Great: *"Agnosce, ô christiane, dignitatem tuam! . . .* Recall, O Christian, how great is your worth!" For you, Jesus came among men; for you, He lived and died; and it is for His sake that you can speak so movingly to God as you call Him, "Our Father." To you He has said: "Servants no longer will I call you, but my friends." The midnight cry, "Behold the Bridegroom comes; go forth to greet Him," is for every human soul.

He is the Bridegroom. He is your Friend. The whole logic of our faith demands that we regard Him as such. This is mysticism; it taps the very roots of faith.

There is little need to show how the preceding maxim is linked to the first. You will indeed be judged, at the end of your life, upon your love; and it is for this reason that you should learn to love as God wishes to be loved. Therefore, and inasmuch as the wondrous things encompassed in mysticism—that *life of union*—must be set forth in our poor human speech, John of the Cross, Prince of Mystical Theology, could not have used a richer formulation of this idea than the one he sets before us: "Take God for thy Spouse and for a Friend with Whom thou walkest continually . . ."

This reverts to a counsel set forth previously to the effect that we should be habitually loving and peacefully attentive to God's presence within us.

What shall we draw from all this? Our only recompense will be love itself. John of the Cross himself tells us: "Then will you never sin; then will you know how to love . . ."

To know how to love—this is the greatest of all arts. And it takes all one's life to learn it. Mysticism is the science of love. We must ever strive towards love. Luther aroused all Christendom with his own cherished notion that justification is by faith alone, independent of good works. John of the Cross, interpreting the true doctrine of the Church based on Scripture and exemplified by St. Paul and in the life and work of all the holy men and women who have been and shall come to be, preached justification by the faith that comes to full bloom in love.

If you love, you have all. "Take God for thy Spouse and for a Friend with Whom thou walkest continually, and thou shalt not sin, and shalt learn to love . . ."

And he adds, in summation: "And the things that are needful shall be wrought prosperously for thee."

These are the very words of St. Paul: *Diligentibus Deum, omnia cooperantur in bonum:* ". . . to them that love God, all things work together unto good . . ." (Rom. 8:28)

This amounts to saying that in love of God, one has all.

Here again I may say that a great many of John's other maxims are variations on the same theme. To cite two at random, let us look, for example, at No. 67:

"Betake yourself to rest, putting anxieties far from thee and caring not at all for whatsoever comes to pass, and thou shalt serve God as He wills and take thine ease in Him."

This is what the soul does when it has chosen God to be its Spouse and Friend, when the soul walks always in His company. Nothing can upset it, nothing can deprive it of peace.

Here is No. 68:

"Behold, God reigns not save in the disinterested and peaceful soul."

Let us consider, however, the divisions into which these counsels are cast.

THE IMITATION OF JESUS CHRIST

Jesus Christ is the only model upon which we can pattern ourselves in our quest of this essential love. Here, John of the Cross shows himself in sharp contrast to some mystics who have seemed to suggest, in an attempt at elevation of thought, that one must go directly to God in all His infinity and transcendence, and bypass the humanity of Christ as though this were the concern only of the small-minded soul—a thought which horrified St. Teresa.

We find among the maxims which have been set down for us by Mother Magdalena del Espíritu Santo—the first member of the convent at Beas to make her sacramental confession to Fray John of the Cross—the following (No. 2):

> ". . . for conquering the desires. Have thou an habitual desire to imitate Jesus Christ in all His works, conforming thyself to His life, whereon thou must meditate in order to be able to imitate it and to behave in all things as He would behave."

This requires careful and thoughtful reading of the Gospels, an habitual searching into the mind and heart of Christ, a resolution to take, in every circumstance, the path we think He would have taken in all our choices. The question: *What would Jesus have done?* is to be uppermost in our minds. I shall turn again to this maxim in the next chapter, which is devoted to the first two books of St. John.

Maxim No. 3 is no more than a development of the preceding:

> "In order that thou mayest be able to do this it is necessary that every appetite or taste be renounced, if it be not purely for the honor and glory of God, and that thou remain in emptiness for the love of Him Who in this life neither did nor desired to do more than the will of His Father, which He called His meat and drink."

The concluding words of this maxim allude to Christ's own words: ". . . My meat is to do the will of him that sent me . . ." (John 4:34).

However, in the life and deeds of Christ there is one central point—the Cross. Even before the question of His being crucified arose—the crucifixion which was to be a scandal to the Jews and, indeed, to the Apostles themselves prior to the coming of the Holy Spirit Who strengthened them—Jesus had proclaimed: ". . . If any man will come after me, let him deny himself, and take up his cross daily, and follow me." (Luke 9:23). And again, He said: And he that taketh not up his cross, and followeth me, is not worthy of me." (Matt. 10:38).

St. John of the Cross would have been untrue to himself had he forgotten this. He returns often to the theme in the course of his counsels:

"He that seeks not the Cross of Christ seeks not the glory of Christ." (*Points of Love,* No. 23).

"Love consists not in feeling great things, but in having great detachment and in suffering for the Beloved." (*ibid.,* No. 36).

"Let Christ crucified be sufficient for thee, and with Him do thou suffer and rest; for which cause do thou annihilate thyself with respect to all things, both without and within." (*ibid.,* No. 13).

And it is the same in the collection of maxims made by Mother Magdalena del Espíritu Santo, as, for example, in No. 8:

"Be strong in thy heart against all things that move thee to that which is not God, and for Christ's sake love thou suffering."

THE THEME OF SOLITUDE

One of the chief themes of the counsels is that of solitude. All the greathearted have been drawn by the mystery of "the solitary soul."

In our own time, this theme has been pursued in the direction of melancholy and despair. Who can forget the words of Alfred de Vigny:

"All unfeeling, sightless, and unhearing,
  I, unnoticed, pass;
  What man has wrought says to me no more than rotted bones,
  As my youth disdains your proffered worship."

Then there is the verse of Sully Prudhomme, as he speaks to the stars in the name of human souls:

"Just as you do, so shines each human soul,
    Far from kindred souls who seem so near
    E'en as each immortal star
    Burns alone, in silence, all the night!"

For certain kinds of Existentialists, man is "set out there" without knowing why. All about him reigns eternal silence. Life itself is an absurdity without an object.

Surrounded by this kind of "Humanism" which denies God, how far are we from John of the Cross? He grants indeed that solitude exists, but for him it is a solitude in which God dwells.

"Live in this world," he tells us, "as though there were in it but God and thy soul, so that thy heart may be detained by naught that is human." (*Points of Love,* No. 61, [4]).

This is a thought which Newman knew very well, whether he had drawn it from John of the Cross or from his own experience.

Never the cause of sadness, fear, or discouragement, it was from solitude that St. John drew all his joy and peace. This most beautiful maxim shows this:

"Oh, how sweet will Thy presence be to me, Thou that art the highest Good. I will approach Thee in silence and will uncover Thy feet that Thou mayest be pleased to unite me unto Thee in marriage [an allusion to Ruth 3:7], and I will not take mine ease until I have fruition of Thyself in Thine arms. And now I entreat Thee, Lord, not to forsake me at any time in my recollection since I am a spendthrift of my soul." (*ibid.,* No. 45).

"If thou be detached from that which is without and dispossessed of that which is within, and without attachment to the things of God, neither will prosperity detain thee nor adversity hinder thee." (*ibid.,* No. 46).

By way of conclusion to these two complementary maxims, this certitude is offered:

"The soul that is united with God is feared by the devil as though it were God Himself." (*ibid.*, No. 47).

And it is on this theme of solitude that John of the Cross paints a charming picture based on the biblical figure of the sparrow that sits alone on the rooftop—*passer solitarius in tecto* (Ps. 101:8).

"The characteristics of the solitary bird are five. The first is that it soars as high as it is able. The second, that it can endure no companionship, even of its own kind. The third, that it places its beak against the wind. The fourth, that it has no definite colour. The fifth, that it sings sweetly. These characteristics will belong to the contemplative soul. It must soar above transitory things, paying no more heed than if they were not. It must be so fond of solitude and silence that it can endure the companionship of no other creature. Its beak must be placed so as to meet the wind of the Holy Spirit—that is, it must respond to His inspirations, to the end that, by so doing, it may become more worthy of His companionship. It must have no definite colour—that is, it must desire to do no definite thing save that which is the will of God. It must sing sweetly in the contemplation and love of its Spouse." (*ibid.*, No. 42).

The final word brings us again to the basic counsel: *Take God for thy Spouse and for a Friend.*

The soul's loneliness is, therefore, to be resolved in the mystical life itself. The soul which loves is fulfilled. It is never alone. "God and myself," said Newman. John of the Cross had reached this point: Whoever possesses God lacks nothing. And everything is wanting to him who does not know God or who becomes estranged from Him.

With God the soul reaches its complete growth. This is one of the important points which John of the Cross treats in his counsels: It is the soul which loves, that is to say, the soul which is with God. Mystical Theology does not lessen man; it raises him to divinity.

THE GRANDEUR OF MAN

As I have pointed out, John of the Cross, even before Pascal, noted that the worth of all the world is less than that of a single thought of man.

"One single thought of a man is of greater worth than the whole world; wherefore God alone is worthy of it." (Maxim No. 32).

The power to think of matters touching on infinity exceeds the power to conceive of finite matters. Therefore, we are unable to understand God; for, as the celebrated Raphael puts it: "Understanding implies equality." But we can, at least, think of God, and thus, overpassing all that is created, go beyond the farthest boundaries of the universe. In John of the Cross's time, men did not have any exact comprehension of the world's dimensions. Today we are scarcely able to do more than set figures to it— hundreds of millions of light years. Our thoughts can, however, go out beyond what we know, and maxim No. 32 of John of the Cross, which Pascal took up, remains as true as ever.

But what John of the Cross saw very clearly is that our very grandeur is the source of our first obligations. We must go out beyond ourselves, lest we become less than we are and stultify ourselves. The man who refuses to go to God, who stops at finite things, does not sin against God alone; he sins even more against himself.

But John of the Cross had an expression worth remembering on the subject of what follows from the grandeur of man:

"The whole world has not the worth of a man's thought, for that thought is due to God alone; and thus whatever thought of ours is not centred upon God is stolen from Him." (*Points of Love,* No. 37).

Let us understand that John of the Cross is not forbidding us all thought of worldly concerns; what he does censure is absorption in them, refusal to go beyond them, unwillingness to bring ourselves to God—without Whom the universe is meaningless.

If we take to heart the words of the Prince of Mystical Theology, how often is God "robbed!" And, after all, who would dare to say that John is mistaken, that he is not arguing in the direct and logical line which stems from faith in God?

There is, moreover, an evident link between this idea of man's grandeur and the basic maxims which we have culled from John's writings.

Because our thoughts can outrun the merely created in order to go to God, our will is endowed with a love proportionate to this gift of our intellect. Because our all lies in love, we shall be judged in regard to love when we come to the evening of life. And it is because of the strength of this love that we have been raised in Jesus Christ to the level of God's friends and adopted sons; and thus, the soul may look upon God as being its "Bridegroom."

Christian Theology teaches us that this is not to be ascribed to any merely natural cause. It is the Holy Spirit who cries out from the innermost depths of our hearts: "Abba! Father!" Christ has made us friends rather than servants and He has spoken to us in those wonderful words: ". . . If any one love me, he will keep my word, and my Father will love him, and we will come to him, and will make our abode with him." (John 14:23).

Inasmuch as the whole matter of mysticism is "union with God," it is rooted in this affirmation of Christ and His promise.

John of the Cross, in common with all Christian theologians, has concluded that God has marked us out to be "gods" with Him.

". . . That which God seeks to do is to make us gods by participation, as He is God by nature, even as fire converts all things into fire." (*Points of Love,* No. 28).

To be gods is, indeed, the ambition of all men. For two centuries man has tried to make himself a god, without God, and, in fact, a god in opposition to Him. Now the result is our daily dilemma. Man is more powerful than he has ever been before; he is also most unhappy and more hopeless.

Mystical Theology, too, is directed to the end that men "become gods," but gods with God, and through God. Thus can the spark of infinitude—which exists within us by the very power we have of being able to think of the infinite—become a reality in us. This is the real end of existence, and all Mystical Theology tends in this direction. Proof enough that it is not something incidental to man, something for the select few, but an end which anyone can reach by the means he has been given.

The grandeur of man, as I have said, outweighs even our own notions of it. John of the Cross has summed it up in a line we should always remember: "Lover transformed in the Beloved."

THE POWER OF LOVE

The one point upon which the maxims are ever insistent is the unique power of love. What this means in effect is that it is not the wisest, not the most eloquent, not the most talented who will best attain the end, but rather the one who knows best how to love.

If we are not great scholars, why should we fear? The holy Curé of Ars, who had great difficulty in passing his theological examinations, is certainly not in a lower place than many of his apparently more brilliant colleagues. The point is that we love. Listen to John of the Cross as he says:

"Love consists not in feeling great things, but in having great detachment and in suffering for the Beloved." (*Points of Love,* No. 36).

How true it is that, in our union with God, He does not ask

that we experience overly refined sentiments, or rise to Him
through erudite thoughts. When we are at prayer, we need not
think of Him as if we were taking a course in theology. He
knows far more than we! All He asks of us is that we love Him
with all our hearts and as best we can.

John of the Cross writes on this subject in No. 9 of *Points of
Love:*

"Have a loving attentiveness to God, with no desire to feel or
understand anything in particular concerning Him."

How can we know that we have this kind of love for God?
John of the Cross tells us in *Points of Love,* No. 27:

". . . souls which are of heavenly texture are also stable, and
are not subject to the generation of desires or to aught else, for
after their kind they are like unto God, and are never moved."

"Humilidad, y Paciencia"

This could well serve as a portrait of Fray John himself. All
who have spoken of him insist on his gentleness, his peaceful-
ness, his humility, his patience—all the qualities that he called
the fruits of love.

Although we may admire his gifts as poet, theologian, and
thinker, we should remember that he did not regard these as his
major gifts. This he clearly indicates in the following:

"God conceives not love for the soul by considering its greatness, but by considering the greatness of its humility." (*Points of
Love,* No. 24).

Although I have cited but a few of John's maxims and *Points
of Love,* I hope that I have given some concept of their richness,
and may thus have awakened in the reader a desire to study them
at close hand so that he may profit more abundantly from them.
What I have most wished to do is give a view of the kind of
teaching John of the Cross gave in the confessional and in his
spiritual conferences with friars and nuns. He tells us that they
requested he write not merely short pieces, as those we have just

glanced at, but a finished and complete account of the soul's ascent to God.

THE STANZAS

But the maxims and *Points of Love* alone did not enflame John's audience with a desire for more. In the forefront of his writings, before considering the treatises, we must place the *canciones del alma*—the Stanzas of the Soul. These stanzas, which we know he composed in his prison at Toledo, were engraved on his mind and heart, fortifying him in his trials until the second of his jailers, Fray de Santa Maria, gave him paper and pen to write them down. The afternoon of his escape, while he was with the Discalced Carmelite nuns of Toledo, he had recited these poems to the enthusiastic sisters, who copied them down.

He recited these verses to them again, no doubt at their request, but at his own insistence as well. This insistence would not have been from vanity, but as a source of the same spiritual teaching as had inspired his maxims. They embodied his own most intimate experience and had become the very breath of his life, as they can be of ours if we are aware of their depth and of the magnificence which inspired them. They are certainly poetry of the highest order; but to John they were, above all else, spiritual nourishment which he freely shared with the souls placed in his care. And as these stanzas seemed magnificent to all who heard them, as he saw the profit which the sisters could draw from them, he did not consider it unfitting, but rather to the contrary, that they be copied down. As a matter of fact, and as we are told by Father Lucien-Marie, Father Andrea de la Encarnación, "after long searching in the convents of Spain for anything which might concern the saint," summing up the results of his work: "I am strongly under the impression that the greater number of the copies which have been made were set down with the knowledge and even under the direction of St. John, for the spiritual consolation of many nuns who had requested that it be done. Actually, it is generally in their convents that most of the copies of these poems are to be found." (St. John of the Cross, *Oeuvres spirituelles*. Ed. Lucien-Marie, p. 1171).

His poems, therefore, played a considerable role in the direction of souls, which John of the Cross was called upon to exercise all his life.

As Father Lucien-Marie puts it, "The Saint's poems, far from being the result of a mere effort at self-relaxation, served, by their religious nature, as a tool of his spiritual direction, and they thus rival, where they do not exceed, the importance of those little jottings by letter which were the seedbed from which his spiritual maxims arose."

Therefore these poems are, at one and the same time, spurts from an inspired soul and instruments of teaching. Nevertheless, they are not mere didactic verse, but are founded on his mystical treatises, although not being restricted to them. One even gets the impression that after he had recited one of his poems and then wished to offer a commentary upon it, he suddenly changed his tone. As the verses were gracious, easy, airy, and full of savor, the commentary would be serious, grave, concise, and almost dry. And, according to all the available evidence, this was deliberate. What might well have occurred was that, after having sung, the saint would suddenly say: "It is a good thing to sing, but let us not lose our heads over music and pretty words; let us be precise, practical, effective. Let us put our hand to work. After we have celebrated the splendor of the espousal which we expect, let us teach the soul how it is to dress in honor of the Bridegroom, and how, crucified by love, it should correspond within itself to the love shown by Christ on the Cross."

It is by the saint's own will that the stanzas are inseparably linked to his treatises. But, if they wonderfully summarize the substance of the treatises and, above all, their glorious conclusion, this should not make us think that the work of preparation and self-abnegation which leads to the supreme end was easy.

The poetry must come first—on condition, however, that it always express the greatness of the "adventure" which it was John's aim to glorify and make loved.

St. John would certainly not have objected to the word "adventure." Life itself is the great and, as John repeatedly affirms, the "happy adventure."

"Oh! dichosa ventura!" he cries out, giving its leading note to the first of his poems. "Oh! happy adventure!" And this "adventure" [Peers translates *ventura* as "chance"] is none other than *the mystical union*.

THE GREAT TREATISES

We have four titles, but, according to the best of the commentators, there are no more than three treatises.

These four titles are, in English: *Ascent of Mount Carmel, Dark Night of the Soul, Spiritual Canticle,* and *Living Flame of Love*.

However, the first two poems actually form one whole work. The second is the conclusion of the first, and without it, the first remains incomplete.

But even when these two are joined into one unit, it does not attain the end to which it points. The two other poems, which are quite distinct by their date and the manner in which they are presented, are necessary to reach the end which has been set.

The four works form, therefore, a structure which is unified. This unity which marks them is the same that marked the saint's whole life. His only wish in living was that he might go to God.

This was the vocation of the religious of Mt. Carmel. In a sense, this is also the calling of every Christian in the state in which God has set him. For this reason, the teaching of the saint is on a scale which no one should limit. There is something here for everyone and, in a madly self-centered world, it is more than ever necessary that we think about the divine transcendence and, by means of mystical love, bring it into our lives that we may become "gods." This is a thought which fascinated Bergson.

THE STANZAS OF UNION WITH GOD

The first of these songs bears the following title in the Spanish edition: *Wherein the soul sings of the happy chance which it had in passing through the dark night of faith, in detachment and purgation of itself, to union with the Beloved.*

I

"On a dark night,
Kindled in love with yearnings—
oh, happy chance!—
I went forth without being observed,
My house being now at rest.

II

"In darkness and secure,
By the secret ladder, disguised—
oh, happy chance!—
In darkness and in concealment,
My house being now at rest.

III

"In the happy night,
In secret, when none saw me,
Nor I beheld aught,
Without light or guide,
save that which burned in my heart.

IV

"This light guided me
To the place where he (well I knew who!)
More surely than the light of noonday
was waiting me—
A place where none appeared.

V

"Oh, night that guided me,
Oh, night more lovely than the dawn,
Oh, night that joined Beloved with lover,
Lover transformed in the Beloved!

VI

"Upon my flowery breast,
Kept wholly for himself alone,
There he stayed sleeping,
and I caressed him,
And the fanning of the cedars made a breeze.

VII

"The breeze blew from the turret
As I parted his locks;
With his gentle hand he wounded my neck
And caused all my senses to be suspended.

VIII

"I remained, lost in oblivion;
My face I reclined on the Beloved.
All ceased and I abandoned myself,
Leaving my cares forgotten among the lilies."

THE POET'S INTENTION

According to the poet, these verses were to be followed by a commentary on its entirety. He has made formal declaration of this in his Prologue:

"In this book are first set down all the stanzas which are to be expounded; afterwards, each of the stanzas is expounded separately, being set down before its exposition; and then each line is expounded separately and in turn, the line itself also being set down before the exposition. In the first two stanzas are expounded the effects of the two spiritual purgations: of the sensual part of man and of the spiritual part. In the other six are expounded various and wondrous effects of the spiritual illumination and union of love with God."

For the first time, then—and for the last, as well—a theological tract was enclosed within a poem, and afterwards explained, line by line, in didactic form.

Such was the plan of John of the Cross and, as we know how the recipients of his treatise had been prepared to receive it, we can understand the manner in which he drew it up. He had sung to them, and then had been lost in wonder. They realized his poem was pregnant with meaning. It was not mere imagination that had brought it into being. Rather, these stanzas were the full fruit of the intellect, the theological knowledge, the soulfelt aspirations of the author, his experience of the life of union with God, all that he intended by the word "contemplation,"—joined as an integrated, whole rather than by a series of distinct acts. The poem needed only a patient and methodical explanation, point by point, symbol by symbol. It is something like the case of Christ's own parables for which the Apostles, who had listened to them, sensed their more profound significance and begged for an explanation.

However, for some reason we do not know, John of the Cross fell short of accomplishing what he had intended. Of the eight strophes or stanzas which make up this poem, he has furnished an explanation for only two. And if, at the very end, he did touch upon the third verse, it was to give no more than a rough sketch, soon to be brusquely interrupted, of the needed commentary. There remain, then, five strophes which have not been explained.

Inasmuch, therefore, as the stanzas of *Dark Night* trace the path of the ascent of Mt. Carmel to perfect union with God, it is as though, having completed the study of *Dark Night,* one found himself at the foot of the slope and continues on to *Ascent of Mount Carmel,* with which *Dark Night* is so closely united.

In order to reach the true summit one must scale further inclines of the hill, aided by two more of the saint's treatises, the *Spiritual Canticle* and the *Living Flame of Love.*

But in these two latter treatises he did not return to the unexplained strophes of *Ascent of Mount Carmel.* He produced further verses as beautiful as the others, and this time was careful to accompany them with a line-by-line commentary.

Nowhere, however, does he go beyond what he had said in *Ascent of Mount Carmel* cited above and in which the climax is to be found, as Father Lucien-Marie insists, in the fifth verse. This should be quoted again as a striking expression of the end to be attained, as embodying, indeed, all that lends meaning and beauty to mystical theology:

> "Oh, night that guided me,
> Oh, night more lovely than the dawn,
> Oh, night that joined Beloved with lover,
> Lover transformed in the Beloved!"

It is not without trepidation that I embark upon the next chapter, *The Mystical Doctrine of St. John of the Cross.* As a matter of fact, it will be concerned with only the first two treatises; but by treating the ten degrees of the scale of perfection, it will make perceptible the whole of the mystic ascent, even to its point of culmination.

I shall try to set forth as much as I understand, and to present to the largest possible circle of readers, in a comprehensible way, a kind of teaching which needs to be popularized without being debased. Nevertheless, I shall not attempt to divest it of its own characteristic notes, even though they belong to another time and to another land.

VII

THE MYSTICAL DOCTRINE OF ST. JOHN
OF THE CROSS

PROLOGUE

We are now about to attempt to follow that path which leads to the mountain's height; it is the high state of perfection we call *"the union of the soul with God."*

Neither experience nor human knowledge avails entirely in this pursuit. But, by the aid of both, the Scriptures can be searched, and in accordance with the teaching authority of the Church an interpretation can be made.

The Scriptures teach us, first of all, that God is *Love,* that He desires our happiness, that He alone is the key. It follows that the only thing that can impede the soul in its striving to attain perfection is its refusal to give itself over to the will of God, and its propensity to behave like a child that will not suffer to be led but thinks, rather, that it is able to carry on unhelped and unguided.

In the first place, one must have a proper idea of the end which is sought: God is this end. He is essentially so, by absolute the mysterious and, sometimes, obscure path of faith—a kind of and evident necessity. But God is invisible. One reaches Him by showing which cannot be seen—and hence we may deduce a primary rule, the very basis of all mystical theology:

Every soul that would reach perfection must pass to it by means of two sorts of darknesses or Nights. These "Nights" are simply what mystical writers term the "purgings" or "purifications" of the soul. Here I shall refer to them as "Nights" because the soul travels in the darkness of deepest night in both states.

Two kinds of Night may be distinguished:

"The first Night is that of the 'beginners,' during the time that God begins to lead them into the state of contemplation."

The second "Night" or second "purification" is that of "those who are on the way," and it endures until that hour when God is pleased to receive them into the state of union with Himself: It is darker and more terrifying than the first.

THE "NIGHT OF THE SENSES"

The first "Night," it may be said, is the night of the senses. In it are put out every light that proceeds from the senses, in order that the soul may be freed from excessive reliance upon the sense perception, which is all-dominant for the majority of men, who accord it too great an importance in their search for the true Reality, too much promise for their souls, and too final a value in the ultimate scale.

That this necessary "Night" may come to be within us, it suffices to rely upon faith, which alone can speak to us of true being, of the absolutely real, faith which teaches us that the real is something quite other than our senses tell us. This is not to say that God will show Himself to our seeing. In this life He does not show Himself to us as He is; at least He does not do so in a clear and direct manner. It is He who is the object of both reason and faith; but, as St. John says: "No one has seen God at any time."

There are, in the "night of the senses," three aspects or three successive acts: (1) the negation of sense perceptibility; (2) the appeal to faith; (3) the discovery of God.

Thus understood, the "night of the senses" is nothing other than the purification of the perceptible appetites or palpable desires. There must be no reaching out for sense consolation, neither the concupiscence of sight, taste, smell or touch, much less any trace of "concupiscence" itself, by which is meant the enjoyment of carnal delights: *This is the night.*

As a marginal note to this outline, which follows closely that of St. John of the Cross, I add the following observations of Father Lucien-Marie in *Oeuvres spirituelles,* pp. 14–15:

"Despite the apparent rigor which has led some to charge the mystic Doctor with a certain pessimism, it is not at all a matter of destroying, in the practice of this strict asceticism, our whole sensitive nature. It is not a question of wholly extinguishing every possible physical sensation. What is in question is the suppression of every voluntary and self-seeking pleasure in any sense-perceptible activity. In most cases, indeed, it is not within our power to suppress the activity in its totality.

"What the saint has in view and wishes may not happen is that anyone 'be devoted to,' 'set his heart upon,' 'be taken up with,' 'love,' or 'take pleasure in,' sight, feeling, hearing, touch, and so forth. He does not aspire to destroy even the least particle of our being—for, in itself, that being, which is of God's own creation, is good—nor even external things—'for they, too, are in themselves good'—but he does seek to root out all voluntary attachment, readily and inordinately enjoyed, to the things which are perceived by our senses."

WHAT SCRIPTURE TELLS US

John of the Cross strongly affirms that he desires no other inspiration than that of Sacred Scripture. But he appeals also to plain reason. This is his method of argumentation: The sensual masks God from us, it distracts us from God, it draws us away from Him. Now God is the Supreme Reality, because He is Eternal.

The "inordinate" love of the soul for a created thing puts that thing on a par with the Creator, and the greater the affection, the more does the soul descend to the plane of what it loves. It then lives only for the senses and by the senses, and it becomes the servant of the flesh. Thus the soul, which is a spirit, sinks to a level lower than that of matter, of which it is made the slave. But herein lies a temptation to be led astray; for, "by comparison to the Infinite Being, who is God, all created being is nothing." The soul, which loves nothingness, is itself no more than nothingness, "even less than nothing."

But here reason encounters the Scriptures, which constantly tell us of the nothingness of all created being: *Fallax gratia et vana est pulchritudo* . . . —"Favor is deceitful, and beauty is vain . . . as we read in Proverbs (31:30). And Jesus in the Gospel has said: ". . . None is good but God alone." (Luke 18:19).

> ". . . the wisdom of this world is foolishness with God . . ." declares St. Paul (I Cor. 3:19).

What are all the passing honors, delights, and riches of the world in comparison with the resplendent soul united to God, the soul which has been *transformed into God?*

Let us hear the author of the Book of Proverbs:

> "O ye men, to you I call, and my voice is to the sons of men. O little ones, understand subtilty and ye unwise, take notice . . . With me are riches and glory, glorious riches and justice. For my fruit is better than gold and the precious stone, and my blossoms than choice silver. I walk in the way of justice, in the midst of the paths of judgment, that I may enrich them that love me, and may fill their treasures." (Proverbs 8:4–5, 18–21).

Has Christ Himself told us anything to the contrary? By no

means. First of all, He requires of all who follow Him that they abandon all else. And this is not the thought of some merely human thinker, however sublime. This is the teaching of One Who is God:

> ". . . every one of you," he tells us, "that doth not renounce all that he possesseth, cannot be my disciple." (Luke 14:33).

Let us reflect on this: Whoever loves anything other than God clearly gives little honor to Him, for he weighs on the scale with God something of infinitely less value.

It is enough to reflect on this to realize how monstrous it is.

THE CONDITIONS FOR UNION WITH GOD

All that has been said, according to the thought of John of the Cross, makes it clear that mystical theology is neither illogical nor unreal. On the contrary, it devotes itself to the pursuit of the unique Reality.

In order that this invisible Reality be approached, three things must be done, in addition to what has already been said: (1) all idols must be cast aside; (2) all earthly desires must be overcome; (3) new ideas and sentiments in respect to God must mark the soul as though it were arrayed in new robes.

> "God permits not that any other thing should dwell together with Him. . . . He permits and wills that there should be only one desire where He is, which is to keep the law of God perfectly, and to bear upon oneself the Cross of Christ."

It cannot be contested that all affection given to creatures weakens the spirit of God within us, for "love for God and love for creatures are two contraries."

> "How, as a matter of fact, can one confuse creature

and Creator, the sensual with the spiritual, the visible with the invisible, the temporal with the Eternal, heavenly sustenance which is pure and celestial with sensual nourishment, the starkness of the Cross with any kind of attachment whatsoever?"

Jesus said, one day, to the Canaanite woman: "It is not good to take the bread of the children, and to cast it to the dogs."

And the Canaanite woman replied that the crumbs were cast to the little dogs who gathered around the table.

Indeed she spoke well—to the dogs belong the crumbs. These crumbs are created things. And when one eats nothing but crumbs he is always hungry. But how dreadful would it be, were these crumbs to deprive us of God!

THE RAVAGES OF CARNAL LUSTS

The carnal lust of creatures is the cause of five serious and inevitable ills of the spirit; these aberrations are: *wearying, tormenting, darkening, soiling,* and *weakening.*

Weariness of soul: The soul is never satisfied, never at peace, never content; hence it is in continual weariness.

Torments and afflictions: These are what Jesus would have us bring to mind when he said, "Come to me, all you that labor and are burdened, and I will refresh you." (Matt. 11:28). By saying *all you* He indicates that there are no exceptions, for He knew very well that for everyone life is a burden and that this burden is crushing.

Darkness and blindness of soul: All who are guided by their senses alone are ever in darkness, life has no meaning for them, they know not from where they came, or where they are going. Their faculties are disordered, devoid of true light, and alienated from their proper and normal activities. A memorable example of this state is found in Sacred History in the figure of Solomon. After he had enjoyed the highest known state of intellectual development, the sun of his wisdom set when he gave himself over to the slavery of the senses.

The soiling of the soul by carnal lusts: The sensual appetites are the channels through which all sorts of sins can enter within the soul and soil it.

The weakening of the soul: Thus wholly wrapped up in the senses, the soul is so weakened that it no longer knows itself to be what it is. Those who are enslaved by the senses no longer believe in the soul or its immortality, or even in God Himself. They glory in their atheism. And even among those who do not reach this dreadful state, weakness is inevitable, for a house divided against itself cannot stand: "The soul that is not at unity with itself in desiring God alone loses warmth and strength in virtue."

Conclusion: "The desires or carnal lusts of the soul are like little vipers which will devour their mothers": *It is evil desires that can destroy the soul.*

How Union with God is Brought About

Obviously, union is achieved through the will: Perfect union with God requires, therefore, a perfect identity of volition, that of God, who is the initiator of all things, and that of the soul, which must, in all things, follow His guidance.

Therefore, what is most necessary is that all desires which are alien to God's will must be repressed. Acts which are quite involuntary are, of course, not in question, although, in the case of souls which are tending toward perfection, even these very acts, which are called "primary motions," will be suppressed. John of the Cross makes this point in one of his maxims. It is clear then, that in order for the soul to cleave to Jesus alone, it is necessary to bypass all else.

Assuredly in this kind of renunciation it is a matter of degree, just as there are degrees in intimacy with Jesus: unruly desires in serious matters are greater impediments to the soul than are such desires in trifling things. Yet all such leanings weaken the spirit, while victories of virtue lend strength. The mystical union marks the attainment of something which is fundamental to what is at the basis of all ascetical endeavor. Thus, Jean Baruzi has declared in his great work, *Saint Jean de la Croix et le problème de l'expérience mystique:* "For John of the Cross, the rules of mortification are mystical rather than ascetical."

ACTIVE MEANS

Active means are employed in this "night" of the sense perceptions which is, by God's grace, the result of our striving and our asceticism. John of the Cross designates three:

Firstly, "let him have an habitual desire to imitate Christ in everything that he does, conforming himself to His life; upon which life he must meditate so that he may know how to imitate it, and to behave in all things as Christ would behave."

This is a rule which we already know, for it has been brought out in the examination of St. John's "maxims."

Secondly, we must renounce every leaning of our senses which is not directed to the honor and glory of God, thus detaching ourselves, for the love of Christ, from all else than the will of His Father, which He called His *meat and drink*.

Thirdly, we will then, as a matter of fact, attain to the "asceticism inspired by mysticism" in which we regard all things from a certain point of view, that is to say, we will "strive always to prefer, not that which is easiest, but that which is most difficult; Not that which is most delectable, but that which is most unpleasing; Not that which gives most pleasure, but rather that which gives least; Not that which is restful, but that which is wearisome; Not that which is consolation, but rather that which is disconsolateness. . . ."

One might, from all this, draw up a pattern of practical action such as John of the Cross, in the somewhat mannered style of

his age, has given us in the following lines, balancing opposite
courses of action:

> In order to arrive at having pleasure in everything,
> Desire to have pleasure in nothing.
> In order to arrive at possessing everything,
> Desire to possess nothing.
> In order to arrive at being everything,
> Desire to be nothing.
> In order to arrive at knowing everything,
> Desire to know nothing.
> In order to arrive at that wherein thou hast no pleasure,
> Thou must go by a way wherein thou hast no pleasure.
> In order to arrive at that which thou knowest not,
> Thou must go by a way thou knowest not.
> In order to arrive at that which thou possessest not,
> Thou must go by a way that thou possessest not.
> In order to arrive at that which thou art not,
> Thou must go through that which thou art not.

Actually, of course, it is by stripping off all things that one
achieves fulfillment. This is why Jesus said, ". . . he that shall
lose his life for me, shall find it." (Matt. 10:39).

THE STRUGGLE OF LIFE

There is nothing which can be done without struggling. This
struggle is no more than what we term the *askesis,* or aspiration
for the very heights of virtue, in which we spend all our energies
to combat and repress our own unruly desires. As I have already
said, in the thought of John of the Cross, asceticism is at the base
of all mysticism, which is as much as to say that it is the prelude
to love. He tells us that it requires a stronger love and a stronger
desire to put to flight lesser loves, lesser desires. One can, therefore, come to know the "night of the senses" only by a love
which is most solicitous, most strong, and wholly active, the kind

of love of which we are told in the poem already quoted at length. This love, which is God's, can be the cause of delight beyond description, even to those who are just beginning to scale the heights. And this is why it is fitting that the soul, before going forth on this great "adventure," should call out *blest and happy!* For it is an adventure that frees the soul from its passions and delivers it from servitude to them.

THE DARK LADDER: THE NIGHT OF THE SPIRIT

The soul that goes out of itself in order to seek God travels, all at once, upon a *dark ladder.* It is the ladder of faith. And it is, despite its darkness, a firm ladder for one who wishes to reach that sublime height of union with the Beloved. By it we enter, at once, into the *night of the soul.*

John of the Cross takes up in great detail why faith should be a kind of darkness. It is by reason of its very nature, for it reaches out into what cannot be seen. Faith, in the memorable words of the author of the *Epistle to the Hebrews,* is "the substance of things to be hoped for, the evidence of things that appear not." It is not wanting in surety because it depends upon God and His word. It opens to us the Real—not, indeed, sensible reality, nor even always rational reality, but Divine Reality—which is, after all, the only thing that is completely real. Faith, therefore, does not speak to our senses, and not in all cases to our reason. It brings us face to face with the truths of Faith in the way that a blind man is confronted by color. If you explain to him what is white and what is red, he will not understand you, but he can believe in the existence of white and red because you have told him of them: *Fides ex auditu . . .* —"Faith then cometh by hearing . . ." (Rom. 10:17). Faith is born of preaching, and preaching has its roots in the words of Christ.

It may, therefore, be said that faith gives light by putting out the sight. It speaks, indeed, of that Truth which is Light; but that truth is darkness itself to unaided reason. Nevertheless, faith is the only road to union with God. With the Psalmist, we can declare: "But darkness shall not be dark to thee, and night shall be light as the day: the darkness thereof, and the light thereof are alike to *thee*." (Ps. 138:12).

If we would attain to that which is beyond all sentiment and sensation, we must leave all sentiment and all sensation, and rely solely upon faith: ". . . For judgment I am come into this world," says Jesus, "that they who see not, may see; and they who see, may become blind." (John 9:39).

What now awaits us is a shining splendor! We must understand what union with God is like. Let us remember that God is everywhere: He is even present to the sinner. It is He who gives life to all that is, and without Him, all would lapse into nothingness, into the Void. However, when we speak of union with God, we have reference to a particular manner of His presence; that is, God, by His grace, brings within us an intensely personal manifestation of His presence. And of this manifestation there is more than one degree. The simple state of grace is only the first stage. What the mystical life really holds out to us is *transforming union,* and this can be defined as *the union of two wills whereby they become one:* a transformation that demands a long self-abandonment to the Divine Will of God. This requires two motions which move in a parallel manner: *The more the soul abandons itself to Him, the more God reigns within it.* Renunciation is not an end in itself: It must be intent on serving God —other than this the effort is futile.

John of the Cross was fond of this comparison which exemplifies the above: If the sun is to shine through a window, that window must be clean. Thus, if God is to enter the soul, the soul must be pure. As the window became light when it was cleansed, so the soul, when it is *wholly* pure, becomes God.

THE THREE THEOLOGICAL VIRTUES

It is through the workings of the three theological virtues that the complete "Night" of the soul is achieved. These virtues purify our three faculties:

Faith purifies our intelligence, our first faculty, by dispelling from true reality all that is alien to God and to the union of the soul with God. *Hope* purifies our second faculty, the imagination, by dispelling all joy and trust in anything whatever save God. *Charity* purifies the will, our third faculty, by dispelling all love other than the love of the one and only Goodness and Beauty, which is God.

Thus, the practice of faith, hope, and charity serves to empty us of mere human concern in the way which Christ instructed when He told us that one loses one's life in order to find it. And this is why St. John stresses this important point.

> "This road to God consists not in a multiplicity of meditations nor in ways or methods of such, nor in consolations . . . but that it consists only in the one thing that is needful, which is the ability to deny oneself truly, according to that which is without and to that which is within, giving oneself up to suffering for Christ's sake, and to total annihilation."

In this, St. John's mystical doctrine has seemed, to more than one reader, harsh and even pitiless. But we should not allow ourselves to be frightened off by his stern words. They are not a matter for daily practice. Life is not, after all, one sequence of tragedies. But in every life there are difficult and trying times, and it is then that the Cross of Jesus rises up before us. For after all, the following of Christ—which is the essence of true religion—is the constant remembrance of the Cross. Let us raise our thoughts up to God. The Creator is, of course, infinitely above all creatures, infinitely beyond even our thoughts of Him. "One can truly unite himself to Him only by the way of faith, which is beyond all understanding." For this reason, Dionysius the Mystic called mystical contemplation "a beam of darkness." As St. Paul has reminded us, we see God ". . . through a glass in a dark manner . . ." (*in aenigmate*) (I Cor. 13:12).

VISIONS AND REVELATIONS

There is a point upon which John of the Cross takes a decisive stand, and that concerns the distrust we should always have concerning all those extraordinary manifestations in which the general public nevertheless finds such satisfaction. One might imagine, from their attitude, that there is no such thing as great sanctity apart from that associated with visions and revelations. This is a patent error, one which should be rectified at all cost.

John of the Cross is concerned with manifestations of this nature only insofar as they may be what we call "gratuitous gifts" or *charismata*. They are manifestations that serve a particular end and which the Church has not rejected. The apparitions of Our Lady to Bernadette at Lourdes are an example of this kind of *charismata*. If we venerate in Bernadette a canonized saint, it is not because of these apparitions, but because she practiced virtue to a heroic degree. It is clear that if Bernadette had drawn cause for self-glorification from these apparitions, she would have fallen into a most dangerous form of self-delusion. John of the Cross had no wish to speak of any of these matters apart from the point of view of the favored soul.

In this question, let us probe the thought of John of the Cross. He tells us that we should avoid and distrust all so-called "supernatural" feelings, whether they be of smell, taste, lights enjoyed, visions experienced, or delights heard. All such things, in his reading of the matter, are, most frequently, sources of Satan's temptation, and they are useless to the normal progress of faith and our union with God through faith alone. Consequently, even though such things may come from God, which is always possible, one must never become attached to them, much less rest satisfied in them, or allow oneself to be disturbed when they cease; nor should we rejoice in their continuance if they do. At best, such gifts can be made use of by beginners. But, if one is to continue on the road to union with God, he must turn away from such things, and even deliberately discard them.

In the same sense St. John counsels distrust of the imagination in the manner in which God is pictured. We should stop striving after this sort of thing; for it will result in nothing but failure to attain the end. God is infinitely beyond our reach, and for this reason the principle obtains that *meditation* ought tend to disappear so that it may give way to *contemplation*.

And, at this point, we touch upon one of the most serious of all problems in Mystical Theology. For this reason John of the Cross now speaks with a special insistence.

MEDITATION AND CONTEMPLATION

The differentiation between these two means of coming closer to God will soon be evident. By God's grace, the soul, in meditating, rejoices in the full flush of its own activity. Imagination, memory, reason, all take part. First, there is set up what we call the "construction of place"; then follows the "enlistment of the faculties." We speak to God as much as we can, even often to the point of not allowing Him to speak Himself, so that we are heedless of what it is that He would say to us. This is "discursive meditation," so named because it is a kind of "discourse" we make to God.

John of the Cross teaches that this *discursive* method is something beginners cannot dispense with. He even says that, from time to time, one should return to this method, in order not to fall into a mere routine of mental prayer.

But he takes great care to point out how the *Spiritual Guide* or *Director*—to whom the soul is in all things to submit itself— may recognize, by signs, when one is to pass on from meditation to contemplation. There are three such signs: First, an inability to achieve discursive meditation; second, a failure of the imagination, even in other fields of its natural activity; third, "The soul takes pleasure in being alone, and waits with loving attentiveness upon God, without making any particular meditation, in inward peace and quietness and rest. . . ."

One can readily perceive how *contemplation* differs from *discursive meditation*.

But in order that one be really called to the contemplative life, the three signs must, necessarily, be present; they cannot be dispensed with.

In explanation of the first sign it may be said that distaste is a sign worthy of consideration. In principle, *quod sapit nutrit;* something which arouses the appetite is something which may be profitably made use of. What tends to good arouses zest in the soul. No doubt, this kind of zest ought not be confused with mere *consolation* which one has no right either to seek or to repulse. However, as soon as the end of meditation becomes attainable without this zest, there is no further need to rely upon it. The end is that the soul becomes with God. Hence, in the case of those who achieve this union "by an act of knowledge, dark, loving, and peaceful, in which the soul places itself to drink in the wisdom, the love, and the full flavor of God," nothing further is to be asked for; there is no further searching required.

The *second sign* is significant in establishing that a distaste for speculative thought about God or the mysteries of faith does not arise from a disposition to retain attachment for the things of this world.

But it is the *third sign* which is of chief importance in determining whether there be in the soul "the knowledge, or loving and peaceful awareness of God."

Yet, it must be recognized that this last characteristic is so subtle, so direct, and so simple that it is often perceptible only with difficulty. This state of the soul very often resembles *a forgetfulness of all things* in which the soul may be plunged, for hours at a time, unaware of the flight of time. This is the state expressed in the words of the *Canticle of Canticles:* "I sleep, and my heart watcheth . . ." (5:2).

The contemplative soul does not turn back again to discursive meditation unless it senses that it is badly established in contemplation. But it is good for it, when it be in the state of "loving awareness of God," with conscious seeing or feeling, to remain so and to refrain from restless striving of the spirit, "in the attitude of one who is content simply to open his eyes just so that he may effortlessly see the light."

What is essential is that "the soul be established in peace, in repose, in true love."

There is no doubt that John of the Cross was not the first to discover what I have been talking about. Dom Georges Lefèbvre, in the work, *La Grâce de la Prière,* compares the doctrine of St. Gregory the Great with that of St. John of the Cross as leading the reader to silent confrontation with God, in peace, in confidence, and in all the wealth of spiritual moderation. Ceaselessly he reverts to one thought—that of simple prayer. Prayer is to be offered to God in single-mindedness, the soul quietly keeping itself ready and open to the action of grace, in entire self-offering, as though it were saying: "Here I am, Lord; do with my nothingness as You will."

It is exactly this disposition which is to be discerned in St. Vincent de Paul as we see him writing to one of his religious: "Rather desire to bear things than to be doing things." And as much is true of Paul-François Libermann, whose doctrine of the "passivity" of the soul, under God's hand, has been strongly brought out by a recent writer, Abbé Blanchard.

We must be quite assured that there is no exercise of the imagination, no kind of intellectual speculation, whether it be born of God, of the devil, or of oneself, which can lead us to union with God. The devil often makes use of the imagination and fancy to confuse and deceive souls. In such instances one believes they have achieved the height of sanctity because they have noble notions about God. Actually, this makes oneself the plaything of Satan. And, after all, it is not worth asking whether or not this or that imaginative fantasy comes from God or

Satan: The better way is to hold oneself in readiness to give "that peaceful and single-minded awareness which in love and gentleness will make possible union with God."

It is to this that John of the Cross constantly returns. And, in his insistence upon it, he forcefully wars against what he denounces under the name of "the spirit of selfhood."

Therefore, the soul is not to search after fancies, visions, or turbulent feelings: It is rather to receive in peace and humility whatever God may send it. Even then, it must not become attached to what it receives, as though it had "a right" to what God may choose to send it. It must not feel regretful if it loses a sense of what God is sending, nor even, when it does feel such a sense, display anything other than reliance upon faith. All else is of no avail.

A First Objection

It may, however, be asked: Why, acknowledge, if all these feelings, visions, illuminations, and things of such ilk are so dangerous, that they can be from God?

The reply is that God treats us according to the nature that He gives us. Yes, He does take hold of our imagination and our sensory perceptions, but He intends these as means, not enduring things, not ends. As a matter of fact, our imaginings, in matters of devotion, are no more than passing things; they come and go, and we know not why. We cannot afford to build upon them. If we had no other foundation the result would be catastrophic. It is for this reason that there are many who turn away from God. Such men have believed, but they have placed their trust in shadows, and when these shadows failed, their faith has failed with them. Thus it is that one sees those who have been believers, devout, and even fervent, pass into a state of indifference and even of hostility to God.

God always makes use of our imaginations and our sense

perceptions in order to raise us to Himself, but only on the condition that as soon as we are able, we ourselves mount to His height. The mystical ascent is made in stages: At the beginning, by listening to sermons, by attendance at Mass, by the reading of good books, by the exercise of the spirit of mortification of the senses, proceeding to the raising of the soul to higher things, through the medium of the imagination at first, as we give ourselves to thought and discursive meditation. All of this is no more than a good beginning. God leads us, ever more and more, to what is within, so that we must, little by little, bid farewell to a reliance on sense perception, the imagination, and finally even to the intellectual preoccupations.

In this sense, I might say that the Liturgical Revival, as we see it in our day, is an excellent thing, and perhaps even more so, the revival of the study of Sacred Scripture. But Christians, whether priests or lay people, must still strive to bring to pass in all fruitfulness a Mystical Revival by the practice of a life deeply oriented toward interior things, such a life of habitual contemplation as John of the Cross teaches us to follow.

St. John has cited in this regard the words of St. Paul: "When I was a child, I spoke as a child, I understood as a child, I thought as a child. But, when I became a man, I put away the things of a child." (I Cor. 13:11).

A SECOND OBJECTION

If all this be true, how can it be that God grants visions, ecstasies, revelations, and such things, particularly to souls already advanced on the path to Him; and how is it that such graces so often are the mark of the highest state of spirituality?

The reply is that God is indeed able to grant extraordinary and sensibly perceptible graces even to those who are in a state of spiritual maturity. But the soul is not to become attached to any of these. It must remain in a state of humble and firm faith. Directors of souls who lay stress upon extraordinary spiritual favors are the blind guides of whom the Gospel speaks: They lead their disciples into the pit (Matt. 15:14). This is actually a great peril to true humility, and more than this, a temptation to a kind of "spiritual gluttony" which inclines one to succumb to the danger of "trusting anyone." Let us therefore always return to this rule: "Place no reliance on visions and revelations, but remain firm in faith alone." It is only by so doing that one can be certain of not being misled. A careful examination of spiritual experiences leads to the following conclusions: (1) The granting of these favors is, of itself, no certain indication of God's pleasure; (2) Self-satisfaction in their possession is a certain cause of His sovereign displeasure; (3) When He does send them to us, it is, so far as He is concerned, to make trial of our humility; (4) It is evident that the demon is often responsible for them in order to work ill to our souls.

A THIRD OBJECTION

But, since all this is so, how can we explain that so much is made, in the Old Testament, of prophecies and revelations, and why Israel is so often reproached for not having "questioned God" through His prophets?

In reply, it may be noted that revelation in the Old Testament was in the process of being given; it had not yet been fulfilled. Consequently, few theological signposts are therein provided; there is nothing really definitive. The prophecies declare what is to be and prepare for it. However, in our era, revelation has been closed. It is completed and irrevocable. The Faith is now fixed. One has only to follow it and to be distrustful of any additions to it. This is why the Church judges with such severity all purported visions, and accounts of apparitions and miracles, and such wondrous events.

Jesus Christ has told us all that we have need of knowing. We need seek no further; if we understand all that He has said, we need look for nothing else.

John of the Cross has emphasized this point at great length and most carefully, doubtless because it seemed to answer to the exigencies of his day. And, to tell the truth, that often unhealthy curiosity which leads men of our own time to tend to spectacular things is in need of the helpful correction which the rules he has provided in this part of his treatise, *Ascent of Mount Carmel,* can provide. They will teach us to distrust the pretended revelations of those who declare "God has said this to me; God has said that to me."

As John of the Cross has written: "I knew a person who had these successive locutions: among them were some very true and substantial ones concerning the most holy Sacrament of the Eucharist, but others were sheer heresy."

Practical Rules

John of the Cross, therefore, formed some very simple and thoroughly logical rules according to which one might determine just what to do in the face of extraordinary manifestations:

It is an *inviolable rule* that ". . . if humility and charity be not engendered by such experiences, and mortification and holy simplicity and silence, etc., what can be the value of them? I say, then, that these things may hinder the soul greatly in its progress to Divine union. . . ."

In the spirit of faith we are apt to have the Holy Spirit shower His gifts upon us. The greater our faith, the more love will He endow us with; the greater our love, the more will He enlighten us. Therefore we must not confine ourselves to *one* revelation, to *one inspiration,* because it has been given to us; we must rather cleave, in faith, to the whole idea of Revelation, which is God's Wisdom and the source of every insight. Let us not give as much value to learned words which lead us into spiritual thoughts, as we do to humble love.

There is another rule which St. John gives us that in substance says: Every thought or interior voice which induces humble and respectful love for God within the soul is born of the Holy Spirit; every thought which engenders self-satisfaction, interior pride, a sense of selfhood, is born of Satan.

To sum up, whatever is demonic is to be recognized by one or another of these signs: There will be either internal unrest and a repugnance to engage in God's service, or overmuch trust in oneself. The means of protection against any kind of illusion is to be convinced always of a desire to hold fast to the faith and to the decision of the Church. Faith is definitively and essentially the path to being one with God.

At all times, John of the Cross grants the possibility of over-whelmingly imperative commands which, in one word, suffice to direct the soul. Such are: "Love"; "Be perfect"; "Walk in My sight." When the soul is enlightened by these divine commands, *it must conduct itself in all humility:* it must fear nothing, but *offer itself unto God,* for His good pleasure. When we have once said to Him: "Speak, Lord, for Thy servant heareth," it is only logical that we receive His answer in all humility. Such will be our reaction when God deigns to infuse into our souls unexpected realizations of His will. The principle is ever the same: *Let us lay ourselves open to His fashioning hand.* This is a principle full of wisdom.

THE PURIFICATION OF THE MEMORY

All that has hitherto been said is concerned with effecting in us that "night of the senses" which leads to the "night of the soul." But, if the soul is to walk this way, in the path of contemplation upon which it has entered, it is necessary that the memory and the will be purged or purified; for the action of faith has served only to purify the understanding.

John of the Cross makes us aware that each of the three theological virtues, faith, hope, and charity, has its own role to play in the "purification" or "night" of the three faculties of our soul, the intellect, the memory, and the will.

According to his understanding of human psychology, which was that of his own age and dates back to St. Augustine, these three faculties embody the activities of the human soul.

The theological virtue of hope is affirmed so that the memory can be purified.

If we are to understand this matter fully, we must realize that, according to John of the Cross, memory comprises all that life tells us, from day to day: It embodies the whole content of daily experience. And it is this which must be cleansed, which must be purified, in order that God alone may reign within us. Herein is expressed that opposition which divides the *Nada* and the *Todo,* Nothingness and All. In order that the memory be purified, it must be stripped of all that it has as its own, it must be made blank so that God may speak. This is exactly what St. Paul tells us when he says, ". . . forgetting the things that are behind, and stretching forth myself to those that are before, I press towards the mark, to the prize of the supernal vocation of God in Christ Jesus" (Philip. 3:13–14).

This is not to say that memory must be cast aside; for the "night of the senses" is not intended to destroy our sensitive nature. Nevertheless, the ideal is that the memory be under God's hand alone and thus rest forgetful of all else.

This subjection of the memory to God is an indispensable thing; for the functioning of the memory lays it open to all perceptible recollection, things which may fill it and darken it by engulfing it in a flood of imperfection, and of venial sins, even of impure thoughts. All such unleashed recollections come from yielding to appetites which grow and demand our subservience. God, however, speaks only when we are at peace within ourselves—as He did in the Cenacle, God comes to us "through closed doors." His first word to us is always *Pax vobiscum*— "Peace be with you."

God's complete domination over our memory is necessary for another reason. Satan will catch hold of it in order to confound us so that he can pummel our minds into despair over old sins and tempt us to new ones; he desires above all else to rupture our union with God, Whom he detests. Therefore, it is impossible for the human spirit to be at rest if the memory is allowed to be active. Great, indeed, are the advantages of emptying it; that is, of *never recalling what is over and done with, so that we may give to God all that is in the present and will be in the future.*

In all this one may easily discern the working of the virtue of hope. Under the impulse of this theological virtue, we place all our hope of happiness in God alone. And, in this way, hope cleanses the imagination, which is nothing other than the direction of memory to the future with the help of past experience.

Once our memory has been purified, it has much more to do in order to conserve the precious recollection of *spiritual principles,* imprinted by God upon it; principles which are readily to be recognized as being *the appropriate means of union with God.* This is, after all, our real end, something which should never be forgotten. The further one becomes detached from things which are seen, things which show no more than a shadow of what really is, the more one becomes enamored of that which is unseen, the more one trusts in God alone.

THE PURIFICATION OF THE WILL THROUGH CHARITY

In this whole process of purification it is evident that much is left to the will; and for it there is still a further purification. This is brought about by the help of divine grace. Yet one might say that the effort made by the will is even more evident than is the action of grace. For this reason the purifications or "nights" achieved in this domain ought be called active purifications or "active nights" or "darknesses."

From the moment that one enters upon the contemplative life, one's effort fulfills itself by the dominating force of grace exercised upon the will, and it is this which makes the "active darkness" become a "passive darkness," as has already been suggested.

Much has to be done to make effective the purification which has just been discussed; much has to be done within the domain of the will itself in regard to certain inner motivations which modern psychology attaches to our sensitivity, but which John of the Cross thought to be seated in the will itself. He calls these motivations carnal joy, fear, hope, suffering, and distress.

Joy is in principle absolutely conditioned by its object: "The will should take no joy in anything unless it is for the honor and glory of God."

The greatest service we can render to God is to follow the precepts of the Gospel. Anything else is valueless and profitless insofar as we are concerned.

Therefore we must guard against placing our joy in anything created, in any such things as earthly riches, which are no more than *vanitus vanitatum*—"vanity of vanities." Moses was well advised to declare in his *Canticle* that the infidelities of God's people arose from the fact that they had become *sated with fatness*. In this very fact alone did they become balky and deny their God. Detachment from worldly riches is therefore the best preparation for the reception of all that God will give to us.

A basic point in the life of devotion is the realization of the vanity of all earthly things. The false joys of this world give rise in their delusiveness to a kind of intoxication of the soul which drives it to forget its own nature, and which destroys in it its inherent capacity for what is divine.

On the other hand, great good can flow from the distrust of false joy: An awareness of the love of God, interior peace, avoidance of occasions of sin, detachment from the vain appearance of worldly things, and all that the love of God requires for its true showing. Every evidence exists that we cannot go to God through our senses. All those things in which the sensory perceptions grant us joy turn us from God and deprive us of godly joy. Such are termed vices, temptations conveyed to the soul through our senses.

On the other hand, when the sensual joys are cast aside and

abandoned, the whole force of the soul is turned toward God. So is progress made in the life of union with Him; so does one prepare for everlasting love.

Logic indicates that all that has been said here in regard to carnal joys is equally applicable to the other sensory appetites which I have named: fear, hope, suffering, and distress.

However, John of the Cross has not thought it necessary to repeat himself on these points; for all can be disposed of in the same manner as he did in respect to carnal joy.

He therefore ends his book *Ascent of Mount Carmel* by two observations of supreme significance.

First, as far as *good works* are concerned, and since it is clear that a will dedicated to God must manifest itself in the doing of good work, John of the Cross again points out the danger which exists in the spirit of selfhood.

Without verging in the least degree upon the heretical doctrine of Luther concerning salvation "by faith apart from good works," St. John of the Cross, who is a theologian infinitely more refined and more dependable than the heavy-minded Saxon, tells us what we should think about good works.

To begin with, he is quite certain that they are fruits of faith, hope, and charity, and that, as such, are necessary and meritorious. But then, and most prudently, John of the Cross actually enumerates seven perils which flow from good works. They are vainglory, the pharisaical spirit, the distrust of our fellows, over-confidence in self, resistance to advice, and so forth. Every one of these is rooted, of course, in the *spirit of selfhood*. On the other hand, he furnishes us with a list of *five advantageous notes,* which are the fruit of our unconcern with the merit of good works: It is by them that we escape from temptation; they free the reason; they make us like unto those who are poor in spirit; they make us humble and prudent, pleasing to God and to men.

In the second place, he discusses *vain observance*. In addition to being prudent about good works, we must avoid anything that resembles vain observance: In other words, the mere doing of things, as it were, for their own sake; for this is superstition. That kind of *searching after charismatic gifts,* which is not born of charity is something John of the Cross warns us against in counseling us to guide ourselves by faith alone. Following along the same line of thought, we are not to give overmuch weight to external things, especially to the veneration of *images,* something good enough in principle, but often disfigured by intemperance in practice. In the Spain of his day—and elsewhere, too—this sort of thing was rather widespread. In the eyes of John of the Cross, images are useful things, provided that their importance be not exaggerated and that they really draw us to the things that cannot be seen by mortal eyes. This is to be applied also to that preference for particular places of devotion. He was hitting, of course, at the undue significance attached to the making of pilgrimages. And he offers similar counsels in respect to sermons; for he who is the best speaker is not necessarily the best preacher; rather is this true of the speaker who is, himself, most saintly and who can best aid his listeners to make the most progress in the direction of holiness.

THE SEVEN DEADLY SINS OF THE SPIRITUALLY MINDED

I have said several times that the second treatise of St. John of the Cross, which bears the title *Noche Oscura,* or *Dark Night of the Soul,* is actually a part of the *Ascent of Mount Carmel,* which I have just attempted to summarize.

As a matter of fact, in the second treatise our author takes up, once more, the chief themes which he had already developed, and he considers them especially from the crucial viewpoint of all that concerns *going from the meditative to the contemplative state.*

I shall pause particularly on the part of this second treatise in which John vividly paints for us the seven deadly sins which lie in wait for "beginners," and which balk them in their progress toward that contemplative life which is the path of those who are already making some progress on the road to perfection. What are these seven deadly sins?

Spiritual Pride. One has scarcely begun the spiritual life when one thinks oneself to be "someone." An inner pride spurs us to undue confidence in ourselves, to the criticism of others: It may even go so far as to become a more or less conscious Pharisaism. It is to be understood very readily that there is only one remedy for this: humility.

Spiritual Avarice. This is the mark of those who have an insatiable taste for readings, for particular practices of devotion and set forms of prayer, for images, for medals and like external things, to all of which they attach an inordinate significance.

Here I may note how great is the good common sense and the noble wisdom of Mystical Theology as taught by John of the Cross.

Spiritual Lechery. This is shown in a desire for consolation and spiritual pleasures. Nothing is more useless to those who would attain holiness than this. It is, again, a manifestation of the spirit of *selfhood.*

Spiritual Anger. This is a deplorable spirit of impatience in the face of one's own imperfections and failures. This is something against which the soul is obliged to struggle.

Spiritual Envy. This is that unworthy feeling which inspires in us a *jealousy of the saints,* causing us to think or to say that they would not have been any more holy than we ourselves had they not been endowed with graces which have been denied to us.

Spiritual Gluttony or Intemperance. This is ever seeking after exciting and favorable impressions, and it leads to:

Spiritual Sloth or Tepidity (*Accedie*). In the grip of this vice, the soul knows only discouragement and despairs of ever attaining the goal.

THE TRIALS OF THOSE WHO ARE MAKING PROGRESS

As a result of the struggle against the defects about which I have been speaking, the soul generally finds itself in a state of "dryness," engulfed in "distaste," but if the soul be strong and faithful, nonetheless firmly *attached to God alone*. Three signs will show that this dryness comes from God and leads us to God: (1) when there is no desire for anything else but God; (2) when one suffers by reason of not loving and serving God; (3) when it becomes impossible to practice discursive meditation.

What is to be done at this point?

The essential thing is that the soul remain at peace and in humility, united to God alone. This blessed weakness which the soul feels within itself is as nothing when set beside "the loving realization that God alone is within the heart."

It is truly here that begins that "adventure happy and blest" —oh! dichosa ventura! It is this which gives us entry to distress but also into the burning heat of God's love:

"On a dark night,
kindled in love with yearnings . . ."

That "dryness" into which the soul has been plunged offers one great advantage: *It makes us conscious of our own nothingness, and it spurs us on to God!*

As a result of this disposition of the soul we come to gentleness and peace, to an habitual fixation of the self upon God, to clear-sightedness and purity of soul, to the practice of virtue.

It would be astonishing if harsh temptations did not now lie in wait for the soul; for we must not forget that Satan is relentless in the pursuit of souls which have entered upon the way of contemplation. And, as all Scripture attests, there awaits those who will travel this way an inevitable and necessary trial.

Dangers similar to those of which I have spoken in regard to "beginners" now await those who are making progress on the way. Such is the belief that one is so "advanced" that one may take vain satisfaction in the fact. Such is the disposition to be deceived by vain fancies, such as visions and ecstacies, or to take pride in one's own cogitations, instead of walking the path of simple faith. Again the craft of the demon fully exercises itself against the soul.

THE SOUL GOES FORTH

We have heard the soul cry out, in a transport of holy joy:

"I went forth without being observed,
My house being now at rest."

The soul has gone out of itself. This is to say that it has left the merely human level of interest, and aided, of course, by grace, is striving to win a place on the divine level, under the impulsion of dominant grace and with nothing but faith as its guide. And this applies, as I have said, to every one of the soul's faculties—to intellect, to memory, to will.

So great is the chasm, so great the unlikeness between fallen human nature and that light of God which is faith, that this passage from one level to the other, this "going out" of the soul into the "dark night" is full of difficult and distressing shapes. Those who are making progress are to expect, here, all sorts of moral suffering. The most bitter to them will be their inability to love and to serve God as they would wish to do. All the saints have walked this way. It is this kind of mystical suffering to which we can apply those Biblical texts of Job, Jeremiah, and David, which we are all too often prone to interpret as though they had to do with physical and moral unhappiness.

What is most necessary now is a complete purification of the sensitive perceptions and of those more subtle self-attachments of the spirit, so that God can reign within us. All the mystical sufferings of the "purgative way," at first, and then, later, of the "illuminative way" stem from this dispelling of all that is unworthy of the divine level.

Here John of the Cross furnishes us with a comparison which has justly become celebrated.

He tells us that if one casts a fagot into the fire, the fire must, first of all, dry it out and purge it so that it can become flammable. Thus it is that God progressively enflames souls. There is at first much smoke, because a great deal of airy vapor has to be burned off. But, when the fagot is throughly engulfed by the fire, when it is glowing at white heat, then there is no more smoke; for the wood has become, so to speak, all fire. It is the same in respect to the soul. At the beginning of the spiritual life there is a great deal of smoke, but as the soul becomes more pure, it bursts into fuller flame and then, finally, it becomes consumed by flame in God.

HOW THE SOUL GOES FORWARD

The time comes when God works, within us, on our understanding and our will, at the same time. But this is not always so. It very often happens—perhaps this is of even more frequent occurrence—that God will work only upon the will and not, to any marked degree, upon the speculative intellect. There have been great saints who have not been "intellectuals." Although there is the well-known case of the Curé of Ars, who is close enough to us in point of time, there are others as well, in the past, such as Francis of Assisi and St. Rita and a great many more, not distinguished for intellectual attainments, but nevertheless burning with most ardent love.

One thing, however, is certain: Whatever be the manner of its advance into the "dark night," the soul does go forth in wondrous security.

This is expressed in the second strophe of *Dark Night of the Soul:*

> "In darkness and secure,
> By the secret ladder, disguised—
> oh, happy chance!—
> In darkness and in concealment.
> My house being now at rest."

And, as the third strophe immediately puts it:

> "In the happy night,
> In secret, when none saw me,
> Nor I beheld aught,
> Without light or guide,
> save that which burned in my heart."

It is pure faith, burning within the heart and incapable of being deceived that makes the soul wholly secure, even though it sees nothing and does not know what will happen to it.

This darkness is the darkness of mystical theology, which is not dependent upon the buttressing of rationality, but is built upon Faith and a close relationship with God.

THE SECRET LADDER

The whole journey of those who are on the way to God is made by the "secret ladder." This is only to say that there are degrees in loving, and that one has to climb for a long time before one reaches the goal. "St. Bernard," as John of the Cross tells us, "has very well said that 'love is a thing of great moment, but there are levels of love.'" One might follow St. Thomas Aquinas here; for in the twenty-eighth chapter of his book on the love of God and of fellow man, he distinguishes "ten degrees of love."

John of the Cross has made this division his own and very clearly points out these degrees.

He goes on, therefore, to describe for us the whole upward advance of the soul from the time it first sets out upon the path of the contemplative life to the point of highest attainment, which is the spiritual marriage of the soul and the Beloved.

In his description of the *ten steps on the ladder of love,* he sets up a whole system of Mystical Theology. No doubt, it may be said that the book which I am now analyzing gives only a rapid survey of this matter; but, in his later works, *Spiritual Canticle* and *Living Flame of Love,* he returns to and perfects the description already introduced in his two earliest works and in his first poem.

To these different degrees I have given names, which are not, indeed, those of St. John, but seem to me to interpret his mind. I take for them full responsibility and leave it to the reader to make his own judgment.

The first degree is the love of self-abasement and of longing. On the first step of the ladder, the soul lies in abasement before God and is smitten with the sickness of love. This is that first point which, in Solomon's Song, the Bride expresses in these words:

"I adjure you, O daughters of Jerusalem, if you find my Beloved, that you tell him that I languish with love." (5:8).

This is not a sickness unto death, but one for the glory of God. Actually, it is through this sickness of love that the soul disentangles itself from sin and from all that is not of God. As the Psalmist puts it, ". . . my spirit hath fainted away. Turn not thy face from me, lest I be like unto them that go down into the pit." (Ps. 142:7).

On this first step the soul is like one who is sick and has no taste for food, for it loses its taste for earthly things. It breaks with all that is past in its life. It enters upon a new world. Now it wants only to please God; only God attracts it. This sickness of love is a great grace and comes from God. It actually brings home to the soul something else said by the Psalmist: "Thou shalt set aside for thy inheritance a free rain, O God: and it was weakened, but thou hast made it perfect." (Ps. 67:10).

It is impossible to begin to mount the secret ladder of the ascent toward God unless we begin with entire detachment from all created things. For this reason I term this love *the love of self-abasement*. It means that, in our eyes, all that is not God is as nothingness. He alone matters, and all things are valueless unless they guide us to Him, bring us closer to Him, unite us to Him. On this first step there is neither savor, nor joy, nor solace, nor light, nor support in anything apart from God. Already, a beautiful kind of love has been attained by the soul; but it is no more than a beginning.

The second degree is the love of the soul's search for God. One passes naturally from the first step to the second almost without knowing it, just as a tree grows without anyone being able to say why. This second step is the unceasing search for God. It is expressed in the words of the Bride in Solomon's Song, where she is made to say: "In my bed by night I sought him whom my soul loveth . . ." (III:1). Psalm 104:4 gives expression to the same thought in the words: "Seek ye the Lord, and be strengthened: seek his face evermore." This search for the well-Beloved then becomes the most compelling thing in all life. The bride suffers many fearsome things: "I sought him," she says, "and found him not: I called, and he did not answer me. The keepers that go about the city found me: they struck me: and wounded me . . ." (5:6–7).

And this is the way Mary Magdalene searched for her Saviour at the tomb; her desire was so great that finally she could not perceive Him. He stood before her and she mistook Him for the gardener. (John 20:14–15).

While on this step of the ladder, the soul looks all about for the well-Beloved, and asks for Him from every passing wind. Should the soul open a book and not find Jesus therein, she shuts it in dismay. So it was that after his conversion no book was pleasing to Augustine unless he could discern Jesus therein. The soul, in this state, has no taste for anything other than the search for the Saviour: it is of Him that it ever speaks and thinks. Whatever the soul may be doing, in the midst even of sleep, in the work of the day, and in recreation, it is always

Jesus who dominates the spirit and fills the heart. This is a state of mind which dominates again and again, even when, after backslidings and failures, the soul mounts once more the secret stair.

I am inclined to see an expression of this degree of love in the first strophes of the *Spiritual Canticle,* which I do not hesitate, therefore, to refer to here as being a natural continuation of the dual work *Ascent of Mount Carmel* and *Dark Night:*

> "Seeking my loves,
> I will go o'er yonder mountains and banks;
> I will neither pluck the flowers
> nor fear the wild beasts;
> I will pass by the mighty and cross the frontiers."

Then follows a moving dialogue between the soul and creatures, but I will cite now only the conclusion, which serves to emphasize that liking for limpid streams which was so marked a feature of John, as we learn from many of those who knew him in his lifetime:

> "O crystalline fount,
> If on that thy silvered surface
> Thou wouldst of a sudden form the eyes desired
> Which I bear outlined in my inmost parts! . . ."

The third degree is the love of work. This is the third step on love's ladder. It is the willingness to *work* in the cause of the well-Beloved and to be spent in this work. This is that state of the soul of which it is written: "Blessed is the man that feareth the Lord: he shall delight exceedingly in his commandments. (Ps. 111:1). If the "fear of the Lord," which is Love's own daughter, has such an effect on the soul, then what will Love itself bring about? On this step, the bride does not take full count of all that can be done for the Beloved. The soul, wholly enflamed with ardent love, finds too little time in which to do all God's work. Jacob was glad to work for seven years to win Rachel.

If human love is so strong, then what will not be done to win divine love? The greatest cause of suffering to the longing soul is that it cannot do better, that it cannot do more and more, for God. The soul wishes to do a thousand times more. And all that the soul does is done freely and without the thought of establishing a title to any recompense. As the Gospel points out, the soul looks upon itself as an unworthy servant. Thus is the soul far from succumbing to the evils of vainglory and presumption. In this state the soul rather fixes all its strength on humility, by feeling itself to be so inadequate and so unavailing in God's service.

The fourth degree is the love which suffers. It will not be a surprise to discover that John of the Cross places on a higher level the love which suffers with Jesus and for Jesus than that which desires to work with and for Him. In many of his maxims it can be noted how frequently he expresses this idea; as, for example, in No. 13 of *Other Maxims:* "Better is it to suffer for God's sake than to work miracles."

On this fourth rung of the secret ladder, the soul therefore agrees, for the sake of the Beloved, to suffer constantly and uncomplainingly. As St. Augustine has stated: "The soul finds all that is burdensome and painful to be quite easy and light to bear."—"*Omnia seava et immania prorsus facilia et prope nulla facit amor.*" (Sermon on the Word of God in Matthew). So, too, does the Bride in Solomon's Song cry out: "Put me as a seal upon thy heart, as a seal upon thy arm, for love is strong as death . . . neither can the floods drown it . . ." (8:6–7).

The spirit is now grown so strong and it holds the flesh in such subjection that the latter seems of no greater moment than does a single leaf of some great tree. The soul's only preoccupation is to serve God and to return thanks to Him. The soul does not even think of any recompense for what it accomplishes or endures. God will, however, say to it, as written in Jeremias (2:2): ". . . I have remembered thee, pitying thy youth, and the love of thy espousals, when thou followedst me in the desert, in a land that is not sown."

The soul which truly loves never recoils from any suffering, and the only thing which really gives it pain is that it cannot love God enough.

The fifth degree is the love of conquest. On this rung of the ladder the soul is so much overcome by its desire to serve God and to be united to Him that every delay, no matter how slight, seems prolonged and grievous. Every time it realizes that its desire has not yet come to pass, it is plunged anew in vehement sorrow. This is what the Psalmist sang of, when he wrote: "My soul longeth and fainteth for the courts of the Lord. My heart and my flesh have rejoiced in the living God." (83:3).

On this step, the bride cannot stop from looking all about for the well-Beloved. The soul would rather die than offend Him or fail in His service. The soul calls out, in the despairing accents of Rachel: "Give me children, otehwise I shall die" (Gen. 30: 1), by which is meant: "Grant that I may win souls to You, grant me victories for You, lest I die. And when I can no more work for You, then let me die indeed."

Here I should be inclined to recall the following verses (VIII–XI) of the *Spiritual Canticle:*

"But how, O life, dost thou persevere,
  Since thou livest not where thou livest,
  And since the arrows make thee to die which thou
    receivest
  From the conceptions of the Beloved which thou
    formest within thee?

"Since thou hast wounded this heart,
  Wherefore didst thou not heal it?
  And wherefore, having robbed me of it, has thou
    left it thus
  And takest not the prey that thou hast spoiled?

"Quench thou my griefs,
Since none suffices to remove them,
And let mine eyes behold thee,
Since thou art their light and for thee alone I wish
  to have them.

Reveal thy presence
And let the vision of thee and thy beauty slay me;
Behold, the affliction of love is not cured
Save by thy presence and thy form."

The sixth degree is the love of the high-flown and rapid journey that leads to God. In the sixth degree, the soul wings its way, with nimble agility, toward God. It has now come to know Him well, and it rushes onward tirelessly in the hope of the Divine Confrontation. This is the love which lends great power to the wings of the soul. The prophet Isaias paints this state of the soul well when he says: ". . . they that hope in the Lord shall renew their strength, they shall take wings as eagles, they shall run and not be weary, they shall walk and not faint." (40:31). And the same thought underlies the words of Israel's great singer: "As the hart panteth after the fountains of water; so my soul panteth after thee, O God. My soul hath thirsted after the strong living God . . ." (Ps. 41:2–3).

The cause of this swift flight, of this great movement of the soul projecting itself ever more and more Godwards is clearly seated in the strength of the love which lies within it. Then it is that the soul joyfully cries out with the Psalmist: "I have run the way of thy commandments, when thou didst enlarge my heart." (Ps. 118:32).

It seems beyond question that this is the same point on the "secret ladder" that is marked by the following verse of the *Spiritual Canticle* (No. XII):

"Withdraw them, Beloved, for I fly away.

Return thou, dove,

For the wounded hart appears on the hill
At the air of thy flight, and takes refreshment."

The seventh degree is the love marked by bold confidence in God. When the soul arrives at this rung of the ladder, it feels itself closer and closer to God. No longer is it in danger of being separated from Him. To Him it dares say all; it awaits all from Him; it hopes wholly in Him.

St. Paul best described this state when he said: "[Charity] beareth all things, believeth all things, hopeth all things, endureth all things." (I Cor. 13:7). And Moses, too, was impregnated with this love, when he said to God: ". . . either forgive them this trespass, or if thou do not, strike me out of the book that thou hast written." (Ex. 32:31–32). Thus did he dare to express fullest confidence in God, trusting even in the pardon of His people who had bowed themselves down before the golden calf. David was inspired with the same thought when he declared: "Delight in the Lord, and He will give thee the requests of thy heart." (Ps. 36:4).

So it is also with the bride in Solomon's Song as she cries out: "Let him kiss me with the kiss of his mouth . . ." (1:1). It is clear that the soul could not speak in such a way unless it felt, as did Esther, that it had found favor in the King's eye. Nevertheless, it does not, for all of that, lose one vestige of the humility that has enabled it to attain this level. The overwhelming strength of its love does, however, gird it with a holy boldness. And this holy boldness is at the root of all it now feels.

Doubtless, it is right to interpret, in this sense and as proper to this degree of love, all that is said in strophes XV to XVIII of the *Spiritual Canticle:*

"Our flowery bed,
  Encompassed with dens of lions,
  Hung with purple and builded in peace,
  Crowned with a thousand shields of gold.

"In the track of thy footprint
The young girls run along by the way.
At the touch of a spark, at the spiced wine,
Flows forth the Divine balsam.

"In the inner cellar,
of my Beloved have I drunk,
And, when I went forth over all this meadow,
Then knew I naught
And lost the flock which I followed aforetime.

"There he gave me his breast;
There he taught me a science most delectable;
And I gave myself to him indeed, reserving nothing;
There I promised him to be his bride."

The eighth degree is the love of the Divine Espousal. In the eighth degree there is brought to pass the espousal of the soul with the Divine Bridegroom. Then it is that the soul cries out in the words of Solomon's Song: "I found him whom my soul loveth . . . and I will not let him go . . ." (3:4).

To tell the truth, were this state an enduring one, it would already be that of heavenly glory; but the espousal is not a really definitive union. The soul has, indeed, found Whom it has been seeking; but it cannot yet perdure in His presence. It has not yet attained the fuller happiness of possessing Him without abatement: It knows Him only at intervals and for short but intense periods. The soul remains what Daniel was —*"vir desideriorum"*—"a man of desires." But does not God greatly love those who burn with desire for Him? In the Book of Daniel God said: "Daniel, thou man of desires [that is to say, a man well loved by God], . . . stand upright . . . (10:11). God is so good that he is willing to accept our great desires to love Him as being the reality of that love. And it is just such desire that marks this eighth degree of love.

I might remark here that all along the path traced by the

rungs of the secret ladder of love, it is the desire of God that brings that love into play. From the very first step, as we have seen, the soul is beset with the desire to love God. By desire it seeks God in the second degree. It works for Him; it endures all for Him; it wishes to win souls to Him; it rushes onward in its flight to Him; it dares to court the state proper to those pure spirits that throng around Him: So much does it do in its desire of Him. Finally, there is brought to be the espousal of the soul to Him, born of that vivid desire the soul has to be His alone.

The ninth degree is the love marked by blandness. In this ninth degree the soul is wholly encompassed by gentle blandness. This is a state characteristic not of those who are on the way to God, but rather of those already made "perfect" in His sight, the state of those who are *burning with love*. This state is found in all the great saints. What I wish to emphasize here, the quality of *burning with love*, is especially familiar to us in the case of Marguerite-Marie Alacoque.

It is the Holy Spirit who brings to birth in the soul this burning flame of all-consuming sweetness, which is the fruit of the union it henceforth enjoys with God. St. Gregory the Great put it very well when, after the Holy Spirit had come upon the Apostles, he said: "Now that they had received the Lord under the form of tongues of fire, they were all sweetly afire with love!" —*"Dum Deum in ignis visione suscipiunt, per amorem suaviter arserunt!"*

What is brought to pass in this ninth degree is beyond expression in words. The higher one goes, the more lacking is human expression in power to depict what passes between the soul and God. Perhaps one might say that our very words enlarge their sense as an attempt is made to speak of each advance. We make use of the same words, because we have no better ones; but their significance is amplified as we pass from the lower to the higher degrees of love.

It is for this reason that it is they alone who have scaled the higher rungs of the ladder of love who can understand what it is all about.

This is even more true as one passes, in the company of John of the Cross, up to the tenth degree.

The tenth degree is the state of the Spiritual Marriage. It is on this tenth rung of the ladder that the ascent upward to perfection has finally been achieved. Neither here nor in the world to come can one mount to greater height. It is in this state that one may say (*Ascent of Mount Carmel*, Stanza 5):

> "Oh, night that joined Beloved with lover,
> Lover transformed in the Beloved!"

In the *Spiritual Marriage* the union of the soul with God is definitively achieved. This is by assimilation of the soul with God. This state plunges the soul directly into the glory of the Beatific Vision, even though it has not passed through Purgatory. Few indeed are the souls who attain to such a state in this life; for it requires the most unspotted purity of heart. Here are fully verified the words of Our Lord: "Blessed are the clean of heart: for they shall see God." (Matt. 5:8). And it is in the same sense that we can best interpret the words of St. John: ". . . we are now the sons of God; and it hath not yet appeared what we shall be. We know, that, when he shall appear, we shall be like to him: because we shall see him as he is." (I John 3:2).

We are not to see here any kind of absorption of the soul into God in the strict sense. There is no trace of pantheism in the authentic mystical theology of one like John of the Cross. The soul remains itself—it is still a finite entity; but God has raised it to a sharing in His own nature which is beyond all understanding. Thus is it made truly divine by the action of divine grace. This I have previously suggested in commenting on one of the maxims of John of the Cross: "And, as we say, this vision is the cause of the perfect likeness of the soul to God, for, as St. John the Evangelist says, we know that we shall be like Him.

Not because the soul will come to have the capacity of God, for that is impossible; but because all that it is will become like to God, for which cause it will be called, and will be, God by participation."

Conclusion

John of the Cross has now run the whole gamut of mystical theology by means of this "secret ladder of love." His great treatise—for the *Ascent of Mount Carmel* and the *Dark Night* form one entire whole—is thus framed by a *Canticle* of eight strophes which already points to the whole upward flight of the soul, and a description of the ten rungs on that ladder of love which takes the soul, little by little, from the foot of the mount to its highest summit.

In his other writings, he gives us many further and delightful embellishments, but he never goes beyond this. The whole essence of his mystical theology is already revealed in this dual work. And it was exactly that doctrine, defined and precise, which he bore within himself wherever he went so that it inspired not only his own conduct but the great work among souls which it was given him to do. I shall now trace out the remaining parts of his life, a life in which we find the best of commentaries on his teaching.

VIII

THE SPIRITUAL GUIDE

(1579–1586)

THE WAY IS OPEN

One question remained at the time John of the Cross was made Rector of the College of the Discalced at the University at Baeza. What would happen in the struggle between the Discalced and the Brethren of the Mitigated Observance? When John escaped from his prison at Toledo, it might well have been asked what would happen to him. The newly appointed Nuncio, Monsignor Sega, who had arrived in Madrid on Friday, August 30, 1577, had shown himself as violently opposed to the "Reformers" among the Carmelites as his predecessor, Monsignor Ormaneto, had been favorable to them. Affairs threatened to turn out badly. The new Nuncio went so far as to describe Mother Teresa as a "disturbed and vagabondish woman, disobedient to the point of contumacy, who, cloaking herself in devotion, thinks up evil doctrines."

His purpose was to place the Discalced under the jurisdiction of the Observants, and consequently totally destroy the "Reform" in root and branch. Happily for Mother Teresa, she had powerful friends both in heaven and on earth. King Philip II, who regarded religious matters as being of prime significance to the welfare of his states, was shocked to see the peril which threatened those who had hoped to renew the primitive spirit of the Order of Our Lady of Mount Carmel. For years complicated negotiations ensued on this subject between the King's Council and the Nuncio. Finally, the hopes of St. Teresa materialized. The Discalced were not made subordinate to the Fathers of the Mitigated Observance, as Father Tostado had wished, but, according to a decision given by Pope Gregory XIII, the two Spanish branches of the Order were separated into two independent provinces which, although they were required to acknowledge the same Superior General, were independent of each other. This Brief of separation was signed by the Pope on Wednesday, June 22, 1580 and sent to King Philip at Badajoz, reaching him in mid-August. But the news had already spread. At Baeza John of the Cross had known of it since the fifth of August. It strengthened him against some of his Discalced brethren who had believed the cause was lost, and he was able to give them renewed courage when it at length prevailed.

Nevertheless, several months were required before the separation could go into effect. The first two commissioners who had been entrusted with the promulgation and carrying into effect of the Papal Brief had died before they were able to fulfill their function. The third one named was the Dominican, Father Juan de las Cuevas, Prior of Talavera.

On Wednesday, January 4, 1581, his authority was confirmed by Rome, and he at once associated with himself Father Jerónimo Gracián. These two convoked a Provincial Chapter of the Discalced at Alcala de Henares, to meet in the following March. All of the Priors were invited to participate and to bring with them some companion of their own choosing. John of the Cross, as Prior of Baeza, was among those invited, and he selected Father Innocencio de San Andreas as his companion.

The Chapter was to be held at Alcala in Castile. It was necessary to travel across La Mancha, which separated Andalucía from Castile. We do not know how John of the Cross made this journey, but he did arrive a day late. On Friday, March 3, under the chairmanship of the Apostolic Commissioner, Juan de las Cuevas, the Bull of separation was solemnly read. The confirming act, therefore, bear neither the signature of the Prior of Baeza nor that of Father Antonio de Jesús, who had contended with John for the title of the "first of the Discalced." Antonio had been detained by urgent ministerial duties.

THE CHAPTER OF ALCALA

After March 4 the deliberations of the Chapter began, and John of the Cross participated in them. The entire town of Alcala was in a holiday mood. King Philip had decreed that all the expenses of the assembly were to be remitted to the Royal Treasury. The assembly was carried out in a magnificent style, truly Spanish, accompanied by religious ceremonies, processions, masses, and public functions. The Chapter proceeded to the election of "definitors" of the Discalced, that is to say of Fathers charged to superintend the observance of their Constitutions. Elected were Father Nicolas de Jesús-Maria Doria, Prior of Pastrana; Father Antonio de Jesús, Prior of Mancera; Father John of the Cross, Prior of Baeza; and Father Gabriel de la Ascunción, a member of the community at La Roda. Without intermission, they proceeded to the election of a Provincial Prior, and Father Jerónimo Gracián was chosen. The *Te Deum* was sung and the whole city rejoiced. That Sunday, March 5, a great academic meeting marked by the intellectual feats of many theologians was conducted, and a great procession was held through the streets of the city. Prayers for the King who had been so generous were offered by all. The Chapter came to an end on Thursday, March 16, having lasted thirteen days. Fray John of the Cross left for Andalucía so that he might return to Baeza.

JOURNEYINGS

But John was not to remain in Baeza for long. Although he had been extremely active and was much in the public eye, he was to become almost an exile. Nevertheless, we have a letter of his, dated July 6, 1581, from Baeza, which contains some surprising lines. John writes to Mother Catalina de Jesús, without knowing her whereabouts, as follows:

". . . Although I do not know where you are, I want to write you these lines, trusting that our Mother will send them on to you if you are not with her; and, if you are not with her, be comforted with me, for I am in exile farther away still and am alone down here; for since I was swallowed by that whale and cast up in this harbor, I have not been found worthy to see you again, nor the saints that are up yonder. God has done all things well, for, after all, desolation is a file, and the endurance of darkness in preparation for great light. . . ."

This is eloquent language. Because he was a man given to renunciation does not mean that he was unfeeling. On the contrary, he seems to have been most sensitive. We should have thought him quite satisfied with his ministry at Baeza, which could not have been more blest. Yet there he found himself a lonely exile. The file of desolation had cut deeply into his soul. Although this Castilian found Andalucía a strange place, he remained there many more years. But he was not to be at Baeza.

During the last days of June 1581, and therefore immediately before writing the letter just cited, he was charged with an important mission to the Monastery of the Discalced at Caravaca where, at the designation of the Prior Provincial, he went to preside at the elections. He did actually superintend them on June 28, and we have his official report on the subject, addressed to Father Gracián.

Soon, however, a much longer trip was to be required of him, but this time it was a journey which would give him the consolation of seeing his beloved Castile again, and his even more beloved friend and collaborator, Mother Teresa.

The question was the foundation of a convent of the Reformed Carmelites at Granada. The Provincial Vicar to whom the matter had been committed had been blundering and unsuccessful. Mother Ana de Jesús, who was approaching the end of her term as Prioress of Beas, understood the reasons for his failure quite well, and she asked the advice of her confessor, Fray John of the Cross, in whom she had unbounded trust. They agreed that if it were possible to have Mother Teresa at the projected Granada foundation, all would go well. But if her collaboration were to be secured, someone she could trust would have to be sent to her and, in the eyes of Ana de Jesús, there was none more suitable than Fray John of the Cross.

A request was therefore made of the Prior Provincial, Father Jerónimo Gracián, that he order Fray John of the Cross to proceed to Avila to see Mother Teresa; Father Gracián agreed to this on Monday, November 13, 1581.

It is easy to realize how happy this made John of the Cross. He would again see Teresa, whom he so greatly respected, and whom he had not seen since the brutal arrest at Avila on December 2, 1577. He set out at once and reached Avila toward the end of November 1581. His interview with Mother Teresa took place in the small parlor at St. Joseph's Convent. We have a letter in which she tells us of her own joy, but in spite of this, she was unable to accept the suggestion that she go to Granada, for she was already committed to establish a foundation at Burgos, in the opposite direction. However, she did appoint the nuns to establish the convent at Granada, and at their head put Mother Ana de Jesús.

On Wednesday, November 29, John of the Cross departed with the necessary letters authorizing the new foundation. Accompanied by the small group of nuns, he reached Beas on Friday, December 8, and gave Ana de Jesús the order to proceed with the establishment of the new house. Preparations were at once begun at Beas. We know how much John was devoted to this community. He willingly agreed to remain there while awaiting a reply from the Archbishop of Granada, who had been requested to permit the foundation of a Carmelite convent in his episcopal city. His answer arrived after more than a month. On Saturday, January 13, 1582 John of the Cross and Ana de Jesús began their journey. As his companion, Fray John selected Fray Pedro de los Angeles, and these two led the seven nuns on the way.

AT GRANADA

After traveling dangerous roads and enduring raging storms, the little group arrived at Albolote, about two and a half miles from Granada, on Friday, January 19. On the preceding evening they had been able to hear claps of thunder, which Ana de Jesús described as "most terrifying." It was not until later that they learned that lightning had struck the bishop's palace, setting fire to the library and to the sleeping apartments of the prelate, as well as killing all the mules in his stables.

As it turned out, however, this was to prove a providential stroke. On the nineteenth, while they waited at Albolote, Fray John of the Cross and Mother Ana de Jesús received very serious news. The Provincial Vicar of the Discalced at Granada told them that the Archbishop had refused to authorize the foundation of a convent of the Discalced Carmelites and that he had nullified the sale of the house which had been selected for the convent. The Vicar was then obliged to take refuge for the time at the residence of a distinguished lady in the town, Doña Ana de Penalosa. John of the Cross could not then foresee all that this lady was to be to him. However, at a later date and at her wish, he was to set down his final piece of writing, *Living Flame of Love,* and it was to her that he dedicated this masterpiece.

Ana de Penalosa secretly received the Carmelite religious and made them welcome at three in the morning; but she did this with such cordiality and made such preparations to receive them that they were at once comforted. She had even gone so far as to set up a chapel in one of the best rooms of her house for the celebration of Mass. After their long trip and the grave uncertainties that greeted them on their arrival, they could not keep from weeping for gratitude at their welcome in this house. In the song of the psalmist, they gave their thanks: *Laudate Dominum omnis gentes*.

To add to their joy they learned that the Archbishop, whose Episcopal Palace had been struck by lightning a few days before, now declared that he would grant them the desired license to establish a convent of the Discalced. However, he refused to receive them or give them any assistance, referring to the heavy damages from which he was then suffering as the result of the storm.

The foundation was set under way at once with the hasty and welcome assistance of Ana de Penalosa.

PRIOR OF LOS MARTIRES

It was a remarkable coincidence that there already existed at Granada a monastery of the Discalced Carmelite Fathers, erected in 1573, and that this convent was then without a Prior. The last incumbent, Fray Agostino de los Rayes, had just been summoned to Salamanca by the Provincial, who had named him Rector of the University College in that city. By right of the new Constitutions, the brethren of this monastery had the power to elect a new prior. Their choice was Fray John of the Cross, despite the fact that he was already Prior of Baeza. According to the Constitutions, if a prior of another monastery should be elected, he was to consider himself in the latter office, providing he had served for two years in his former incumbency. These provisions applied to John of the Cross, and he therefore now became Prior of the Carmel of Granada, which was called the Monastery of Los Martires. It was delightfully situated on a hill, to the southeast of the Alhambra, and not far from the well-known

Gardens of Generalife. The nuns from Beas found refuge in the
old Palace of the "Gran Capitan," Gonzalo Fernández de Córdoba, the famous emulator of Bayard.

The community at Los Martires was not large. Fray John
accepted novices, and their testimony during the enquiries pre-
paratory his beatification furnishes us with a detailed account of
his life at Granada. Among these novices were Fray Juan Evangelista, who was to become John's most faithful companion during the nine years of life remaining to him, and who often acted
as his secretary and amanuensis; Fray Alonso de la Madre de
Dios, a nephew of the Archbishop of Granada, who was later to
be Novice Master there and, afterwards, Prior at Ubeda; Fray
Martin de San Jose, who believed his master so holy that for
more than thirty years he carried a cincture which John had
worn and by means of which cures, considered to be miraculous,
were wrought; Fray Miguel de los Angeles, who died as Novice
Master at Granada with the reputation of sanctity; and Fray
Agustín de la Concepción, who had been present at the establishment of the foundation at Baeza and who was a favored witness
of certain ecstasies of John of the Cross.

Alonso de la Madre de Dios had, originally, thought of going
among the Carthusians, and had even taken some preliminary
steps in that direction. But when he came into contact with the
Carmelites, he hinted, in the midst of a half-serious, half-jok-
ing conversation, that he would prefer to become one of them.
Once he had been received into the house, he fell prey to violent
self-reproach, as though he had attempted to deceive everyone,
Carthusians and Carmelites alike, by contradictory promises. He
dreamed of fleeing to some place where he was unknown, where
he might hide the shame of a liar. Happily, he was taken in
hand by John of the Cross, who had discerned his troubled state
of mind. With some difficulty, the consent of the Archbishop was
secured for the young man's entry into the Carmelite Order.
During his first two days in the house, the food seemed so dis-
tasteful to him that he could eat nothing; but finally, hunger

triumphed over his reluctance, and afterwards he manifested so great an appetite that John of the Cross, who understood everything, said laughingly to him: "Come, my brother, do not attack the food with such gusto!"

Sometime later, during the Prior's absence, Fray Alonso committed a serious fault against the Rule. He was punished for this by the Superior's deputy, and when John of the Cross returned, he was told of what had happened. When Fray Alonso passed in front of him, he confined himself to saying, "Fray Alonso, repeat what you did before." These words were so terrifying to the poor friar that he shut himself up in his cell and applied the discipline so vigorously that he was months in recovering from the blows he had showered upon himself in the spirit of penitence.

After he had completed his novitiate and had been ordained, Alonso was named Novice Master by John of the Cross. Following this, he underwent great trials: He fell into spiritual darkness, and doubts, and his whole soul seemed so enmeshed by fear that he did not think he would survive. At this time John of the Cross, who, as we shall see, had been named Provincial Vicar for Andalucía, was making his round of visitations. When he returned, Fray Alonso hastened to confide to him all his troubles, but John of the Cross only smiled and said, *"Ande, bobo, que no es nada!"* "Run along, you dunce; it's nothing!"

Suddenly the depression lifted and Father Alonso was cured of all his anguish.

JOHN OF THE CROSS AND HIS PROCURATOR

There are many similar anecdotes about Fray Juan Evangelista. He had won the entire confidence of John of the Cross and had been made Procurator from the beginning; that is to say, he served as the *Econome,* or Treasurer, of the community.

It is interesting to see a great mystic in daily life. Teresa of Avila showed the world that she was quite capable of coping with material affairs. John of the Cross was no less an organizer than she. He brought about renovations and enlargements in his monastery, although, naturally, funds were short. One day, when the Procurator had nothing to give the community to eat and no money with which to buy food, he went to the Prior to ask his permission to go and beg money from some of the benefactors of the monastery.

"May God forgive you, my son," Fray John answered. "Shall we not pass a day—and even longer—in patience if it should please God to test our courage? Go now, and return to your cell and put your troubles in the hands of Our Lord."

The Procurator obeyed, but remembering that there were some invalids in the house, he again faced the Prior. Once more John of the Cross told him to return to his cell. The Procurator was upset and still not convinced. Mealtime was approaching. What would the brethren say as they came to an empty table? Finally, he cried out:

"Father Prior, it is tempting Our Lord to wait: He wishes us to do all that we can. Will Your Reverence allow me to do what is necessary to obtain food for the brethren?"

"Very well, then," said John of the Cross with a laugh. "Choose a companion and you will soon see that God will make you ashamed of your lack of faith."

The Procurator obeyed at once. But he had scarcely left the monastery when he ran into an official of the Court, who said to the priest:

"Where are you off to now, Father?"

"I am going to beg for food."

"Well, indeed; let Your Reverence look at this. I have here a judgment of the Court to the effect that a fine which has been imposed upon a lawbreaker is to be applied to the use of your monastery."

And he handed him twelve gold pieces. The Brother Procurator was stupified. He returned hastily and told his Prior what had taken place, but John only said:

"How much more merit you would have had had you remained in your cell until God sent you whatever was necessary, rather than running about in such excitement. Learn, my son, to trust in God."

On another occasion, John's help was asked in a case of demoniac possession. A young girl of noble lineage was in the power of Satan. The Father Prior went to her, taking with him Fray Juan Evangelista (who has passed these facts on to us). After the Prior saw the possessed girl, he remained apart in prayer. Out of the mouth of the unfortunate girl came the words of the demon: "I can do nothing against this wisp of a friar. I have never been able to trip him up, although he has pursued me all over, at Avila, at Torafe, and now here!"

When the Father Prior returned, the brother told him what the demon had said in praise of him; but John of the Cross said hurriedly: "Be quiet, my brother; do not believe what the demon says, for all his words are false."

These are certainly all minor incidents, but they have been gathered from the process of beatification, and they show us this great mystic in the midst of the events of the workaday world. So also may we see him in the accounts which follow.

THE DAILY LIFE OF A SAINT

John of the Cross, although outstanding and honored among all who knew him, selected for his own use at the Monastery of Los Martires the poorest, the least convenient, the narrowest of chambers. The house had been greatly embellished and enlarged, but it was his wish to remain in the older portion of it. In his cell were only a figure of Christ in wood, an image of Our Lady, a Bible, and a Breviary. There were no other books. For a bed he had a poor pallet on which he lay during the relatively few hours he allotted to sleeping. A motto from the Psalms summed up the whole spirit of the place: *Quid mihi est in coelo et a te quid volui super terram?*—"For what have I in heaven? and besides thee what do I desire upon earth?" (Ps. 72:25).

There is, however, one slight detail which, in its simplicity, tells us all we need know: In this miserable room there was a small window which looked out on the garden. Fray Luis de los Angeles tells us that when he was in his cell, Fray John spent much time in prayer at this window. He says that he often found his Prior in this position, for John would gaze upon the flowers by day and the stars by night.

How much this helps us understand some of the lines of John's *Spiritual Canticle,* as when he says of the flowers (Stanza 5):

"Scattering a thousand graces,
   He passed through these groves in haste,
   And, looking upon them as he went,
   Left them, by his glance alone, clothed with beauty."

Thus does he express the splendor of the night (Stanza 15):

"The tranquil night,
   At the time of the rising of the dawn,
   The silent music, the sounding solitude,
   The supper that recreates and enkindles love."

All this is, indeed, in character with the great poet we know John to be.

JOHN AS A SUPERIOR

Even ten years before, while he had been Confessor at the Convent of the Incarnation at Avila, his reputation for sanctity sometimes frightened some of the sisters. They thought that he would be unbending and austere. One nun, in fact, did not dare confess to him until one day, partly reassured, she knelt trembling before him and naïvely made avowal of her fear of him at the same time she told him of her sins.

"But I am no saint," John of the Cross said to her. "And even if I were, you ought not to fear, for the more holy a confessor is, the kinder and gentler he is, and the less will your faults astonish him, for he knows very well what human weakness is."

At Granada he conducted himself in the same fashion. Father Fernando de la Cruz, who knew him then, declared: "He treated all the religious with great charity and love. No doubt, he was firm: He corrected their slightest faults, as was his duty. When necessary, he would inflict the penance imposed by the Constitutions—the discipline of the rod. But when the penance had been effected, it was he who would affectionately cover up the shoulders of the delinquent and return the doffed habit, sometimes kneeling down to kiss the scapulary and to ask a blessing, all of which filled the heart of the offender with worthwhile regret for the fault committed."

Least of all was he the suspicious type of superior, forever snooping about and spying upon his subordinates to catch them at fault. Having confidence in his brethren whenever he gave an order, he allowed full freedom in its fulfillment. He did not seek to surprise his sons. On the contrary, he was careful that they knew of his approach by the quiet rustling of the Rosary he carried, so that those at fault would be alerted. He was never heard to raise his voice in reprimand to anyone, nor was he known to speak in anger or to show his irritation. When he found it necessary to issue a reprimand, it was in so kind and gentle a manner that it was obvious his only desire was to correct the fault without pain to the culprit. Whenever possible, reprimands were given privately. He knew how to gain willing acceptance of the penances which were imposed to ensure true repentance. Never did he show distress before any brother who might show a spirit of rebellion.

One day, when he was dealing with such a rebel, he was met with angry and bitter words. But the Prior was not upset. He pulled up his hood and threw himself face down on the ground. He remained in this penitential position until the young religious had finished his tirade. Then he arose and kissing his scapulary, said: "I accept this for the love of God." So greatly did this impress the angry young religious that his ill-feeling was at once dispelled and, overcome with shame, he repented. The humility of the Superior had won a victory over the arrogance of the subject.

Moreover, it is evident that John of the Cross regretted any occasion which demanded severity. It was his wish that the rest of the community should ask pardon for the guilty member. One day, after he had punished one of the brethren by commanding him to stay in his cell until evening, it was John himself who went about seeking the others, since none had come forward to intercede on behalf of the delinquent.

However, this kindness never degenerated into weakness. John never forgot that religious discipline must be inward rather than outward. He knew every one of his religious intimately. He saw them individually. Usually in the evening he would go about the house learning the state of the brethren's souls, particularly their prayer habits, the temptations which they suffered, and the progress they were making in union with God. It can be understood, from the exposition I have already attempted of the principles of Mystical Theology as interpreted by John, how he would direct others in a certain way and to what end he would point. He knew, most of all, how to adapt general principles according to the needs and aptitudes of individuals. In a community not everyone marches along at the same pace toward perfection. A good superior, such as John, is able to say to each one just what is fitting and to give the kind of advice needed.

In Nature's Garden

At Granada, as it had been at Calvario, John liked his community to enjoy the outdoors, and loved to lead the brethren into the open fields. To someone who once asked him why he made these excursions, he replied that it was better for the brethren not to be too much confined indoors. Usually he would have them climb the hill behind the monastery and then lead them as far as the foothills of the Sierra Nevada, upon which grew various species of plants, orange and olive trees among the chestnuts and pines; and on some bare summits the snow gleamed.

When they arrived at the place he had chosen, they would pause in contemplation of the magnificence of the countryside. Then he would tell his brethren to scatter out, saying:

"Today, each of us will go alone to the heights, that we may spend the day in prayer and solitude, praising the Lord after our own fashion."

Sometimes, also, he would get them engaged in some quiet game or sport, and then withdraw to spend the time before they were to eat in prayer.

More than once, when his religious went to look for him, they found him in ecstasy kneeling before a sprig of herb or a bunch of thyme.

He loved the sight of running water and would sit on the bank gazing into the waters, and at the little fish who darted about.

"Come and see," he would cry out, "come here and see how these little creations of God's hand know how to praise their Master . . ." And then, as he would fall into a state of ecstasy, his brethren would respectfully withdraw while their Prior continued to praise God in His creation.

Does this not remind one of Francis of Assisi? Such has been the thought and impression of one of the most recent biographers of St. John of the Cross, Gilles Mauger, who in a book published in 1959 wrote something of which I heartily approve: "St. Francis and St. John are assuredly the two saints who have most savored the beauty of nature and who have best voiced its poetry . . ." I share, too, M. Mauger's astonishment "that some should, wrongly indeed, paint the *gentle* St. Francis as opposed to the *harsh* St. John, as though they were contrasting the sun-flooded horizon of Umbria to the dreary landscape of Castile."

What I most love about John of the Cross is his deep and consistent humanity. He was a man who knew how to win the heart. His religious regarded him with veneration, but it was a veneration shot through with the affection of sons for their father. Whenever he returned from a journey they would gather about him, kissing his scapulary and asking for his blessing.

Not only did he allot time for the outings which I have described, but he established real festivals, which were called by the brethren *huelgas,* or holidays. On these days, although he did not relax his own practice of self-denial, he made certain that his spiritual sons had more abundant and more appealing fare than on ordinary days. He loved to please them by telling stories he made up at their request or which he formed from the Scriptures, with his own inspiring commentaries. At other times, seated in the midst of them, he would ask them questions and draw out their replies. One day he asked the most artless of the lay brothers:

"Fray Francisco, what is God?"

"God," replied the simple brother, "God is someone whom one loves."

And John of the Cross was so taken with this reply that he repeated it and enthusiastically explained it, thus making everyone see its charm.

There was a monitor appointed among the brethren, known familiarly as the *alguacil,* or detective, because he was charged with keeping watch over conversations. Whenever they would become too frivolous, this person would cast himself face down on the ground, to indicate that the subject should be changed.

Although John of the Cross set himself against the abuse of images, medals, and such external showings of devotion, this did not mean that he did not respect the celebration of liturgical solemnities. He was particularly fond of the Christmas festival, which was the occasion for delightful rejoicing at his monastery.

JOHN AND THE CARMELITE SISTERS

It will be recalled that when Fray John of the Cross, Mother
Ana de Jesús and their companions reached Granada, they could
find no place to stay except in the home of Doña Ana de
Penalosa, and it was there that John visited them. Thus between
Fray John and Doña Ana there arose a friendship based on the
respect and confidence she felt in him and on his own interest in
her spiritual development. By chance, a smattering of their conversations have been preserved for us. One day, when one of
the sisters wished to speak to him, she found him seated in the
attitude of a confessor with Doña Ana kneeling before him
in tears. The sister heard John, whose eyes were uplifted, cry
out in resolute accents: *"Nada! Nada! Hasta dar un pellejo y otro
por Cristo!"*—"It is nothing, nothing! One must give the whole
self and more for Christ!"

Later, when the nuns found a place in the town where they
could set up a convent, John of the Cross visited them regularly
to hear their confessions and confer with them; these conferences
were a source of spiritual delight to them all. No doubt, it was in
the early days of his life at Granada that there occurred an
episode over which he was more inclined to laugh than be
annoyed. As he walked along the streets one day, a woman with
a child in her arms threw herself on him, crying out that he was
the father of the child whose mother was a young lady of noble
lineage. The woman's clamor attracted a crowd. Everyone wanted
to know what the religious would say in reply to the accusation.

Undisturbed, John asked:

"How old is this child?"

"He is exactly one year old."

"And from what place does his mother come?"

"She was born in Granada, and has never left it."

"In that case," replied John of the Cross, to the accompaniment
of much laughter from the surrounding crowd, "this is indeed a

miraculous child, for I have not been in Granada a year, and this is my first trip."

At the Convent of the Discalced Nuns the first to receive direction from John, whether in the confessional or in the parlor, was the Prioress, Mother Ana de Jesús. For Mother Ana and her nuns he was to compose that book which some of his admirers prefer above all his works—the *Spiritual Canticle,* from which I have already given numerous quotations and to which I shall return in the following chapter.

All the other nuns also wished to confess to him. Confession in the eyes of John of the Cross was no mere avowal of transgressions: It meant a true kind of spiritual direction, fitted to each of the souls who came to him for help. He possessed the gift of the discernment of spirits, as did the Curé of Ars, and knew in advance all that his penitents would tell him when they came to confession. He would, therefore, immediately question them about the problems they wished to submit to his judgment. As these nuns were later to say, "In a word, he understood the soul." He treated all the nuns with the same degree of respect and attention, whether they were intellectual or ungifted. As before, he wrote little notes to them all. Sometimes these would be by way of commentary on one or another of the stanzas of his poems, for as one of the religious said, they had as much respect for his writings "as for those of St. Paul."

His spiritual direction was so certain, so firm, so well-suited to the capacities of each one of them that, in this highly privileged convent, great progress was made along the path to holiness.

The sisters who served at table were astounded at his abstemiousness when they waited on him. They were unable to make him accept any of the choicer foods, and contended among themselves for the honor of eating whatever would be left over from his frugal repast. In their fond eyes it seemed as if these crumbs were relics.

Naturally, they desired even more the nourishment they received from his spiritual conferences. He occasionally was even willing to speak to them about trifling matters and, as with the members of his own monastery, to entertain them with stories. But this would be for no more than a few minutes, and by one of those rhetorical devices which he termed "anagogic"—in the sense that they were elevating and suggestive of higher things—he would suddenly cry out: *Lift up your hearts and think rather of the life that is to be forevermore!* At this appeal all would be drawn to recollection, while he himself was plunged into the ecstatic state.

Sometimes too, it seemed that with him they would be enshrouded by the supernatural. Even when he was absent, Fray John of the Cross knew what was going on among his spiritual daughters at the Carmel. One day some question arose concerning the profession of one of the sisters, Augustina de San José, who was about to be received. At the last moment some unexpected difficulties made the whole community hesitate to approve her profession. The Prioress, therefore, sent a messager to Los Martires to ask the confessor's advice. But, as the messenger was about to ascend the hill which led to the monastery of the brethren, he met John of the Cross who was coming down the path. John said to him, "Go and tell the Mother Prioress that I know why she has sent for me, and that I am already on my way to her." He was soon at the Sister's convent and in a few minutes had settled all the difficulties so the novice was able to make her profession according to plan.

Another time John of the Cross found that he could not go to visit the religious, and therefore sent Fathers Pedro de la Encarnación and Juan Evangelista in his place. They had no sooner arrived at the square near the convent than they were met by a distinguished, white-haired man. He seemed about fifty years old, and was impressive and venerable in appearance. Coming up to the religious and standing between them, he asked:

"Whence come you, my Fathers?"

"We are from the house of the Discalced Carmelites," replied Father Pedro.

"Your Reverences are well advised to offer your spiritual services to these sisters," said the gentleman, "because their Order is one with which Our Lord is well pleased; and the King also thinks highly of it. For these reasons it flourishes."

Then he put another question to them:

"My Fathers, why is it that this Order shows so much devotion to St. Joseph?"

"It is because our holy Mother, Teresa de Jesús, has always been one of his clients and because he has always helped in the establishment of her foundations, she has placed them all under the patronage of St. Joseph."

Then this mysterious person declared:

"And many further favors will be granted. I want your Reverences to promise me that you will always foster the sisters' devotion to this saint, for all that they ask of him will be granted."

Suddenly the stranger disappeared. When they returned to the Monastery of Los Martires the religious told what had happened to the Prior. Fray John of the Cross did not seem surprised, but merely said to them:

"Be quiet! Do you mean that you did not recognize him? It was St. Joseph. Yet it was not for you that he came, but rather for myself. I have been wanting in due devotion to him, but I shall do better in the future."

This anecdote is all the more noteworthy because we know the holy distrust which he had for all accounts of apparitions and visions.

This distrust is illustrated by another remarkable occurrence.

THE STIGMATIC OF LISBON

On Sunday, May 1, 1583, a General Chapter of the Discalced Carmelites was held at Almodovar. John of the Cross attended in his capacity as Conventual Prior of Granada. In obedience to the prescriptions of the Constitutions, Father Jerónimo Gracián, the Provincial Prior at the Chapter, had offered "correction," that is to say, an official reprimand to the Conventual Priors subordinate to him. He reproached John of the Cross for not having devoted more attention to "seculars" and for therefore being responsible, as he said, for a decline in the amount of alms offered to his monastery. Fray John humbly received this reprimand on his knees. Then he modestly intoned the usual formula, *Benedicite,* to indicate that he wished to offer an explanation. When permission to do so had been granted, he said:

"My Father, if during the times when I might have been making such visits to seculars, I remained in my cell praying the Lord to inspire the hearts of benefactors, and if God does indeed so furnish our monastery with all that it needs, what should I have gained by making these visits unless obliged to do so by specific necessity or by the urgings of charity?"

The Provincial Prior had nothing to say against this reasoning, and the entire Chapter agreed with John of the Cross.

Other points were brought up for discussion in this meeting. Once again two factions were displayed—those who desired a development of the active life of the brethren, and those who wished, rather, to emphasize their contemplative function. Father Jerónimo Gracián belonged to the first group. He was devoted to preaching and excited much admiration by his efforts. Among those who took the opposing view was Father Nicolas de Jesús-María Doria, of the noted Genovese family. He and his followers wished to stress the life of contemplation, as did John of the Cross. But John was distressed to see such contentions within the Order, especially as he realized that there would be trouble between Father Doria and Father Gracián.

In the spring of 1585, another General Chapter was set for Friday, May 10, at Lisbon. However, it was now Doria's turn to preside, for he had been elected Provincial at the expressed wish of Gracián. The latter's nomination of Doria seems to have disturbed John of the Cross, for when Gracián proudly spoke to him of having been responsible for Doria's election, John said to him: "Your Reverence has made Prior Provincial a man who will deprive you of your habit."

It was a prophetic statement, for such dissension eventually rose between Gracián and the new Provincial Prior that Gracián was finally expelled from the Order and died in 1614 at a monastery of the Fathers of the Mitigated Observance in Brussels.

The most significant incident at the Lisbon Chapter Meeting concerns the celebrated stigmatic, Sister María de la Visitación, of the Dominican Convent of the Annunciation in Lisbon.

Everyone came to gaze upon her. She had the stigmata of Christ in her hands, in her feet, and in her side. She was considered to be a saint. Her case afforded as interesting a point of discussion among theologians as has that of Theresa Neumann in our own time. The majority concurred in the opinion that what had been wrought in her was miraculous, and there was great excitement. Almost alone, John of the Cross maintained a careful reserve. This attitude surprised his brethren, and they were ready to reproach him for it. One day Father Agustín de los Reyes, who had preceded John as Prior of Granada, met the latter at Lisbon in the interval between two sittings of the Chapter. John was walking along the beach carrying his Bible. Agustín invited him to see the stigmatic, and it is most interesting to observe the reaction of John of the Cross. He had not seen Sister María but we know that he was guided by certain principles. In his view, the guide of a Christian is faith alone. He felt no need for any new wonders. The Gospel was, to him, sufficient. He had taken his stand, and he would not go to see this nun. To the insistent appeals of Father Agustín, he therefore said only:

"Why do you want to go see something which is false? Say no more, for you will see what the Lord will choose to bring to light."

Father Agustín, however, was unconvinced and went off to see the wounds of the nun while John remained in prayer, reading his Bible as he walked by the sea.

But this was not the only time he had been solicited to visit the Convent of the Annunciation. Even before he had left

Granada both religious and seculars had urged upon him the importance of making such a visit. Everyone felt it would be absurd to go to Lisbon and fail to see Sister María de la Visitación. And at Lisbon itself, the Fathers who were attending the Chapter of the Order were all of the same opinion. Father Ambrosio-Mariano went so far as to say that the absence of Fray John of the Cross was causing so much astonishment in the city that it verged on the scandalous. This is much the same attitude that has been aroused among our contemporaries in respect to the case of Theresa Neumann. Father Mariano declared: "It is because she does not agree with you that you do not wish to go to see her," and all the other Fathers agreed with him. Everyone went to see the stigmatic, and many were anxious to bring back some relic as a memento of their visit. John of the Cross alone resisted this temptation. And he returned from Lisbon without having once set foot in the Dominican Convent of the Annunciation.

However, after he returned to Granada, he found that his own companion on the journey, Father Bartolomeo de San Basilio, had an impressive array of souvenirs of the stigmatic: linen stained with her blood, flasks of water she had used to wash her hands, portraits of her wounds. John made him send all these back, and when the religious of the Monastery of Los Martires pressed him with enquiries on the subject of the Portuguese nun and asked him for relics, he firmly declared:

"I have not seen her, nor do I wish to see her because I would be ashamed of my faith did I believe that it could be linked with events of this kind."

The sweeping nature of this statement should be noted.

As a matter of fact, it came to be recognized that the nun in question had deceived all her admirers. After the Inquisition had made its declaration in her case, John of the Cross was able to speak more freely than had been previously possible. He told his brethren that although he had always been of the opinion that she was not inspired by an "good spirit," he had never wished publicly to say so as he preferred to leave in God's hands the declaration of the truth.

THE CHAPTER OF PASTRANA

After stopping in Malaga at the request of the Carmelites there, Fray John of the Cross returned to Granada. But he was not to remain there long. The new Provincial Prior, Father Doria, who had been in Italy when he was elected, arrived in Spain and convoked a new General Chapter to be held at Pastrana on Thursday, October 17, 1585.

Since the journey from Granada to Pastrana was a long one, Fray John set out either late in July or early in August, taking as his companion Fray Luis de San Gerónimo, formerly a member of the house at Calvario and now at Granada.

En route John planned to stop at the Carmelite monastery at Caravaca, and it was there that he received a letter asking him to go to Baeza to settle some difficulties which had arisen there. He went and although he felt the matters were trivial, he set them in order and started once again for Pastrana.

During this journey he made his confessions to Fray Luis who was—as he avowed after John's death—very much embarrassed by having to give his Superior absolution. This was because he found no matter for confession in the accusations which John made against himself. The imperfections which he avowed could not even be considered venial sins. The confessor, to be certain that some matter for absolution might be elicited, had to require his penitent to accuse himself of the "little fibs" which he had told as a child.

On the appointed date, October 17, the Chapter was opened at Pastrana. Father Doria had arrived armed with a plan for reform. He stated that the convents and monasteries of the Discalced had multiplied to the point where they would have to be divided into several provinces or sub-provinces. He suggested a division into four, having at the head of each one of the Definitors General of the Order, with the title of Provincial Vicar. The first sub-province was to be formed of Navarra and Castilla-la-Vieja, under Father Gregorio de Nazianzene; the second, consisting of Castilla-la-Nueva, would be under Father Juan-Battista; the third, Andalucía, would have Fray John of the Cross as Provincial Vicar; and the last, comprising Portugal, would be under the care of Fray Jerónimo Gracián.

Having caused these arrangements to be adopted by the Chapter, Fray Doria, a rather crude person who wished to contradict all that his predecessor, Gracián, had practiced, outlined his administrative program. He did so quite categorically by shouting at them:

"There must be rigorous observance of the Rule, my Fathers, rigorous observance! We are on the road to losing everything because of what Your Reverences can see now going on . . . My Fathers, I could not be easy in my conscience did I not reiterate this again and again. Let it be well understood that this will be the burden of my speech, it will be my care; it will be my object—my motto. And, as I trust in God, I believe that, even after my death, my bones will rattle against one another in the tomb, crying out: 'Keep the Rule!; Keep the Rule!'"

There was nothing ambiguous about this declaration of policy. Fray John was too thoroughly imbued with a sense of religious obedience not to accept it faithfully, but his attempts to carry it out were, of course, to be made in accordance with his own kind and loving character.

JOHN AS PROVINCIAL VICAR

When he left Pastrana, John had a new title; Provincial Vicar of Andalucía, as well as continuing as Prior of Granada. This meant that it would be his duty to visit, at least once a year, the monasteries of his province: Granada, El Calvario, La Penuela, Malaga, Caravaca, Seville, and Gualdalcazar. He had the same jurisdiction over the women's convents in Andalucía and a part of Murcia.

At Seville, where he went first in the discharge of his new office, he stated that he had found some abuses to correct. It will be remembered that the Discalced were divided on the question of knowing whether the active or the contemplative principle of living should dominate their work. Gracián had been an advocate of activity; Doria of contemplation. At Seville there were several young religious who had attained reputations as preachers. Two of these were Fray Diego Evangelista and Fray Francisco Crisostomo. On their tours of duty as preachers, both spent long periods of time outside their monasteries. Fray John drew their attention privately to the dangers to which their way of living—today we would term it their "activism"—exposed them. He told them that they must lead retired lives more in conformity with Carmelite requirements.

The two men resented his reprimand and became antagonistic toward him. Later, when the occasion arose, they did not hesitate to put this antagonism into action.

ON THE ROADS OF ANDALUCÍA

All this meant a new kind of life for John of the Cross. Most of the time he was traveling between monasteries. If the distance was short, he would walk with the companion required by the Rule. For longer trips, he went by horse or mule. He never carried much luggage, and there would be one mount for the two men so they would take turns riding. When his turn came, John would sit upon the mount and read his Bible or, more often, recite verses from the Psalms or the Song of Solomon, the books of the Bible that were special favorites of his. On other occasions he would be so deeply immersed in prayer that at the slightest false step on the part of the beast he would fall out of his stirrupless saddle. Fray Diego de la Concepción, his usual companion,

tells us that it was necessary to have someone walk beside him
to avoid accidents.

During the enquiries marking the process of the beatification
of the saint, many episodes which occurred on these picturesque
journeys were brought forth, and have thus been preserved for
us. Fray Jerónimo de la Cruz particularly recalled one day when
they had stopped at an inn so Fray John of the Cross might find
some food for his mount. The innkeeper asked Fray Jerónimo,
"Who is the brother who stopped here to feed his mount?"

"And why do you ask such a question?" replied Jerónimo.

"Because there is no doubt that he is a saint."

And all who saw him thought the same.

On these journeys, John practiced the same penances, the
same mortified manner of life, as he did in the monastery. He
slept in his cloak on the ground. One day Fray Evangelista
noticed that he was wearing drawers made of knotted rope, and
remonstrated with him because of his health and the tiresome
nature of the journey.

"Son," he answered, "it is relaxation enough to go on horse-
back; we must not take our ease all the time."

These incessant journeys were not without their own adven-
tures. One day they came to an inn where not even bread was to
be had. Fray Martín de la Asunción, who was with the saint,
complained about the lack. John of the Cross exhorted him to
bear the fast joyfully, but when a fortunate traveler came in
bearing provisions and invited them to join in his meal, Fray
John accepted without hesitation, and all went well.

Another time, they were passing through a wilderness said to
be infested with bandits. Fray Martín listened as the Prior spoke
of the dangers which lurked there.

"What would you do," asked John, "if we should fall among
robbers who would harm us?"

"By the grace of God, our Lord," replied the lay brother, "I
would bear it patiently . . ."

"And why," demanded Fray John, "do you speak with such

tepidity rather than with a zealous desire to suffer martyrdom for
Our Lord Jesus Christ? We should be able to convince them to
do even more to us, even to putting us to death for Christ, our
Redeemer! . . ."

Again, when John was with Fray Martín en route from
Bujalancia and Córdoba, they came upon a woman of ill repute
plying her trade in the road. John of the Cross spoke to her of
modesty, of her soul, and of God; of Jesus Christ who had pur-
chased her by the blood He shed upon the Cross. So greatly did
his words shame her and so strong was their effect that the poor
wretch fell senseless in the road. People gathered hastily about
her and cast water on her face. Soon she recovered and asking
for pardon, begged to go to confession and promised to be good in
the future. Fray John consoled and encouraged her. He sent her
to the nearest town, Córdoba, with a message to the Discalced
Carmelites there to allow her to make her confession at leisure,
as from all appearances it would require some time.

It was later ascertained that she did go, that she sincerely
reformed her habits, contracted a decent marriage, and became
a member of the Third Order of St. Francis.

On one occasion while Fray John and Fray Martín were traveling between Granada and Jaen, they arrived at an inn at Benalua
to find two men fighting with knives. One of the men was already
dripping with blood. From his mount, Fray John called out to
them:

"In the name of Our Lord Jesus Christ, I forbid you to continue fighting!"

Then he cast between them the hat he had been wearing. The
two men stopped in great surprise and stared at him. John of the
Cross lectured them, begged them to pardon each other and be
at peace. He was so successful that they embraced each other to
signify that they had become reconciled. The people of the inn,
who had vainly tried to separate the two adversaries, were astonished at such power and felt that they had witnessed a miracle.

Another time, accompanied by Fray Pedro de la Madre de

Dios, the Provincial Vicar came to a river which had overflown its banks. Four muleteers were standing there, not daring to risk the violent surgings of the water. Fray John, however, went straight in, although his companion hesitated and his mule staggered in the swirling waters. In the meantime, John safely reached the opposite bank and called to his companion that the waters were subsiding. Then he pressed on to an inn about a mile and a quarter away. When he arrived he found that the innkeeper's son had stabbed a man and the victim was dying. He found that the dying man was an apostate religious, that he had cried it aloud and had asked for a confessor. Fray John heard his confession and told him not to cry his woes abroad lest he bring shame to the Order to which he belonged. Then he helped him prepare for death. John was personally convinced that it was the Divine Hand that had impelled him into the raging stream, without waiting for the waters to subside, for had he paused, the unfortunate man would have died without receiving the Last Rites.

This conviction was all the stronger because during the time he was crossing the river, he felt as though he were being borne along by the Holy Virgin who had grasped the corner of his hood.

We are told of many other occasions when the protection of heaven guided John.

Once while on a journey he was overtaken by night and in the darkness fell down a cliff which edged the road. He could not understand how he was able to grasp some branches and climb back to the edge, but some days later, when he came to the convent of which Mother Ana de Jesús was Prioress, she questioned him:

"What kind of a journey did Your Reverency have? Were you in any danger?"

"And why do you ask me that?" he returned.

"Because while I was at prayer one day, I saw you in great danger, and I besought Our Lord on your behalf."

Fray John told her of his adventure at the edge of the precipice. Together they computed the time and found that it was at the very instant when he had been about to tumble down the side of the precipice that the nun had been praying for him.

"Well then," he said, "it was you who dragged me up the side."

It was in May 1586 that John of the Cross, as Provincial Vicar, presided at the establishment of a Carmelite foundation at Córdoba. The ceremonies were carried out in the splendor with which the Spaniards of that day delighted marking such occurrences. The ever-growing prestige of John of the Cross helped matters connected with the new establishment considerably.

Shortly afterwards, Fray John went to the Monastery of Gualdalcazar, which had been founded on Sunday, March 24, 1585, by Father Gracián. But while he was there, John fell gravely ill. He suffered from terrible pains in his side and his lungs were affected. The physicians declared that nothing could be done and that death was near. But John had means of information which were denied the physicians, and told Fray Martín, "The hour of my death is not yet, despite what the doctors may say. Even though I am to suffer much more in this illness, I shall not yet die. I am not quite sufficiently well-shaped by life's chisel to become a stone in the holy building which is on high."

When Fray Martín attempted to apply the ointments the physicians had prescribed for John's body, he found that the saint was wearing next to his skin a girdle the points of which were embedded in his flesh. Fray Martín wanted to remove this, but John consented only on condition that it be kept secret. When they took off the girdle, the blood flowed copiously. It is hard to understand how John could bear such suffering; but such a man as the Curé of Ars would have thought it all quite natural.

As John had foretold, he recovered perfectly and resumed his travels.

Here again, it is of prime importance that we interrupt our narrative to point up the significance of these anecdotes.

We have seen that he was constantly moving, but during the intervals he was fulfilling obligations of visitation at convents and monasteries. What took place during these canonical visits? Doubtless, each time there were held the customary ceremonies, but more important to us is the spiritual vitality which he imparted to others wherever he went, and the means by which he succeeded. I intend to explore this in the next chapter, which is definitely one of the most important in the book.

IX

THE LAST GREAT WRITINGS

Two Great Masterpieces

From what I have pointed out in previous chapters on the Maxims and the treatises which are actually parts of the *Ascent of Mount Carmel* and the *Dark Night of the Soul,* it should be possible to describe what John of the Cross communicated to those who met him on the roads of Andalucía, and what he brought into the convents and monasteries he visited. His writings embody the most vital expression of his holy life. They sum up all that he had to give to others, which was the best of himself.

But since the point at which I left the discussion of his earlier writings, two other treatises were added. These are even more vocative of John's life than the earlier works; they are, in fact, his masterpieces.

I shall take up first his *Spiritual Canticle* and then *Living Flame of Love.*

These two works complement each other, and the subject of both is the same. In the eyes of John of the Cross there was only one focus of interest: *union with God through love.*

In *Dark Night of the Soul* he had made his preliminary

flight—the eight strophes of the *Stanzas of the Soul* sketch out in advance all the stages which are later developed in the detailed description of the ten rungs on the secret Ladder.

But he never felt that he had finished with these steps, and he loved to turn back to them—to say more of them, to paint their varied beauties, and to show them in their upward mounting ascent, their inner logic, as the way to the final end.

Concerned with all these points, the saint had composed his *Poems* in his prison cell at Toledo, and they had helped him to bear the dark hours of his captivity.

From the first moment they heard these *Poems,* the Carmelite nuns of Toledo, found themselves held in rapt attention. He had recited them to the nuns on the day of his escape, and they had copied them down.

I cannot lay too much stress on the importance of this fact. From the time of the saint's escape, his *Poems* played an important role in his work as director and visitor to the convents and monasteries. They were flaming embers which he scattered abroad wherever he went. He is the poet and the theologian of the one love that matters—the love of God, the only love which does not deceive and which raises us to the state of gods. Insofar as he is a poet, he has shown that he knows how to give to his own elevations of soul a form so exquisite that his words become deeply embedded in the hearts of those who hear them. I do not intend to embark now on a literary study of John's poetry. My point of view is both removed from and alien to literary criticism. If I sometimes speak of a "mannered" style in regard to some forms of expression he used, it is merely to enable us to see him against the background of his time and country. What I am chiefly concerned with is the lasting, essential, and eternal, in other words, that in his poetry whch is enduringly valuable for all times and all places, that which will conduct its readers straight to the everlasting God.

This indeed was his only aim, and in speaking of his works

on this basis, it is in order to be faithful to the spirit of St. John.
Well might he have spoken the words of the French poet:

"What is the worth of all that fades, all that does not endure?"

Wherever he went, people expected of him, they desired to
know from him, the secret of love. And even in our time—perhaps more than ever before—this is what we seek when we
turn to his writings.

It is from such holy curiosity, from a like hunger and thirst
for divine love, that the poems and later the treatises came to be.

THE SPIRITUAL CANTICLE

The *Spiritual Canticle* was born in John's prison cell at Toledo;
it grew and matured, one might say, from one convent or
monastery to another. First at Toledo, then at Beas, and finally
at Granada, to name only the principal locales where it developed. It was only natural that, some day, he would be asked for a
particularized commentary, verse by verse, on this poem, especially after what he had done by way of commentary on the
Stanzas of the Soul, and which can now be read in the *Dark
Night of the Soul.* At Granada, Mother Ana de Jesús asked, on
behalf of her nuns, to hear him explain the meaning of his poem.
It was in answer to this filial request that he drew up his
commentary, excusing himself for attempting to treat a subject
which is ineffable. This is what he has to say in his Prologue:

"Forasmuch as these stanzas, religious Mother, appear to
be written with a certain degree of fervor of love for God,
Whose wisdom and love are so vast that, as is said in the
Book of Wisdom, they reach from one end to another, and
the soul which is informed and moved by Him has to some
extent this same abundance and impetus in its words, I do
not now think of expounding all the breadth and plenteous-
ness imbued in them by the fertile spirit of love, for it
would be ignorance to think that sayings of love understood

> mystically, such as those of the present stanzas, can be
> fairly explained by words of any kind. . . ."

He thus makes it clear that, for him, the final word of mystic love will never be said on earth. All our babblings to this end are no more than unworthy approximations.

"For who can write down," he goes on, "that which He reveals to loving souls wherein He dwells? And who can set forth in words that which He makes them to feel?"

These souls will remain limited. And it is for this reason that recourse is had to symbols, to figures of speech, and to poetic impressions.

Following the Prologue, the saint sets down the complete poem. Very recently, Dom Chevallier, whose competence in the subject is well known, has once more supported two ideas about this poem: first, that the original version numbered but thirty-eight verses, of which the first thirty originated in the Prison at Toledo, the remaining eight being added later at Beas; second, that of the two versions of the commentary which we possess, it is only the shorter of the two which is authentic. But his feeling on this is not shared by everyone.

I shall not enter here into the discussion of problems of textual criticism. My aim is to clarify somewhat the mystical theology of St. John of the Cross rather than to become enmeshed in the controversies which have sprung from so abstruse a work.

Very often after 1578, John of the Cross had given sketches of his ideas in his conversations with the Carmelites at Beas or elsewhere. In 1584 he gave to Mother Ana de Jesús, at her request, a series of notebooks, his attempt to set the whole thing down. The brother who served as his copyist at the Monastery of Los Martires in Granada was delighted by these chapters. And when, in her turn, one of the sisters under Mother Ana de Jesús was given the book to reproduce, her soul, too, caught fire from the writing.

It is this kind of effect which we must take note of. I have already pointed out that John of the Cross excelled in "casting wood into the fire." No one has striven better to make God loved than he did in his lifetime. And it is through his writings that he still continues to do this. One reads him not for the beauty or for the deep learning displayed in his *Poems* or in the explanations which he has appended to them, but for the sake of the warmth which emanates from them.

Even in John's own day, the celebrated rigorist Father Nicolas Doria, a man from whom he would have to suffer much, said of him:

"The words of Fray John of the Cross are like grains of pepper which arouse the appetite and warm the palate."

The numerous manuscript copies of this particular work attest to the enormous influence which it has had. It is even more remarkable when one remembers the sufferings John of the Cross endured even in his last days and the fact that the nuns, indignant over his mistreatment and to avoid questioning about him, burned entire chests of his writings that they might not fall into the hands of the tormentors. Those remaining copies were read and reread in all the religious houses, not only by the sisters, but by the brethren as well.

We must remember that this *Spiritual Canticle* was intended solely for use by the Carmelites. It was not officially published until 1630, thirty-nine years after the saint had died. However, one of the witnesses at the process of beatification tells us that, as early as 1615, a translation under the patronage of the Dean of the Cathedral of Bordeaux was in preparation. In 1621 a French translation by René Gaultier appeared in Paris. In 1627, the Infanta Isabela, Governor of the Spanish Low Countries, had the Spanish text printed for the first time at Brussels even before the Order itself had done so. This was the Spanish text which Mother Ana de Jesús had brought into France when she went there to establish the Carmelite nuns at the invitation of Cardinal de Bérulle.

Ever since 1578, the date of the first oral commentaries of St. John, the *Canticle* has enriched souls and aroused intense spiritual devotion in numerous convents and monasteries. From our point of view, the best way to learn of the spiritual climate in these religious houses is to read and reread this work and others like it.

THOSE FOR WHOM THIS WORK WAS WRITTEN

While we should not limit this work to religious, neither would it be helpful to every individual. It has nothing to say to those who are unconcerned about their souls or union with God, nor was it written for beginners. Rather, it is addressed to those who have already made some progress in their spiritual life.

St. John has stated this precisely in his Prologue, adding:

> "But I shall leave aside the commonest of them and note briefly the most extraordinary, which come to pass in those that, by the favor of God, have left behind the beginners' state."

He goes on to explain that there are many treatises for "beginners" and that, at the request of Mother Ana de Jesús, he intends in this book to discuss higher states of prayer inasmuch as "Our Lord has granted the favor of drawing you forth from these beginnings and leading you farther onward into the bosom of His Divine love."

It is not surprising that we should be able, while scaling the higher rungs of the secret Ladder, to cite the most important and meaningful strophes of the *Spiritual Canticle,* for they describe some of the higher steps of the mystical ascent.

Is this to suggest that all those who dare not aspire to the highest stages of prayer life should avoid reading the *Spiritual Canticle?* I think not, for, after all, should one forbid the denizens of the plains to take pleasure in accounts of those who climb mountains? No, I certainly do not think this should be the case, and surely John of the Cross did not. When he wrote *"O dichose ventura!*"—"Oh, happy chance!" in regard to the soul's effort, he really felt that there is no comparable adventure in mortal life. Don Chevallier puts it forcefully when he says:

> "But beginners will ask: 'Does he say, in effect, that this kind of joy is beyond my efforts, that I am too weak for its enjoyment?' . . ."

This is, indeed, an objection, but he offers a reply to it.

> "We may grant the hypothesis that the *Spiritual Canticle* is concerned with those who are almost perfect as well as those who have actually attained perfection. While my own eyes are barely open, they remain blinded, just as if I had fixed them on the sun . . ."

He then goes on to say:

> "Although it is true that the sun blinds us when viewed in its full glory, it is also the sun which leads and inspires us through those things which it shines upon. One can reach it through them. . . . So it is with the *Spiritual Canticle,* what it reveals to us of the works of love. These works are beyond us, and will probably continue to be beyond us during our days of mortality. But it is enough that we have an idea of them, to know that they are real so that we may come to a true estimation of passive purification, of active mortification, and even of the first stirrings which self-dissatisfaction arouses in the soul. The fire of the *Spiritual Canticle* is enough to do this. It wakes us from the dangers of habitual indifference. This is a fact of experience which should surprise no one. According to God's ordinance, light comes from above; whatever is below depends upon what is above it."

The *Spiritual Canticle* is designed at least to arouse in us the wish for Divine love even if we are incapable of plunging into it fully. No one comes close to a fire without being warmed by it. The *Canticle* is intended for all who wish to love God.

A Summary Analysis

I cannot embark upon a detailed and complete study of the *Spiritual Canticle,* but I shall indicate some of its more important aspects.

The *Canticle* is a dialogue between the soul and God.

In the first four strophes the soul gives vent to its anguish during its search for the Beloved. It asks creation about Him, and the fifth strophe is creation's reply. (This section was quoted above.) In His hasty passage over all created things, the Beloved has only glanced at them, but this is enough:

". . . looking upon them as he went,
  Left them, by his glance alone, clothed with beauty."

The soul again takes up the strain, and from the sixth to the thirteenth strophes, it repeats its great desire to find its Beloved. It wishes to find *Him,* not a mere messenger. The created things can do no more than stammer out His divine name, and the soul cries (Stanza 11):

"Reveal thy presence
  And let the vision of thee and thy beauty slay me;
  Behold, the affliction of love is not cured
  Save by thy presence and thy form."

This is the end of what may be termed the first part of the *Canticle.*

The second part comprises the thirteenth to the twenty-seventh strophes, and it might be called *The Betrothal.* Full of unique beauties, I find most significant the manner in which the holy writer expresses his sense of finding his Beloved everywhere. Although in the earlier part, he seemed to repulse created things as being no more than messengers of God and to desire only a direct conversation with God, he now finds the Creator in His creation. This indicates, to my mind, a most valuable note in the understanding of the character of John of the Cross. I have said that he was no less enamored of the beauties of creation than was Francis of Assisi. We might try comparing the latter's *Canticle of the Sun* with those strophes of the *Spiritual Canticle* in which John of the Cross describes all that his Beloved means to him, how he sees Him and where he finds Him.

In the following lines, after the words "My Beloved," we should sense that there follows some such mental expression as "I see Him in . . ." or, "He is for me . . ."

"My Beloved, the mountains,
  The solitary, wooded valleys,
  The strange islands, the sonorous rivers,
  The whisper of amorous breezes,

"The tranquil night,
  At the time of the rising of the dawn,
  The silent music, the sounding solitude,
  The supper that recreates and enkindles love.

"Our flowery bed,
  Encompassed with dens of lions,
  Hung with purple and builded in peace,
  Crowned with a thousand shields of gold.

"In the track of thy footprint
  The young girls run along by the way.
  At the touch of a spark, at the spiced wine,
  Flows forth the Divine balsam.

"In the inner cellar, of my Beloved have I drunk,
  And, when I went forth over all this meadow,
  Then knew I naught
  And lost the flock which I followed aforetime.

"There he gave me his breast;
  There he taught me a science most delectable;
  And I gave myself to him indeed, reserving nothing;
  There I promised him to be his bride."

It is easy to see that every one of these figures, every one of these symbols, is employed in a hidden sense, and the understanding of them will come from John of the Cross's own commentary.

The *Canticle's* theme is the soul's espousal with God. St. Thérèse of Lisieux understood this and was particularly fond of the next strophe:

> "My soul has employed itself
> And all my possessions in his service:
> Now I guard no flock nor have I now other office,
> For now my exercise is in loving alone."

We should remember this, for its meaning will soon be clarified.

The twenty-eight to the fortieth strophes, which complete the *Spiritual Canticle,* are concerned with the spiritual marriage representing the highest rung on the mystical ladder.

We have now reached the tenth and last rung on the ladder. No higher eminence can be attained in this life, and there are few souls whose love will bring them this far or even near it.

The Essential Meaning of the Spiritual Canticle

It seems to me that the essential point in the richness of the *Spiritual Canticle* lies in a statement made by John of the Cross with regard to the following lines:

> ". . . the affliction of love is not cured
> Save by thy presence and thy form."

We should note particularly John's commentary, for he tells us why this doctrine means so much to him and to all who can grasp it:

> ". . . love's sickness has no other cure save the presence and the form of the Beloved. . . ."

This sentence sums up the most profound thought which can be gathered from a theological giant. The whole message of the

Gospel verifies this teaching; the First Commandment enjoins us to love. John of the Cross tells us, in one of his most beautiful maxims, that as the sun sets upon our lives, there is but one point upon which we shall be examined: the matter of love.

He develops the thought thus:

"The reason that love's sickness has no other cure save the presence and the form of the Beloved, as is here said, is that, even as the pain of love differs from other sicknesses, so its medicine differs likewise. For in other sicknesses, according to sound philosophy, contraries are cured by contraries; but love is not cured save by things that are in harmony with love. The reason is that the health of the soul is the love of God, and thus, when it has not perfect love, it has not perfect health, and is therefore sick, for sickness is naught else than lack of health; so that, when the soul has no degree of love, it is dead; but, when it has any degree of love for God, howsoever small this may be, it is at least alive, though very weak and infirm by reason of the little love that it has; and the more its love continues to increase, the more health it will have; so that, when it has perfect love, its health will be complete."

The whole argument proceeds with impeccable logic. Mystical Theology is, in essence, the art of bringing the soul to its best state of health. Far from being an accessory adjunct, a singularity, or an imaginative fantasy, it is the very core of the human condition. It is important that we understand the human condition as the desire for God. The saints are, then, the only ones who can be regarded as perfectly normal, for they alone are fulfilling the desire of life, the human condition—union with God. Sanctity is the secret of religious and moral health; it is the secret of eternity; it is the secret of men becoming gods by uniting themselves with God.

In the Garden of Eden, Satan whispered to Eve: "You shall be as Gods." But, in a wholly different sense and in a proclamation infinitely more assured, John of the Cross declares: "You shall be as gods"; for his meaning is that only in God and by God's working within us are we to attain this state of deification.

Thus I return to the conclusion reached in my summation of the mystical doctrine of John of the Cross, which establishes the convincing unity of his teaching—the teaching which he spread among the convents and monasteries while he was Provincial Vicar in Andalucía. He never ceased to preach this in one form or another from the very beginning of his ministry.

As one reads the depositions made at the enquiries prior to John's beatification and canonization by those who had known him in life, one realizes that in all the convents and monasteries where his influence was felt, his doctrine kindled hearts with divine love. As Father Lucien-Marie observes, even the lowliest of the lay brothers "died with words on their lips which are worthy of being parts of John's poetry." Moreover, it was not the Carmelites alone who were nourished by his poems. Lay people, rich and poor alike, vied with one another for copies of his manuscripts.

THE INFLUENCE OF ST. JOHN OF THE CROSS TODAY

But do we dare claim that what was delightful to the best minds of a bygone age has an appropriate message for our own time as well?

Father Lucien-Marie, writing in 1945, believed that it has:

> "If words have any meaning, it is clear that the concepts expressed by St. John of the Cross are of universal worth, and that, if he were writing in our own day, it is likely that he would again emphasize the universal character of these concepts.

> "Heroic measures of correction are called forth by evils which are beyond the ordinary. Even more formidable

among our contemporaries than their insatiable appetite for carnal joys is that concept of life which knowingly and bluntly calls itself atheistic and accordingly searches after material things—the joys of this life, and mere physical activity, have attained the proportions of a religion. Men have created myths which are more pressing in their exactions upon them than is the God for whom they have made them a substitute. There are even a few—and we see them around us today—of whom it may be said that materialism constitutes in their view a kind of spirituality. Human self-sufficiency, the conviction that mechanical progress is an unlimited force, and trust in scientific positivism—all have their devout beliefs, their forms of worship, their rites. And such people are so far from being ashamed of themselves that they glory in what they have themselves raised to the status of an absolute. One thinks of two hard sayings in the Gospel: . . . yet the Son of man, when he cometh, shall he find, think you, faith on earth? (Luke 18:8), and . . . because iniquity hath abounded, the charity of many shall grow cold. (Matt. 24:12)."

There is no other way of counteracting the effects of such aberrations than by a revival of mystical love among men. We become ever more conscious of God's presence in our souls through love as we take up the last of John of the Cross's writings, *Living Flame of Love*.

Rarely has a title been so well suited to a book. It is the shortest and the greatest of all the saint's works. This is all the more remarkable because he wrote it for someone other than a religious—Doña Ana de Penalosa, the lady who was of such assistance to him and Mother Ana de Jesús when they first arrived in Granada.

Doña Ana was not a native daughter of Granada. She had been born at Segovia where she and her husband, Don Juan de Guevara, had been large property owners. Upon his death, Doña

Ana had come to Granada. When John of the Cross met her for the first time, she was experiencing great troubles. She was not only a widow, but had also lost her only daughter. These tragedies affected her so deeply that she ran the risk of falling into a mute and rigid resignation which would have deprived her of love of the Cross and of the great advance in spirituality to which God was calling her through suffering. But her charity saved her. She threw her house open, but it was God who opened her heart. Taking courage from the nuns who were to stay in her house for a time, and from the enlightening counsels of John of the Cross, she literally found a new life in prayer—a life of love led in God's light.

Doña Ana lived with her widowed brother, Don Luis de Mercado, who was an important official in Granada, and had undertaken the education of his daughter, Inez. John of the Cross immediately became Doña Ana's confessor and spiritual director. When the sisters saw John with Doña Ana and Inez, they said: "Here are St. Jerome, St. Paula, and Eustochium."

For some years, John of the Cross had been directing the conscience and assisting the spiritual growth of this remarkable lady who was mounting the rungs of the mystical ladder. Doubtless, Doña Ana expressed a desire to have for herself some verses describing the higher reaches of mystical love, and it seems to have been in 1586, while he was Provincial Prior of Andalucía, that John of the Cross composed *Living Flame of Love*. He had already drawn up his *Spiritual Canticle,* of which the title in his own manuscript was *Exposition of the stanzas which treat of the exercise of love between the Soul and Christ the Spouse.* . . .

THE STANZAS OF THE SOUL MADE PERFECT

In the Spanish text, this great poem is entitled *Stanzas of the Soul in the Intimate Communication of Union of the Love of God*.

Although the *Spiritual Canticle* runs to forty strophes (or

thirty-eight, according to Dom Chevallier), *Living Flame of Love*
has but four. It is the first line which has given the work its
definitive title.

I

"Oh, living flame of love
   That tenderly woundest my soul in its deepest centre,
   Since thou art no longer oppressive, perfect me now if it
      be thy will,
   Break the web of this sweet encounter.

II

   "Oh, sweet burn! Oh, delectable wound!
      Oh, soft hand! Oh, delicate touch
      That savours of eternal life and pays every debt!
      In slaying, thou hast changed death into life.

III

"Oh, lamps of fire,
   In whose splendours the deep caverns of sense which were
      dark and blind
   With strange brightness
   Give heat and light together to their Beloved!

IV

   "How gently and lovingly thou awakenest in my bosom,
      Where thou dwellest secretly and alone!
      And in thy sweet breathing, full of blessing and glory,
      How delicately thou inspirest my love!"

When Doña Ana received this subtle and profound poem
from her spiritual father, it was natural that she should wish to
have the theological explanation of it. There is a slight resem-
blance here to the Parables of Christ. Every time He told a
Parable His disciples were struck with admiration, but they also
felt incomplete and unsatisfied. They had, indeed, glimpsed a
magnificent light, but it contained meanings beyond their discernment. In this lies the charm of symbols, comparison, and

figures, which from the beginning of time have been the stuff of which poetry is made.

The Apostles' most pressing request of Jesus was that He explain His Parables, and Doña Ana made a similar request of John of the Cross. As it had been at the request of various nuns that the saint had written the commentaries which made up his earlier writings, so also it was to be with Ana de Penalosa. John of the Cross gave in to her pleading and wrote the commentary for *Living Flame of Love*. With the aid of Fray Juan Evangelista, the saint's faithful companion and secretary, its preparation took but two weeks, despite all the duties with which John was burdened.

We are told that many of the strophes of the *Spiritual Canticle* as well as much of its commentary were written while their author was kneeling. No doubt, we would be correct in thinking that such, too, was the case of this new work, which is so closely linked to its predecessor and which might be said to attain to higher regions of insight.

One day Sister Magdalena del Espíritu Santo asked if God had inspired the lines of his *Spiritual Canticle,* and he replied simply, "Daughter, sometimes God gave them to me and at other times I sought them."

Certainly this was also true of *Living Flame of Love*.

THE PROLOGUE

Like the works which preceded it, this treatise includes a *Prologue,* which is worth careful study inasmuch as here, as in all his prologues, the saint very clearly sets forth his intention:

"I have felt some unwillingness, most noble and devout lady, to expound these four stanzas which you have requested me to explain, for they relate to things so interior and spiritual that words commonly fail to describe them . . ."

A statement to this effect, it will be recalled, is also found in the Prologue to the Commentary on the *Spiritual Canticle*. Here, therefore, we find ourselves in the same stream of ideas. The difficulty of describing such states of the soul increase as one goes forward and mounts higher on the mystical ladder.

Nevertheless, he set himself to the task because it had been requested and also because he felt that, with the prayers of Doña Ana, spiritual help, without which he could do nothing, would guide him.

"Wherefore," he declares, "my part herein will be limited to the defects and errors that this book may contain, for which reason I submit it all to the better judgment and understanding of our Mother the Roman Catholic Church, under whose guidance no man goes astray. And, with this preamble, relying upon Divine Scripture, and making clear that all which is said herein is as far removed from all that there is to say as is a picture from a living person, I shall make bold to say that which I know." This first part of the Prologue should not be considered as a mere rhetorical preparation. John writes with great prudence of his intentions. He is concerned with the greatest of divine gifts: Christ's promise that the Father, Son, and Holy Ghost will come and dwell with those who love Him (*cf.* John 14:23).

In the fifth stanza preceding *Ascent of Mount Carmel*, John of the Cross had touched lightly on this subject in that wondrous line:

"Lover transformed in the Beloved!"

We find this deification, which is the most dazzling hope of man's heart, everywhere, and it will be the subject of *Living Flame of Love* just as it had been of its predecessors. But now, one finds that one is carried on to the end; that is, to the very heights, to that "swallowing up of death into life," to the rending of that web that intervenes between ourselves and the face of God.

Once again, John of the Cross takes up his favorite comparison of the fagot in the fire. At the beginning, as we know, the fagot smokes a great deal, but there are few flames. Then when it is well enkindled, this state is reversed: there is no more smoke, for the fagot is all fire. At the end of the process of which it has been a part "it glows much more and becomes more completely enkindled, until it gives out sparks of fire and flame."

Here St. John presents the entire theme of his treatises: the state of burning love in which the soul is so transformed in its inner parts that, because of its unity with this burning love and the inner fire that flames so brightly, it becomes a fire of love itself.

It may be said that, with this, we have reached the loftiest peak of Mystical Theology.

ANALYSIS OF THE POEM

In the opening verse the most significant line is:

"Break the web of this sweet encounter."

When one nears the point to which love is leading, there is no reason to fear death, for it is then that one earnestly asks of God that the thin thread, the shadowy "web" that holds one to the world, be rent.

This plea of the soul as expressed in this line makes me think of another celebrated poem by John of the Cross. I think it well to refer to it here, for it expresses the same thought under a new form.

The theme is based on the following words of a song of which we know no more:

> "I live yet no true life I know,
> And, living thus expectantly,
> I die because I do not die."

On this theme John of the Cross composed the following eight verses. They are marked by that mannered style so characteristic of the refined taste of his age and by that charm which springs from a certain balance held between contraries:

I

"Within myself no life I know
And without God life cannot be;
Then, since there's neither life for me,
What can my life be here below?
A thousand deaths I undergo
And for my true life here I sigh,
Dying because I do not die.

II

"This life that has been giv'n to me
Is but true life's negation—nay,
'Tis death that comes with each new day,
Until I live, my God, with Thee.
Hearken, O Lord, to this my plea.
No longing for this life have I
Who die because I do not die.

III

"Absent, my Lord and God, from Thee,
What gain I as I draw my breath?
What taste I, but the pains of death,
The sharpest that I e'er did see?
Yet, living perseveringly,
For my unhappy lot I sigh,
Who die because I do not die.

IV

"The fish that leaves the river's brim
Finds mingled suffering and gain.
At first he suffers death-like pain,
But at the last death comes to him.
And, as my wretched life burns dim,
'What death can equal this?' I cry:
'The more I live, the more I die.'

V

"I gaze on Thee, to assuage my pain,
  Beneath the sacramental veils,
  Yet even here my spirit fails
Because Thy Self I cannot gain.
With deeper anguish I remain,
Who see Thee thus imperfectly
And die because I do not die.

VI

"And if, O Lord, I seek for joy
  In hopes of seeing Thee above,
  Then fears of wandering from Thy love
With doubled grief my hopes alloy.
Thus hope my soul would e'er employ
While fear is ever standing by:
I die because I do not die.

VII

"O save me from this death-like case,
  My God, and give true life to me.
  Hold me no more, but set me free
From straitest bondage in this place.
Look how I yearn to see Thy face,
And how I grieve so utterly,
Dying because I do not die.

VIII

"My death I'll mourn unceasingly,
  Lamenting life that still is mine,
  What time my sins, as I repine,
Detain me here when I would flee.
And oh, my God, when shall it be
That I may gladly, truly cry:
'Now live I and no longer die!'"

We may be certain that it was just such thoughts which sang within John's soul and in the souls of many of those whom he had aroused to spiritual reality, and we know this singing continued up to the moment of death.

In the commentary which John of the Cross provides for the first of his strophes, he reaches the high point of his exposition when he affirms that the true Christian, although he may appear to eyes of men unwise to die of illness, does, in fact, find a way, by God's grace, to die of love.

DEATH BY LOVE

The following passage is one of the most unforgettable written by John of the Cross (Stanza I, Exposition, Section 30):

"Therefore it must be known, with regard to the natural dying of souls that reach this state, that, though the manner of their death, from the natural standpoint, is similar to that of others, yet in the cause and mode of their death there is a great difference. For while the deaths of others may be caused by infirmities or length of days, when these souls die, although it may be from some infirmity, or from old age, their spirits are wrested away by nothing less than some loving impulse and encounter far loftier and of greater power and strength than any in the past, for it has succeeded in breaking the web and bearing away a jewel, which is the spirit. And thus the death of such souls is very sweet and gentle, more so than was their spiritual life all their life long, for they die amid the delectable encounters and sublimest impulses of love, being like to the swan, which sings most gently when it is at the point of death. For this reason David said that the death of saints in the fear of God was precious, for at such a time all the riches of the soul come to unite together, and the rivers of love of the soul are about to enter the sea, and these are so broad and dense and motionless that they seem to be seas already. From the beginning to the end, their treasures unite together to accompany the just man as he departs and goes forth to his kingdom, and praises are heard from the ends of the earth, which, as Isaias says, are the glories of the just man."

THE SECOND STROPHE

In the three final strophes of this poem, John of the Cross gives a beautiful description of the interior acts of the soul that has reached that degree of intimacy with God which had been pointed to in the first strophe.

And it is here that one can best see the variety of expression characteristic of a true poet.

When he speaks to us of a "sweet burn," of a "soft hand," and of a "delicate touch," we would have difficulty in discerning that he is here concerned with the activities of the Three Persons of the Blessed Trinity in the soul which loves God. We would be even more incapable of discerning the part appropriated to the activities of each of the divine Persons, which nevertheless remain common to all three. The commentary explains to us that the "sweet burn" refers to the devouring action of the fire of the Holy Spirit; the "soft hand" is that of the infinite goodness of God the Father; and the "delicate touch" expresses the Son's love of us.

But the most moving line of this second strophe is:

"In slaying, thou hast changed death into life."

It is for this reason that the soul loves to reiterate the final line of the first strophe:

"Break the web of this sweet encounter."

THE THIRD STROPHE

The most remarkable part of his commentary on the third strophe is the long digression which the saint introduces on the guidance of the soul.

Nowhere else does he treat this problem with more feeling and strength. Nowhere else does he more eloquently deplore the insufficiency which marks many men as spiritual directors.

I shall lay some stress on these points inasmuch as they concern matters which, from all the evidence, concerned him very deeply.

We know that it was the summit of St. John's ambition to make God loved, but he wished this love to be the kind that God wants. In this love there are many degrees and we have heard John of the Cross list and describe ten of them. Not every soul walks the path of love to the end, because although God is generous in His gifts to souls, each soul, as it ascends to God, meets a conflict which is life itself.

John of the Cross tells us that souls who have the wish and the means to reach the higher rungs on the ladder of love will encounter three enemies: an inadequate spiritual director; Satan; and the soul itself when it lacks courage.

He then takes up the damage caused by these three adversaries of mystical perfection. I shall not linger over what he has to say about the attacks of the demon, neither shall I linger on the weaknesses of the soul itself. What he has to say is very much to the point, but it is all well known. The more penetrating of his pages are those which he devotes to poor spiritual directors.

These blind shepherds are all who have insufficient knowledge of the ways of divine love, those who have not kept abreast of the upsurging of mystical love and who, therefore, seek to confine, at any cost, the souls in their care to the same low plane on which they themselves live.

John feels that the passing from discursive meditation to contemplation, which he has mentioned in all his earlier works, is so important that he regards any director who, in ignorance of what the contemplative life is, is the cause of incalculable harm when he attempts to fetter a soul to discursive meditation and counsels against contemplation as though it were no more than intellectual laziness and sloth. This kind of director robs the soul of all the endowments with which God wishes to enrich it when He brings it to the state that we call "passivity," that is to say, the state wherein it is completely at the disposal of God's indwelling action.

Hear what John of the Cross has to say of such directors (Stanza III, Exposition, Section 43):

"Although the gravity and seriousness of this evil cannot be exaggerated, it is so common and frequent that there will hardly be found a single spiritual director who does not inflict it upon souls whom God is beginning to draw nearer to Himself in this land of contemplation. For, whenever God is anointing the contemplative soul with some most delicate unction of loving knowledge—serene, peaceful, lonely and very far removed from sense and from all that has to do with thought—so that the soul cannot meditate or think of aught soever or find pleasure in aught, whether in higher things or in lower, inasmuch as God is keeping it full of that lonely unction and inclined to rest and solitude, there will come some spiritual director who has no knowledge save of hammering and pounding with the faculties like a blacksmith, and, because his only teaching is of that kind, and he know naught save meditation, he will say: 'Come now, leave these periods of inactivity, for you are living in idleness and wasting your time. Get to work, meditate and make interior acts, for it is right that you should do for yourself that which in you lies, for these other things are the practices of Illuminists and fools.'"

Thus, bad directors are those spiritual guides who fetter the soul, who are unaware of the gifts of the Holy Spirit, who close up the ways that lead to the higher rungs of the secret ladder. At great length, in great detail, and most convincingly, John of the Cross belabors this treason—and that word is not too strong (Stanza III, Exposition, Section 53):

> "These spiritual directors . . . fail to understand souls that are now walking in this solitary and quiet contemplation, becasue they themselves have not arrived so far, nor learned what it means to leave behind the discursive reasoning of meditations, as I have said, and they think these souls are idle. And therefore they disturb and impede the peace of this quiet and hushed contemplation which God has been giving their penitents by His own power. . . ."

These spiritual directors "offer a great insult and irreverence to God, by laying their coarse hands where God is working."

John of the Cross, whom some have wished to represent as a severe and harsh spiritual director, is here claiming for souls that holy liberty proper to God's children. One of his biographers has pointed out that it would not be suspected that John could be so talented a critic and pamphleteer. Gentle as he was, when the needs of souls, the spouses of God, were concerned, he could become as implacable and vigorous as one could wish.

THE FOURTH STROPHE

In the final strophe of *Living Flame of Love,* there is another passage which it is important to note.

In commenting on the line, "Where thou dwellest secretly and alone!" John of the Cross brings out all that every Christian should know about God's presence within his soul. There are great differences in this presence of God, Who is in all that exists. But we would do well to follow the words of St. John (Stanza IV, Exposition, Section 14):

"The soul says that He dwells secretly in its breast, because, as we have said, this sweet embrace is made in the depth of the substance of the soul. That is to say that God dwells secretly in all souls and is hidden in their substance; for, were this not so, they would be unable to exist. But there is a difference between these two manners of dwelling, and a great one. For in some He dwells alone, and in others He dwells not alone; in some He dwells contented and in others He dwells displeased; in some He dwells as in His house, ordering it and ruling everything, while in others He dwells as a stranger in the house of another where He is not allowed to do anything or to give any commands. Where He dwells with the greatest content and most completely alone is in the soul wherein dwell fewest desires and pleasures of its own; here He is in His own house and rules and governs it. And the more completely alone does He dwell in the soul, the more secretly He dwells; and thus in this soul wherein dwells no desire, neither any other image or form or affection of aught that is created, the Beloved dwells most secretly, with more intimate, more interior and closer embrace, according as the soul, as we say, is the more purely and completely withdrawn from all save God. And thus He dwells secretly, since the devil cannot attain to this place and to this embrace, neither can the understanding of any man attain to a knowledge of the manner thereof. But He dwells not secretly with respect to the soul which is in this state of perfection, for it feels this intimate embrace within it. . . ."

One might say that this passage sums up the whole of St. John's mystical doctrine, and his spiritual testament is contained in the following lines (Section 15):

"Oh, how happy is this soul that is ever conscious of God resting and reposing within its breast! Oh, how well is it that it should withdraw from all things, flee from business and live in boundless tranquillity, lest anything, however small, or the slightest turmoil should disturb or turn away the bosom of the Beloved within it. . . ."

He brings his treatise to a close by reiterating his declaration that this divine action within the loving soul surpasses all human language and thought.

I think we can now feel that we know what John of the Cross, Provincial Visitor for his Order in Andalucía, brought into each convent and monastery he visited during the course of his many trips. And now I may resume the narrative of his outward life in order to bring it to that "death by love" which he has so well described and which should be the lot of every Christian worthy of the name.

X

FINAL CONFLICTS: JOHN'S LAST TRIALS

(*1586–1591*)

THE INTERNAL AFFAIRS OF CARMEL

We left John of the Cross about the middle of 1586 when, as Provincial Vicar, he was traveling a great deal to monasteries and convents. While he was in Córdoba early in August of that year, he received a message from the Provincial, Father Doria, sumoning him to a meeting of the Definitors of the Order to be held at Madrid on Wednesday, August 13. He and Father Gracián set out immediately, but did not arrive in time for the opening meeting, although St. John's signature appeared from August 16 on in the *acta* of the Chapter. The absence of the two men seems to have been regarded overseriously by Father Doria, for although he thought highly of John of the Cross, he disliked Father Gracián. Here was laid the germ of an ever-growing misunderstanding which was to affect the final years of St. John's life seriously and unpleasantly.

There were three chief matters for discussion at the meeting: (1) The changing of the liturgical rite proper to the Order; (2) the establishment of a Procurator General of the Order at Rome;

(3) the printing of the writings of Mother Teresa of Avila, who had died in 1582.

On the first point, the members were divided. Father Doria wanted the Roman Rite to be adopted. John of the Cross and many others were strongly attached to what was called the Liturgy of Jerusalem, which had up until that time been identified with the Order. The Provincial's feelings carried the day. On the other hand, the decision to publish the writings of St. Teresa and to return her body from Avila to Alba de Tormes, where she had died, was unanimous. Finally, as Provincial Vicar of Andalucía, the assembly entrusted John of the Cross with the task of founding a monastery of the Discalced in La Manchuela.

On his return to Andalucía, St. John went to the Convent at Malagon, where he spoke to the nuns on his favorite subject—the path of prayer. From Malagon he went to La Manchuela where, because of his prompt and prudent manners, the monastery was started with a minimum of difficulty. He appointed as Vicar Fray Eliseo de la Martires. (We shall return to him later, for he has left us with the most realistic portrait of John of the Cross.)

The latter part of November 1586, Mother Ana de Jesús left her post as Prioress of the convent in Granada to start a new foundation at Madrid. John, therefore, returned to Granada to preside over the elections held by the nuns. On Thursday, December 18, John was at Caravaca where a convent had been established by some religious who had long claimed kinship with the Carmelites there. Although the Prioress of Caravaca, Mother Ana de San Alberto, wished to establish a Carmelite convent, John of the Cross gave her no answer other than to urge her to pray for guidance. Then an incident occurred which was directly responsible for the establishment of the convent. One day, John said Mass for the sisters. While he was at the altar, Mother Ana de San Alberto noticed a light emanating from the tabernacle and playing around him. Later, at Communion, she saw that his face was "shining like the sun" and that "tears of joy" flowed from his eyes. After Mass, Mother Ana went to the confessional which opened off the sacristy and said to the saint:

"Why was the Mass so long?"

"How much time did I take to say it?" asked John.

"For the enjoyment of heavenly joy, there is never too much time," replied the Prioress.

"My daughter," said the priest, "Our Lord has spoken to me and said: 'Tell the Prioress that I will arrange the foundation here . . .' Therefore, my daughter, do all that you can, for Our Lord will not let you fail."

FURTHER JOURNEYINGS

During the following year, John traveled widely. On one trip, while engaged in the establishment of a monastery at Bujalance in Andalucía, he was urgently called to Madrid by the Vicar General of the Order, Father Doria. Always prompt in obedience, John wished to start out at once despite the fact that the weather was cold and miserable. His breathren tried to insist that he wait for two or three days, but John would not hear of it; his Superior had spoken and requested his obedience; for John, this was the voice of God. In spite of his exhaustion, he set out early the next morning, not returning to Andalucía until March. An important Chapter Meeting of the Order was called for Saturday, April 18, at Valladolid, and as one of the Definitors of the Order, he had to attend it.

Contemporaries called this meeting "the great Chapter." There were forty-six of the most prominent members of the Order in attendance, and the subjects under discussion were extremely important. (There was even a rumor that the prophet Elijah in person had shown himself to the assembly!) Father Doria created a council to which was given authority over the laws and customs of Carmel. This action alarmed the nuns and was later to have serious results.

Fray John was deprived of his offices as Provincial Vicar and

Definitor, but he was elected Prior of Granada for the third time. Although he pleaded with the Chapter to allow him to return to the life of a simple religious, his request was ignored, and he had to return to Granada. However, in June 1588, a General Chapter was convened at Madrid for the purpose of organizing the new Council. As Prior of Granada, Fray John attended this meeting. It opened with the election of four definitors whose duties were to be concerned only with the *acta* of the Chapter. John of the Cross was the first to be elected. A vote was then taken to fill the office of Vicar General of the Order, and once again, Father Doria was chosen. (Under the authority of the Carmelite Superior General in Rome, who had supreme jurisdiction over the Order, the Vicar General had power over only the Discalced; the members of the Mitigated Observance were not affected.)

The Chapter then turned to the election of the six members of the Supreme Council who were to have the title of Counselors.

As one of the Counselors, Fray John was elected to the third level of rank and named Prior of Segovia, which lies in Old Castile about ninety-two miles from Madrid. It will be recalled that John of the Cross, who originally came from that province, had always regarded himself as an "exile" in Andalucía, despite his many years there. And now what Mother Teresa had never been able to obtain for him under the regime of Jerónimo Gracián as Prior Provincial of the Order, was conceded to him under the less benevolent rule of Nicolas Doria. However, there was a particular reason behind this nomination.

JOHN AS PRIOR OF SEGOVIA

The establishment of a great monastery of the Discalced at Segovia had been under consideration with the understanding that it would be a residence for Vicar General Doria, the Council, and the Counselors. Father Doria had charged the Prior Provincial of Castile, Father Gregorio de Nazianze, with the preparations for the acquisition of buildings and land for the future monastery. On Saturday, May 3, 1586, the new Carmel had been solemnly inaugurated with seven religious in residence. On Thursday, September 25, it was raised to the status of a Priory, and Fray Gaspardo de San Angelo was chosen to head it. But soon it became evident that the monastery was far too small to fulfill adequately the projects which had been hoped for. And when the question arose of making provision for the Council and its members, it became obvious that considerable enlargement was essential.

Because of Fray John's close friendship with Doña Ana de Penalosa, therefore, Father Doria appointed him Prior of Segovia in the hope that he would be able to persuade her to help.

It will be recalled that Doña Ana and her husband, both natives of Segovia, owned a large amount of property there. Now she wished to put this property and her wealth to the best possible use. Although she had thought of building either a convent or a hospital, when Fray John suggested establishing a monastery for the Discalced, she agreed.

John of the Cross thus once again demonstrated that the highest kind of mystical living had not destroyed those practical qualities which are needed for everyday living.

John had wide experience in setting up new foundations, and now, as he had done so often before, he took charge of the manual labor for the new foundation. As soon as he had said morning Mass, he joined the workers and gave example to all during their long day. Not only did he hasten the work by his presence, but he was also able on one occasion to help them in a way that all understood. One of the workers was severely hurt by a great stone which fell, crushing two of his fingers. When John came up and asked what had happened, the workman showed him his crushed hand. The Prior took it between his own and, stretching the shattered fingers, restored them so quickly to their shape and suppleness that the man was able to go back to work immediately.

It was during the course of this construction that Juan Evangelista, who had accompanied his Prior from Andalucía, said to him:

"God bless me, my Father; Your Paternity is happy to go about among all this lime and stone."

"My son," replied Fray John, "do not be surprised; I have always found it easier to deal with stones than with men."

Soon the great work came to an end. John of the Cross was happy to be able to add to the monastery garden a wide plain which stretched out to the nearby mountains. From the higher points of the new property magnificent views could be enjoyed. There were also some rocks which formed natural caves. John of the Cross had always loved grottos; according to what we read in the final strophe of *Living Flame of Love,* he saw in them the symbol of man's human faculties, originally empty and awaiting fulfillment from the love of God.

Whenever he could withdraw from the management of the affairs of the monastery, the Prior of Segovia loved to climb up the hillside and, going into one of these caves, devote himself to prayer. All about him was peace. The sky above was brilliant, the horizon glorious. He could close his eyes and become lost in prayer. Never did he feel less alone than when he was with God. If one of the brethren came to seek him because his presence was required at the convent, John would sometimes say:

"For the love of God, let me be; I am not made to deal with the world."

Even when he did come down to the house, he remained so absorbed in prayerful thought that he seemed scarcely to follow the conversation.

Nights were always, for St. John, better than the days for that sweet contemplation he so loved. Juan Evangelista tells us that more than once he found him under the trees of the garden, plunged into prayer with his arms spread out in the fashion of a cross. He would be so rapt in God that he would not even notice his secretary's coming. If he could not go into the open, he would lean on his elbows at the little window of his bare cell, just as he had done at Granada, and lose himself in contemplation of the stars. Juan Evangelista would thus find him in ecstasy and carefully avoid upsetting him. Sometimes this state of rapture would last until morning, and when he came out of it, the Father Prior, on seeing Juan at his side, would say: "What are you doing here, and why have you come?"

He did not, however, allow any of his obligations to suffer. Not only did he continue to superintend the work of completing the monastery—work which continued until he left Segovia—but he also fulfilled his duties as Counselor, especially during the absence of the Vicar General, Father Doria, who had undertaken a series of visitations of the convents and monasteries of the Order beginning Saturday, September 16, 1589. In his absence, which lasted for three months, John presided over the Council and was required to attend to all the needs of the Carmelite nuns and friars who were subject to it.

There were establishments of convents and monasteries to be arranged; rules to be promulgated for the nuns; occasional elections to be presided over; and, of course, there was the superintendency of the printing of the works of Mother Teresa. Certainly, Fray John was not the only one concerned in these projects, and while there is no way of knowing how great a share he took on, we may assume, by what we know of him, that he did all that was necessary—if not more—and that he was never in the position of being reproached for having failed to fulfill his obligations.

DAILY LIFE AT SEGOVIA

We are indebted to John's intimate companions for precious details concerning his daily life at Segovia. Actually, these were to be the last peaceful times he would enjoy, for he was then highly esteemed by all his associates. The persecution which was to last to his death, however, was not far off.

Just as he had done elsewhere, and especially at Granada, he had reserved for his own use the smallest and poorest of the monastery cells, and, as at Granada, he had only a wooden crucifix and a figure of Our Lady. There was a hard pallet for the night. A folding board attached to the wall served as a table. If John wished a book, he borrowed it from the monastery library. His own possessions consisted only of his Bible and his Breviary, neither of which ever left him. If the Protestants of that time had cause to deplore Catholic neglect and ignorance of the Bible, John of the Cross could not be reproached on this point. The Bible had always been his most constant companion, and he frequently cited it in his writings.

There is an anecdote which illustrates a special side of his character. Just above the door of his cell was a protruding wooden beam. Fray Barnabo noted one day that a beautiful pigeon was perched on this beam, and that it did not mingle with the other pigeons. Fray Barnabo pointed this out to Fray Juan Evangelista who, in his turn, was quite struck by it. It was a source of wonder in the monastery, especially when Juan Evangelista maintained that he had previously seen the same pigeon in Fray John's cell at Granada, far to the south.

They all spoke to the Father Prior about the bird, but he said merely:

"Don't disturb it."

However, the brethren so venerated Fray John that they could not help but think this some kind of significant miracle.

As it had been at Granada, John's rule was at once paternal and energetic. He held all to the strict observance of the Rule and at the appropriate time corrected those who failed. One Easter Sunday while the Prior was celebrating Mass, the priest who had been appointed to preach the sermon advised him that he was unprepared, but Fray John went on with the service without showing any sign of impatience or dissatisfaction. After the Mass, the defaulting preacher expected to receive a reprimand, but none was forthcoming. Shortly afterwards he was told that some close friends had called to see him and were waiting in the monastery parlor. When he went to ask the necessary permission of John of the Cross, however, the Prior refused, and the priest understood that this was the penalty he was to suffer for his fault. It was so opportune and appropriate that he had the good grace to accept it as being fully merited.

On another occasion, acting in accord with the provisions of the Carmelite Constitutions, the Prior was obliged to administer the discipline to an offending religious. While we do not know the circumstances, there has been preserved the following remark of the offender, which was made immediately after the infliction of the penalty:

"I trust, Reverend Father, that I shall one day see in heaven the hand that has just disciplined me."

Among the religious John of the Cross showed a special love for the lowliest, for the lay brothers, the novices, and the students. He personally shared in the housework they had to do—the sweepings and scourings, and the dressing of the altar in the chapel. He was known to divest himself of a new tunic in order to give it to one of the less favored among his religious. When food was scarce, he was careful to halt the expenditures for embellishment of the monastery lest his spiritual sons lack the necessities of life.

However, just as at Granada, he was more concerned with spiritual than with temporal matters. And he was not only the chief guide chosen by his religious brethren, but was also the spiritual director of the leading men of the town. Notable among them were Don Juan de Orozco y Covarrubias, Archdeacon of Cuellar and Canon of the Segovia Cathedral, one of the chief among the friends of Carmel, as well as Canon Diego Muñoz de Godoy, who held the academic rank of Master of Arts. Both of these men were great servants of God. However, Don Juan de Orozco, when nominated to a bishopric, accepted the office despite the contrary advice of John of the Cross; but he was soon so filled with disgust he resigned. A third Canon of Segovia was one of John's most faithful disciples—Dr. Villegas, who was to become Confessor to the nuns of Carmel for a period of more than twenty years. These men could speak tirelessly together of the things of God for as long as five hours at a stretch.

He also continued as spiritual adviser to Doña Ana de Penalosa, who lived in a simple house which had been prepared for her near the monastery. John of the Cross often went to see her, and all the servants of the house would gather to listen to him speak of God and of the way to sanctity. Among them was a fifteen-year-old girl, Leonora de Vitoria, who was later to serve as a witness at the process of beatification.

One day at the monastery great flashes of light were seen emanating from the confessional in which John of the Cross was seated. This phenomenon occurred three times, but when he was questioned about it in the confessional, he refused to discuss it. On other occasions, rare perfumes were wafted forth from the same confessional.

Remarkable conversions were effected by John's assistance, as, for instance, that of the young Angela de Aleman, and that of a woman possessed, who had been sold to Satan and was delivered from this bondage by the Prior of the Carmel.

THE CHRIST OF SEGOVIA

It was at Segovia, and probably toward the end of his sojourn there, that there took place one of the best-known incidents in the life of St. John of the Cross. I refer to his moving dialogue with Christ carrying His cross. All the biographers have reported this. In Father Crisogono's book no less than twelve or fifteen witnesses, all in perfect agreement, are cited on this subject. In truth, all these testimonies derive their value from a single source, which is, however, one of great worth. Actually, the fact became known through the account of it by John's own brother, Francisco de Yepès, for whom John of the Cross had the greatest affection. He saw in him a true friend of Our Lord, a man very far advanced along the ladder of holy love. Knowing either by divine revelation or by a presentiment based upon human calculation that he would not see him any more in this world, he had invited him to visit Segovia. Francisco, therefore, spent some days with him, being greeted with much attention and many proofs of fraternal affection. After two or three days, he thought of returning to Medina del Campo, but his brother held him back by saying: "Do not be in so great a hurry about going off, for you don't know when we shall see each other again."

Francisco, therefore, agreed to prolong his stay at the monastery. After supper one evening, John of the Cross took Francisco by the hand and led him into the garden. It was spring—probably in 1591, the last springtime of John's life. Although winter at Segovia is sharp and often snowy, the springtime is delightful. As the two brothers walked alone in the garden, under the starlit sky, John of the Cross made the most astonishing confidences to his brother:

"I would like to tell you," he said, "something that took place between Our Lord and myself. In this monastery we have a crucifix, and one day as I stood before it, it struck me that it would be better placed in the Church, because I wished that it might be venerated not only by the religious but also by those who came from outside the monastery. And I therefore made the change. After the crucifix had been set up in the Church, in as good a location as possible, I was, one day praying before it when Our Lord spoke to me and said:

" 'Fray John, ask of Me what you will, and I shall grant it to you in return for your service to Me.'

" 'My Lord,' I said to Him, 'what I will ask of You is that *You visit me with affliction so that I may suffer for You, and that I may be misunderstood and thought of as being of no account.*' This is what I have asked of Our Lord; but His Majesty has done otherwise so that I suffer much by reason of the immerited honors which have come to me." [Very often the reply of the saint is abridged and given in the following form: "O Lord, to suffer and be misunderstood for Your sake." It is actually in this form that it is given in the Breviary Lessons on St. John's feast day. The original Spanish text is as follows: *"Señor, lo que quiero que me deis es trabajos que padacer por vos, y que sea yo menospreciado y tenido en poco."*]

In this account there is one expression that requires explanation. Francisco de Yepès speaks of a crucifix. But the incident actually concerns a painting which still exists. In it Christ is seen carrying His cross upon His right shoulder. His head is pierced with the Crown of thorns and blood is flowing. The face breathes forth the most profound and noble sorrow. The eyes are all but closed and the mouth slightly opened as though Christ were saying to John of the Cross the words which have been set out above. There are not many souvenirs of John's own time which are more evocative than this.

"O Lord, to suffer and to be misunderstood for Your sake."

These are the words of one who understood Christ's love for us. And thus does the love which desires to respond to Christ's love express itself.

John of the Cross thought that he had been surrounded with too much honor, but since he knew that he would not see his brother again in this life, it may well be that he may have also thought that his prayer would soon be heard: "O Lord, to suffer and to be misuderstood for Your sake."

We shall see how this came about.

AT THE CHAPTER MEETING IN MADRID

At the Vigil of Pentecost, early in June 1591, a General Chapter of the Discalced Fathers was held in Madrid, under the chairmanship of Father Nicolas Doria. As a Consultor of the Order, Fray John attended this Chapter.

Before his departure for Madrid he paid a visit to Mother Maria de la Encarnación, Prioress of the Convent at Segovia, to whom he was much devoted. She told him that it was the hope of all her spiritual daughters that John would be named their Superior by the Chapter.

"My daughter, if only you knew how different are my own ideas! I will say to you that, while I have been praying for the success of this Chapter, it seemed to me that I was taken by the scruff of the neck and cast into a corner! . . ."

Had he had a true revelation? This may be doubted. It can be deduced from his attitude that John of the Cross must have been aware that he was likely to encounter the displeasure of the Vicar General, Father Doria. At the Chapter held on June 10 of the preceding year at Madrid, he and Father Doria widely disagreed on two points: the question of the spiritual direction of the Carmelite nuns, and the place in the Order of Father Gracián.

The nuns had been greatly distressed ever since Father Doria had created the Council and given it power to deal with both the male and female branches of the Order. They were all much attached to the Rules and customs which they regarded as an inheritance from their late foundress, St. Teresa. They wished all these Rules and customs to be preserved. While they hoped always to be under the spiritual direction of one of the Carmelite Fathers, they disliked being subject to the Council. Fearing interference by the Counselors, they immediately acted to meet the threat. By authorization of Father Doria, to whom they had not explained in detail all that they intended to do, they had recourse to Rome in order to obtain from the Holy See a decree which would forbid any change in their Rules. On Tuesday, June 5, 1590, Pope Sixtus V granted the desired Brief to their representative, a priest who was a relative of Father Doria. However, the carrying out of the terms of this Papal Brief was vested not in Father Doria, but in two papal commissioners who were not even Carmelites.

Offended by this action, Father Doria coldly suggested to the Chapter at Madrid that the Fathers withdraw completely from the spiritual direction of the sisters. This would have been an act of revenge, and John of the Cross openly opposed it. Springing to the defense of the sisters, he stated that they most heartily wished to continue under the spiritual direction of the Fathers of Carmel, but that they did not grant anyone the right to interfere with their own Rule. His authority was so great that the Chapter was much impressed by his plea, but Father Doria came to the false conclusion that John of the Cross had inspired the steps which had been taken by the nuns at the Court of Rome in opposition to his own plans. Meanwhile, he had been at some pains to have the Papal Brief annulled, and at this moment was near success. Nevertheless, he still suspected John, and relations between the two became even more strained, particularly since he also suspected that Fray John disapproved of the measures he had taken against Father Gracián. As a matter of fact, it is quite certain that even if John of the Cross had agreed with Father Doria in all the other matters, he still would have been opposed to the way the conflict between Father Doria and Father Gracián had exceeded all limits of decency, as well as Father Doria's extreme measures against Gracián.

It was in such an atmosphere that the General Chapter opened in June 1591. Among the members of the assembly was Fray Diego Evangelista, attending as a representative from the Province of Andalucía. This was the young preacher whom John of the Cross had reprimanded when he was on a Provincial visit in Andalucía, and the reprimand had aroused in him a bitter hatred for John.

John of the Cross knew that the greater part of the Chapter members were opposed to him. He knew, moreover, or he could at least guess, that even if the majority had been on his side, the greater number of those who criticized Father Doria behind his back for his severity and officiousness would, nevertheless, vote as Father Doria wished because they feared him.

The meeting, therefore, proceeded unfavorably for Fray John.

The first matter of business was the election of Counselors and Definitors. John of the Cross was not re-elected. Father Diego Evangelista was elected in his place. The followers of Father Doria particularly wished to avoid naming John "Commissionary of the Order to the Nuns," as the Sisters themselves had wished and hoped for. Father Doria realized that by depriving John of the Cross of his former offices, he would be ineligible for this particular charge.

If, by this action, he had hoped to silence John on the discussions concerning the spiritual direction of the nuns and Father Gracián's position in the Order, he was mistaken, even though the discussions were a repetition of those of the previous years: John was the only member of the Chapter who tried to defend the sisters and Father Gracián. Since he won no support from anyone, he accomplished but one thing: Father Doria became convinced he must be excluded from every post of honor or influence in the Order. Moreover, Doria, fearing any reproach from Fray John or his friends, thought to avoid any embarrassment if John could be sent off to Mexico. Actually, this was a matter under discussion. The Fathers who made up the Mexican Province of the Order were asking for assistance and, as they were greatly undermanned, had requested that ten more priests be assigned to them. When the question came up in debate, John of the Cross, who was always foremost in self-sacrifice, had actually volunteered to accept such a mission. The Definitors, who saw here a clear and happy solution to all the difficulties, accepted the saint's offer on Tuesday, June 25. He was named to head the projected expedition according to a document drawn up in regular form and dated at that time.

However, Father Doria had been successful in his efforts at the Roman Curia. By a Brief obtained from Gregory XIV, the document which the nuns had received from Sixtus V was annulled. No longer was there any question of a commissionary to the nuns being named, and therefore the danger that John of the Cross might occupy this post was dispelled. Father Doria, who was perhaps a little ashamed of the steps which had been taken against John, abandoned the idea of sending him to Mexico and wished to rename him Prior of Segovia. Now, however, Fray John refused. When Father Gregorio de San Angelo, a Definitor and Secretary to the Board of Definitors, informed him of the new decision about his future, he humbly replied:

"Father Gregorio, do not be distressed because I have no office; for I will regard it as a great mercy granted me by God in order that I may be concerned only with my own soul."

But Father Doria was insistent. Therefore, John of the Cross wrote from Madrid to Mother Ana de Jesús on Saturday, July 6: "What I beg of you, daughter, is that you beg the Lord to continue his favor to me, for I still fear that they may make me go to Segovia and not leave me wholly free, although I will do what I can to escape from this also. . . ."

When Father Doria understood that Fray John of the Cross would not willingly return to Segovia as Prior, he decided that he should go to Andalucía. But, contrary to the opinion of most of the older biographers of St. John, this was not because John of the Cross had asked it. Rather, it was because he thought he might leave for Mexico from one of the ports in that province. John of the Cross seemed to be under the assumption that this was still the plan. This is confirmed by the fact that scarcely had the decision been made when John charged Father Juan de Santa Ana, who had accompanied him to the Chapter, to go in haste to Andalucía to seek recruits among priests to go with him to New Spain, as Mexico was then known.

How worthy of our admiration is the state of John's soul in the events which I am about to describe. On the same day he wrote to Mother Ana de Jesús, he wrote also to the Prioress of Segovia, Mother María de la Encarnación, who was a spiritual daughter of Ana de Jesús.

In the extant fragment of this letter to the Prioress of Segovia, there is a truly magnificent phrase:

". . . As to my affairs, daughter, let them not grieve you, for they cause no grief to me. What I greatly regret is that blame is attributed to him who has none; for these things are not done by man, but by God, Who knows what is meet for us and ordains things for our good. Think only that God ordains all. *And where there is no love, put love and you will find love.* . . ." (italics mine)

Once again, in the time of tribulation, John is able to raise himself above passing things. He knows that love is the beginning and the end of all things, that it must be seen in all things, and that, in vesting ourselves in it, we make certain that we shall not be deceived and shall find it everywhere.

It would seem that Fray John had prolonged his stay in Madrid as the two letters quoted above are addressed from there, and it was in that period he learned he was the victim of unjust spying. Doña Ana de Penalosa and her brother, Don Luis de Mercado, were also in Madrid at that time, and it was natural that John, as her confessor and spiritual director, should visit her. According to the Rule of the Carmelites, a priest must always be accompanied by a companion when making visits. On this occasion, he learned that Fray Cirilo Pinán, who was named to accompany him, had received orders not to allow him out of his sight during the time they were at Doña Ana's house. This order had been given to Fray Cirilo secretly by one of the Definitors. When they came to the house, Fray John of the Cross went with Doña Ana into the Oratory to hear her confession while Fray Cirilo remained respectfully in the outer chamber; but, to his great embarrassment, John of the Cross told him that he should carry out his orders and not allow him out of his sight. He therefore made Fray Cirilo sit on a stool at the open door of the Oratory so that he might at least see Fray John during the lady's confession. This is a seemingly insignificant detail, but it indicates the lengths to which his enemies went in their injustice to Fray John. From that time on, he was to be spied upon and while he was in Andalucía, the new Provincial Vicar, Fray Diego Evangelista, made one enquiry after another with a view to casting doubt upon the moral character of John and on the nature of his spiritual relationship to the nuns. The nuns, of course, were indignant at such suspicions, and I have already mentioned that they burned a number of his writings and his letters rather than undergo the indignity of such injurious inquiries.

This was the beginning of John's Calvary. He had asked: "Oh Lord, to suffer and to be misunderstood for Your sake." His prayer had been heard.

XI

CALVARY AT THE LAST

(1591)

Farewell

When the time came for John of the Cross to "drink his chalice," he did so with such courage, such "self-abnegation," and such a "love of the Cross" that it is understandable why the Church, in the Collect appointed to be said on his feast day, lays such stress upon these two virtues: "O God, Who didst give to holy John, Thy Confessor and Doctor, a wondrous spirit of self-abnegation and a love, all abounding, of Thy holy Cross, grant that we, ever following his example, may thus obtain the glory that endures forevermore. . . ." (*Missale Romanum,* November 24)

It was not only for the benefit of others that John had preached so well the renunciation taught by the Gospel, which was at the root of all his mystical teaching. I have said that his writings were the very expression of his life. This is apparent not only in his prayer to Christ while he was in Segovia, but also in the way in which he accepted the persecution which was to last to his death.

As soon as Father Doria's decision was made to send him to

Andalucía, Fray John went to see the Carmelite sisters in Madrid. One of the nuns tells us that he had a joyful appearance, a look of angelic peace upon his face. When he told them that he was to go to Andalucía but could not tell them the exact monastery, one of the nuns, knowing him well and understanding the kind of trial in store for him, cried out:

"Oh! where then is our Reverend Father to go?"

And the saint replied:

"My daughter, I am better off among stones than among men."

There was another painful farewell to make. He went to see Ana de Penalosa and said simply to her:

"May God be with you, my daughter, for I am going away."

At these words Doña Ana began to weep and reproach him for leaving her, but St. John said:

"My daughter, do not be disturbed; for it is you who will come to seek me and will bring me back . . ."

Neither Ana nor anyone else understood these mysterious words, but five months later, when John of the Cross lay dead in Andalucía, and Ana de Penalosa and her brother Don Luis de Mercado went to carry his body from Ubeda to Segovia, where he was buried, many remembered what the saint had said in veritable prophecy.

Finally, John went to see the parents of Jerónimo Gracián, who lived in Madrid. Gracián, too, had suffered persecution at the hands of Father Doria and had been forced to leave the Discalced. But before his death, he was able to find refuge with the brethren of the Mitigated Observance. Soon an attempt would be made to take the habit of the Discalced away from John of the Cross as well.

After leaving Madrid, John returned to Segovia to complete the preparations for his departure and to visit the sisters. Mother Maria de la Encarnación saw him come into the parlor, and later declared that it pained her so much to see how he had failed that she could not refrain from saying:

"May God help us, my Father! In what state does Your Paternity come to us! . . ."

But when she went on to speak of the affronts to him by the members of the General Chapter at Madrid, he interrupted her, saying:

"We will not talk of that."

And he would allow nothing further to be said about it. To one of the friends of the Carmelite monastery who asked when he would see him again, St. John replied firmly and almost prophetically:

"Nevermore on this earth shall we see each other again; but we shall meet in heaven."

With these thoughts in mind, he bade farewell to his beloved monastery at Segovia, to the garden and the little grotto where he had found retirement on the hills around the monastery grounds, to Christ carrying His Cross, the Christ Who had spoken to him, to the chapel of the monastery, and especially to the sisters at the convent who were so dear to him and who would not forget the words and example by which he had taught them holiness.

Two Months at La Penuela

John of the Cross set out for Andalucía, which was about one hundred fifty miles from Segovia, in the latter part of July. No monastery had been assigned him as a place of residence. As far as he knew, he was supposed to be on the point of departing for Mexico, but no one discussed the change in plans with him, or any plans for that matter. So he stopped at the first monastery he reached early in August. This was La Penuela, one of the lowliest, the poorest of all. On his arrival, he wrote to the Provincial Prior of Andalucía, who was none other than his old companion at Duruelo, Father Antonio de Jesús. His letter is typically humble and submissive:

"My father, I am come as the subject of Your Paternity.

What is Your Reverence's pleasure that I do, and where do you wish me to go?"

Amiably, the Provincial replied at once that he might choose whichever monastery he wished to live in and go there immediately.

But John of the Cross insisted that he wished only to obey, not to choose:

"My Father, I am not come to do my own will, nor to choose where I shall live. Let Your Paternity indicate where you wish me to go, and there I shall go."

To the great satisfaction of the monks of La Penuela, who regarded him as a saint, it was decided that John of the Cross was to remain with them, and there he would have died had it not been that the medical resources he was to need were lacking in that mountain fastness, and they were obliged to send him to Ubeda.

There are a good many testimonies about the kind of life he led during the two months he was at La Penuela. One of the Fathers, who was then living at the monastery, recorded that John wrote an admirable little book about the miracles attributed to the statues at Gualdalcazar, but the book has not been preserved. It undoubtedly was destroyed with others of the saint's works because of the persecution to which he was subjected. All we can know is that he must have treated the subject in the tone as his great writings which we have, that he would have discussed true and false miracles, and that he would have put the reader on guard against the evil spirit, by which we might understand him to mean, against an unhealthy taste for wonders.

On the other hand, it is certain that he reworked his masterpieces, *Spiritual Canticle* and *Living Flame of Love*.

But John of the Cross did not spend all his time at work in his cell. Early in the morning he would go alone into the monastery garden where he would kneel in prayer by a clear stream or commune with God in the natural works of His creation. If the summer heat did not drive him back to the house, he would remain in the garden for long periods, for now that he had no official duties, he could devote himself, with a joyful heart, to contemplation. Yet, like the least of the novices, he would do nothing without his Prior's permission. The last view, then, that we have of John of the Cross before his final illness is that of a man still before the face of the unseen God, but surrounded by the things of visible creation, offering to the Lord the homage of all nature.

Sometimes he would go on priestly missions to places as distant as the little village of Linarès, about seven and a half miles away.

In the accounts we have of his stay at La Penuela there are some episodes of a miraculous nature—or such as were believed by the religious of the place to be miraculous. One day the monastery was threatened by a fire. The brethren had been burning some dried herbs when the wind changed course and the fire began to spread rapidly in the direction of the monastery. Soon the danger became so great the religious urged that the Blessed Sacrament be taken to a place of safety. But John of the Cross was opposed to this. He recommended rather that they gather in prayer around the tabernacle, and he threw himself on his knees before the flames. The fire advanced toward him, but he did not move. Instead, it was the fire that yielded for when it reached him, it went out. John then rose and told the frightened monks to open the doors and windows of the church so that the air might be cleared.

Another time, a tornado burst upon the mountain during the evening. The monks saw all their vineyards and olive groves being destroyed, but John of the Cross told them not to be upset. Then he went outside, uncovered his head, and lifting his eyes to heaven, made four great signs of the Cross in the air, one in each direction. Suddenly the tempests ceased as though Christ had spoken to the elements through the mouth of his servant and said: "Peace; be still." One witness, Fray Francisco de San

Hilarión, tells us that the religious were struck with wonder and gave thanks to God.

There was another incident thought to be miraculous. This was the unexpected cure of the lay Brother, Juan de la Madre de Dios. Although Juan's work of cultivation of the property made him indispensable to the community, they had been obliged to send him to Baeza for medical care. Fray John of the Cross, however, insisted that the brethren instruct him to return to La Penuela. They obeyed, although they did not understand. When the lay Brother learned at Baeza that it was Fray John of the Cross who had so commanded him, he did not hesitate, but leaving his bed, returned feeling so well that if the brethren had allowed it, he would have been back at work within the hour.

THE DEFAMATORY PROCESS OF FATHER DIEGO EVANGELISTA

It is a strange thing that, even as these wonders were being wrought at La Penuela before the eyes of all the religious there, in the other parts of the Province of Andalucía the most ignominious kind of enquiry was taking place under the direction of the Definitor of the Order, Father Diego Evangelista. Although he was a young man, thirty-one years old, he was egotistical, suspicious, and bitter. As we have mentioned earlier, he had received a reprimand from John of the Cross when, as Provincial Vicar, he admonished Father Diego for the pride he took in his preaching ability. The young friar hated John for this affront to his ego. Now that Father Doria, intent on disgracing Fray Gracián, had appointed Father Diego to draw up charges against his enemy, the vengeful young friar saw an opportunity to disgrace John of the Cross as well.

A fragment of one of John's letters which has been preserved gives us an idea of the view he took of the matter. It is dated from La Penuela and is addressed to Mother Ana de San Alberto, the Prioress of Caravaca:

"My daughter: You will already know of the many trials that we are suffering. God allows this for the glory of His elect. In silence and hope will be our strength. Commend me to God, and may He make you holy."

Once he had described the bare cross as "a beautiful thing." Now the time had come when he was to cling to that cross with all his strength.

Although great trials are not the same for all, God always chooses to allow us those trials which most affect us. For John of the Cross, the very core of his being was his perfect purity in God, and it was on this point that Diego wished to attack him. He sought to cast aspersions upon John's relations with the nuns to whom he had been and was spiritual director, as though his deep love for them, although wholly supernatural, had been sullied by unholy desires.

At La Penuela, John was advised to appeal to Father Doria, but he refused. Despite his sorrow and his shame—shame not for himself, but for his persecutor—he would not complain, nor would he allow anything to be said against his defamer.

One day, one of his sons said to him: "Oh, my Father, how does Father Diego Evangelista dare so to persecute Your Paternity? . . ."

"These words of yours give me more pain and chagrin than does anything else," was the vigorous reply of John of the Cross.

Father Diego, therefore, was not faced by any resistance on John's part. But he found it quite otherwise on the side of the nuns. He sought in vain to trap them by promises or threats; he futilely tried to twist words from their statements into a sense which would make the most natural actions seem suspicious. But the sisters became frightened that Father Diego would fabricate some evil accusations and, in their indignation, they gathered together all of John's writings in their possession and burned them.

The most deplorable part of the whole affair was not the re-
volting method of Father Diego Evangelista, for he was a man
whose lack of judgment was so great it made him the victim of his
own evil leanings, but the complacency with which Father
Nicolas Doria and the whole Board of Definitors of the Order
regarded Diego's actions. Not only did they give him a free
hand but, even after John's death, when they sent him on a
mission to Italy, he continued his work of defamation without
censure.

It was Diego who, when he saw a nun weeping at the news that
John of the Cross had died, cried out:

"Had he not died, I would have deprived him of his habit, and
he would never have died in the Order."

Another fragment from one of John's letters, which was written later from Ubeda, indicates that he knew what Diego had
in mind. To Fray Juan de Santa Ana he wrote:

". . . do not let this worry you, son, for they cannot take
the habit from me save for incorrigibility or disobedience, and
I am quite prepared to amend my ways in everything in which
I have gone astray, and to be obedient, whatever penance they
give me. . . ."

JOHN'S DEPARTURE FROM LA PENUELA

While the defamatory campaign was in progress, Fray John was
attacked by the illness which was to prove fatal, although it did
not prevent him from dying from that "death of love," his ideal
for any Christian worthy of the name. The illness began with an
inflammation of the left leg which led to a fever.

At first, he paid no attention to it, but soon the remarks of his
brethren obliged him to submit to treatment. At this time, another
one of the fathers, Francisco de San Hilarión, also fell ill and it
was decided to send him to Baeza since the monastery of La
Penuela had no facilities for medical care. Fray Francisco

suggested that John of the Cross go with him, but in his humility and desire to be wholly self-denying, Fray John replied:

"Your Paternity may indeed go to Baeza, but I am too well known there. As for me, I shall soon go to Ubeda, for there I am unknown."

This was all the more heroic for he had been the founder of the University College of the Carmelites at Baeza, and the Prior of that college, Fray Angel de la Presentación, was devoted to him. There were others at Baeza who also loved him, and it was from this that he turned aside. The saints have their own way of solving human problems.

But even to go to Ubeda required a categorical order from his superiors.

Even then, he said only:

"Since it is for obedience's sake, let us go."

He wrote to tell Doña Ana de Penalosa, and this letter has been preserved in its entirety. It is dated September 21, 1591, less than three months before his death, and in it are revealed his most intimate feelings:

"Jesus be in your soul, daughter. Here at La Penuela I received the packet of letters which the servant brought me. I greatly appreciate the trouble you have taken. Tomorrow I go to Ubeda to cure a slight bout of fever, for I have been having attacks of it daily for over a week, and if it does not go, I think I shall need medical aid; but I go with the intention of returning here again, for in truth I am deriving great good from this holy retreat. . . ."

And he ends with the following lines:

"Give my daughter Doña Inés [Doña Ana's niece] my many greetings in the Lord and pray both of you that He may be pleased to prepare me to be taken to be with Him.

"Now I can think of no more to say, and so, on account of the fever, I stop, though I would gladly go on."

Surely he was in the deepest state of interior peace, yet he still thought that he would be able to return to La Penuela. Thus it would seem that he had not been the recipient of any personal revelation concerning the place and date of his death.

AT UBEDA

Although he had intended to leave the next day, September 22, he did not actually depart until a week later. The trip was long and was marked by a curious incident. John of the Cross was mounted upon a mule brought expressly from Ubeda and which was led by a young boy. The day was very cold and the road much traveled. After they had covered about seventeen of the twenty-five miles to Ubeda, the travelers came to the Bridge Ariza over the River Guadalimar. The sick man felt tired and had no desire to eat. Although the boy had asked him several times along the way what he would like, each time he had answered that there was nothing. However, when they came to the bridge, to the amazement of the youngster John of the Cross suddenly cried out:

"Ah! If only I had some asparagus! . . ."

The boy thought: "What an idea—to have asparagus in the last days of September!" He looked about him. There, upon one of the pillars of the bridge, stood a bunch of asparagus. John of the Cross did not seem surprised.

"Go and get them," he said to his companion, "and put some coins on the stone for the owner of this asparagus." The boy obeyed, and that evening, the whole monastery of Ubeda saw the bunch of asparagus. Father Bartolomeo de San Basilio has affirmed that he saw it himself. That night, while the monastery cook was preparing the asparagus—and it was all the sick man ate—John told the story in a light and pleasant manner as though it were nothing at all unusual, and the only remarkable feature was the boy's amazement, but everyone in the monastery stayed convinced that the story of the asparagus was the pure and simple account of a miracle, a kind of Providential intervention on John's behalf.

The Monastery of the Carmelite Fathers at Ubeda, which had been founded in 1587, was small and poor, but Fray John was joyfully greeted by the brethren, for many of them had formerly worked under his authority. In particular, Father Alonso de la Madre de Dios, the sub-Prior at Ubeda, had been his first novice at Granada, and several brethren were known to be friends of John of the Cross.

But the Prior, Fray Francisco Crisostomo, did not welcome John. He was a good preacher but a man of rough character and was disliked at Ubeda. Alonso de la Madre de Dios has described him as being very rigid and especially hostile to those whom he regarded as saints. "It might be said of him," Father Alonso goes on to remark, "that he led his religious to perfection, but as it were by means of a cudgel—a *palos*." But Fray Crisostomo's dislike of John of the Cross was animated by another reason, similar to that of Fray Diego Evangelista. He, too, had been reprimanded by John when, as Provincial Vicar of Andalucía, he had occasion to censure Fray Crisostomo for his open taste for success in the pulpit to the detriment of the interior life.

Fray Crisostomo had set aside for the sick man the smallest and barest of the cells, and insisted that Fray John attend all the community exercises as though he were in perfect health. On one occasion, when John of the Cross excused himself for not being able to go to the Refectory with the others, the Prior forced him to go and then, in the presence of the entire community, severely reproached him.

Under these conditions, it was not long before the inevitable occurred. The illness from which John suffered grew worse and, soon after his arrival, he was so exhausted that he fell on his pallet and could not rise from it.

JOHN'S LAST ILLNESS

The sickness was a virulent inflammation of the skin, centering around the foot. Nowadays we know that this affliction is of microbic origin and is due to a streptococcus infection. Although it is not serious for a strong person, in the case of one such as John of the Cross, who was so weak, it could become very serious. The illness formed five cruciform wounds at the core of the inflammation, the central and largest wound at exactly the point where one of the nails pierced Christ's foot. Fray John regarded all the wounds not only with resignation, but with a kind of joy, for he saw in them some sharing of Our Saviour's wounds. And the largest wound spurred him to the greatest devotion, according to an eyewitness, Fray Agustin de San José, who had been one of John's obedientiaries at Granada.

The surgeon, Ambrosio de Villareal, decided to cut into the leg in order to cleanse it. At that time, a surgical operation was a terrifying thing. Anesthetics were unknown and the surgeon cut and probed in John's leg in such a way that even those who were merely observers almost fainted.

"Sir Doctor, what are you doing to my leg?" asked the patient very gently.

"I have just opened the foot and the leg, and Your Paternity asks me what I am doing!"

"If he must cut further, let him do so," Fray John then said to the Infirmarian, Fray Diego de Jesús. "Let him cut as he will, and may all be according to the will of Our Lord Jesus Christ."

The surgeon went on with his work, even driving his scalpel into the bone. During all this butchery the sick man lay quietly with his hands joined over his breast, as was his custom when he was at prayer. He never complained.

But during the days that followed, an even more remarkable phenomenon than John's patience occurred. Pus rushed forth in such abundance from the wounds the surgeon had opened that whole cups had to be filled with it, and yet this liquid gave forth a most agreeable scent. This perfume naturally permeated the bandages used to cover the wounds. The laundresses were two young girls who were so pleased that they disputed with one another for the honor of washing the bandages and their mother, Doña Maria de Molina, was obliged to require them to take turns at their work. One day, when some of the bandages did not give forth the strong and pleasant odor to which the girls had grown accustomed, they said that either the sick priest had died or these were not his bandages. They spoke to the Brother Infirmarian, who did not understand them at first, but then admitted that the bandages of John of the Cross had been mixed up with those of another priest who was suffering from a wound in the shoulder.

At length, when they returned his own linens to him, the two young girls sent messages to the sick man through the Brother Infirmarian. One of them, Catalina de Salazar, asked him to tell John that she wished to become a nun, and asked that he pray for her. Fray John replied, through the same intermediary, that the Lord did indeed wish her to do this, but that it could not be for three more years. As a matter of fact, three years after John's death Catalina de Salazar did become a Carmelite sister under the name of Catalina de San Alberto, and all these details were revealed by her own deposition during the process of John's beatification.

On the whole, although John of the Cross had chosen to go to Ubeda rather than to Baeza on the ground that he was unknown in Ubeda, this reason was not entirely verified inasmuch as there were some brothers at Ubeda who thought highly of him and had known him for a long time. But on the whole, his presence in the village soon became a matter of note. It was learned that the Carmelite monastery possessed a saintly man. The surgeon had been quick to glorify the unbelievable virtues of his patient. He said that he had seen in him that courage, strength, and kindness which declares spiritual truth. No one but a saint, he said, could have borne so horrible a sickness as John's.

When in time bits of flesh clung to John's bandages, the surgeon asked the two laundresses to keep some bandages for him so he might apply them to other patients by way of remedy.

There were benefactors of the monastery in the town of Ubeda who sought to do some service for the sick man, such as preparing food for him. They talked with pleasure about little details concerning him. The most favored were those who succeeded in obtaining permission to visit him. Later on, the testimony they offered was assembled during the process of John's beatification and they all had some small fact to relate concerning either a remark, a prophecy, or a bit of advice which he had given them. But they also told of the constant hostility of the Prior, Fray Crisostomo, who bewailed the expense which Fray John's illness was causing the monastery, and even more, the visits which John received and the marks of honor which were showered upon him. The attestation made by the Prior of La Penuela, Fray Gabriel de la Concepción, is worthy of note. He had come to see the patient and listened to the Prior's grievances. In reply, Fray Gabriel de la Concepción pointed out that there were many benefactors of the Ubeda monastery, and that their gifts compensated for the trifling expenses which John's illness had caused. He even went so far as to offer to repay them from the revenues of his own monastery at La Penuela, and, as a matter of fact, when he returned home, he sent four loads of wheat for the brethren and six fowl for the sick man.

But Fray Crisostomo continued his unkindness to John. He shifted the blame, which he knew he should assume himself, to the sick man and was as disagreeable as possible to him. Fray Bernardo de la Virgen, who generally attended the sick man, stated that Fray Crisostomo never entered the cell without making some harsh remark about John. He even went so far as to dig up forgotten matters with which to reproach him. He forbade the lay brothers to visit him without his express permission, and one day even forbade the bandages to be sent to the laundry. When the Infirmarian complained to John of the Cross, the latter said, with his habitual kindness:

"Don't distress yourself, my Brother, let the matter rest in the hands of God and pray that He may help us."

When the friars complained in his presence that the Prior had not given him his necessities, he was always ready to excuse him, for he would never criticize the treatment being given him. When Fray Crisostomo claimed that Ubeda was poor, John replied:

"May God be blessed. The day will come when this monastery will have all that it needs."

HELPFUL INTERVENTION

In the midst of all this unpleasantness, relief came from an unexpected source in the person of the lay brother, Bernardo de la Virgen, who had given John such affectionate care.

The Prior had noted his attention to John of the Cross and formally relieved him of his office as Infirmarian, categorically forbidding him to see John again. But Bernardo was not daunted and, as the Rule permitted, wrote at once to the Provincial Prior of Andalucía, Father Antonio de Jesús, to inform him of the affairs at Ubeda. Although Father Antonio had not cherished the title "Father of the Reform" being given to John of the Cross rather than to himself, his feelings for him were above this smallness and, in the present contingency, he did his duty. Whereas the Vicar General had allowed full freedom to Fray Diego Evangelista to sully John's reputation, Father Antonio reacted vigorously to the harshness of Fray Crisostomo. He hastened to Ubeda at once, where he severely rebuked the Prior for his evil conduct. He ordered the brethren to be allowed full liberty to visit the sick man, and restored to Fray Bernardo his charge of the sole care of Fray John. He told him to buy whatever things were necessary and promised that the Province would recompense his expenditures.

The Provincial Prior's visit took place on November 27, and coincidentally, it had been on November 28, 1568, that, with John of the Cross, he had inaugurated the monastery of Duruelo.

"Father," he said to Fray John, "tomorrow it will be twenty-four years ago that we began our first foundation! . . ."

Although the good man was mistaken by a year, he was so happy to reminisce about the past that he started to retell the history of those blessed days in such terms that John of the Cross hastened to stop him by saying: "Father, is this your way of keeping the promise you gave me long ago that while we lived we would never talk of these things? . . ."

At these words the Provincial Prior stopped. But the friars began to question him and he let first one detail drop and then another so that finally John of the Cross smilingly remarked: "He finished by telling the whole story! . . ."

CLOSE TO DEATH BY LOVE

John's suffering continued to increase. Not only were both his legs affected, but a large, deep wound appeared on one of his shoulders. This wound was discovered only by chance because whenever he could, he tried to pretend he was better so as not to concern his nurses. It was a gradual disintegration and yet the sick man never complained, even as he slowly became partially paralyzed. Soon they were obliged to suspend a rope above his bed so that by grasping it, he was able to move slightly. He scarcely had strength to speak, but from time to time could be heard murmuring some short aspiration in prayer or recalling a phrase from the Bible.

"All the time he was in bed," states Fray Bartolomeo de San Basilio, "he seemed to be sleeping, save that occasionally he was heard to repeat these words: *Haec requiyes mea in saeculum saeculi:* 'This is my rest forever.' This he was heard frequently to repeat when his pain was at its greatest. . . ."

Often he would say to Our Lord:

"My God, grant me more patience, more love, and more suffering."

Yet God alone knows if there was any suffering that he lacked. Besides that caused by the illness itself, the medical treatment was excruciatingly painful. He was hacked at, he was cauterized; he was literally cut up into pieces. In those days the cure was often worse than the disease.

After December 6 he began to ask daily what day it was. In the evening of the seventh, at First Vespers of the Immaculate Conception of the Virgin, the sores became more painful and John's fever rose. The physician told the sub-Prior, Father Alonso de la Madre de Dios, that there was no hope and advised him to speak to the sick man so that he might prepare himself for death. The priest agreed but only on condition that the physician remain.

"Father John," said Fray Alonso, "the physician tells me that Your Paternity is approaching the end. Commend yourself to God."

"I am dying," replied Fray John. Then joining his hands on his breast, he cried out in joy: *Laetatus sum in his quae dicta sunt mihi, in domum Dominum ibimus:* "I rejoiced at the things that were said to me: we shall go into the house of the Lord."

This was indeed that great desire of death which he had described as being the mark of the true Christian—who would not wish for such a death!

On Wednesday, December 11, he asked for the Holy Viaticum, which he received with great fervor.

"I am going out of this world," said John of the Cross to the Infirmarian, Fray Diego, who was always at his side. The brother was greatly moved, and throwing himself on his knees beside the bed, asked for his blessing. Fray John excused himself, but the brother took his hand, kissed it, and then put it on his own head so that the dying man might bless him.

"Fray Diego," said John of the Cross, "do you really want me to die?"

And the good young brother replied that, since it was God's will, he did, for His will should always be accepted. Fray John told him always to act and think in this way.

Up until this time he had kept a packet of letters, most of which concerned the defamatory process against him, at his bedside. He also had many documents to refute the atrocious calumnies which were directed against his honor. On December 12 he asked Fray Bartolomeo to bring him a candle and, in his presence, burned all the letters.

(Three years later the successor of Father Nicolas Doria burned the whole dossier which Diego Evangelista had drawn up against St. John.)

Fray Antonio de Jesús frequently came to visit the sick man. One day, in order to encourage him, he said:

"Father John, be of good heart; put your trust in God, think of all the good we have done and the trials we have suffered in starting the Reform."

The dying man quickly replied: "Do not say that! Do not say that to me! Rather speak to me of my sins!"

And then, at once, he closed his eyes in meditation.

On December 13, John felt that his end was near and he asked the Infirmarian to call the Father Prior. When the Prior had come and in the presence of the Infirmarian, who later reported this incident, John of the Cross asked Father Francisco Crisostomo to forgive him for all the trouble and expense he had caused by his illness. And then he added: "My Father, here beside me is the habit of the Virgin which I have worn! I am a poor man, and I have nothing to wear to my grave. I beg Your Paternity for the love of God to give me this habit as an alms."

And then he asked the Prior for his blessing.

Father Crisostomo was quite moved. He asked pardon of the dying man, and said that, if he had not taken as good care of him as he should have, it was because of the poverty of the monastery.

"Father," replied John of the Cross, "I am content with all, and I have received more than I have deserved. But do not be concerned about this monastery, for a time will come when it will lack for nothing. Put your trust in Our Lord."

Father Crisostomo could not restrain his tears and went out weeping. Three times Fray Bartolomeo de San Basilio saw him return and kneel by the bed of the sick man. Finally he asked him to give him his Breviary as a remembrance.

"I have nothing to give to Your Paternity," replied John of the Cross, "for all that I have is yours: You are my Superior."

JOHN'S LAST MOMENTS

Fray John himself asked for the sacrament of Extreme Unction. He held a crucifix in his hands and kissed the feet of the image of Our Lord several times as he said aspirations. He would not allow anyone to tell him that he had been a good workman for the Savior. "No," he said, "I have never done anything that was worthy of Him."

At this time he suffered such cruel agonies that he begged Fray Antonio de Jesús to excuse him for not answering because his pain was so great.

Late in the evening he asked the time and, when told it was ten o'clock, asked them to retire and promised to let them know when his time came. Then he again became immersed in prayer.

For a second time he asked what the hour was.

Fray Pedro replied: "It is now half after eleven."

At these words the face of John of the Cross was suffused with joy and he cried out:

"The time is near! Call the Fathers."

In a few minutes, the religious, who numbered fourteen or fifteen, came into the cell, each one holding a lighted taper, and ranged themselves along the wall of John's cell. A lay brother, Francisco, stationed himself at the bedside of the dying man. One of the Fathers asked John how he felt. Raising himself up by the rope, he said:

"I feel better. Let us say the *De profundis* together."

Then he intoned the first verse, to which all responded. John recited it to the end.

He requested that they also recite the *Miserere,* and finally, the psalm, *In te Domine speravi.*

During this time, Fray Francisco thought that he saw a circle of light about John's head. This light enveloped the dying man completely and was more brilliant than the twenty candles which burned in the cell.

After the recitation of the Psalms, Fray John rested for a moment and gave himself to prayer. Then he asked that he be allowed to adore the Most Holy Sacrament. When they brought It into his cell, he spoke words in the presence of the Host which reached out to the hearts of all. As the Holy Sacrament was borne away John cried out:

"Soon, O Lord, I shall see You again with more than these mortal eyes!"

For the last time he asked: "What is the hour?"

"Soon it will be midnight."

"At that hour I shall be before God, Our Lord, saying Matins. . . ."

Several of the religious then wished to begin the prayers for the dying, but as they began to open their Breviaries, John stopped them. He exhorted the brethren always to keep the Rule and to obey their Superiors.

Father Alonso reminded him that it was Friday, and that on Saturday the Holy Virgin of Carmel would come to seek him in Purgatory. But John of the Cross smiled and replied that at midnight he would be saying Matins in heaven. Then the Prior began the prayers *Commendatio Animae;* but John of the Cross asked that they read some verses from the *Canticle of Canticles*. During the reading he was heard to say:

"What precious pearls."

Soon the dying man amiably dismissed all who were with him:

"Go," he said; "it is time to close the monastery. Remember that I must go to say Matins in heaven . . ."

They obeyed him. In the cell there remained only some of the benefactors of the monastery and the father of the two girls who had washed the bandages.

Finally, at midnight, Fray Francisco, too, left the room to ring the Matin bell.

When the monastery bell chimed, the saint asked:

"What is it that rings?"

"That is the Matin bell . . ."

Then, as though he had been waiting for a signal longed for and much desired, John of the Cross cried out in joy: "Glory to God! For I must go to say Matins in heaven."

Then he took his crucifix into his hands and said very deliberately:

"In manus tuas, Domine, commendo spiritum meum."

And with these words, which were those of Jesus on the Cross, John quietly died—the "death of love." His face, which had always been tanned, became white and transparent as light, and from his sore-covered body there gushed forth the perfume of roses. It was Saturday, December 14, 1591.

AFTERWORD

THE SEVENTEEN COUNSELS OF ST. JOHN

OF THE CROSS

Twenty-nine years after the death of John of the Cross, there died in the Monastery of the Discalced in Mexico an exemplary religious who had known him well. He was named Fray Eliseo de la Martires, and he had made his religious profession at the Monastery of Granada while John of the Cross had been Prior there. When the preliminary enquiries were made into John's sanctity, Eliseo had been among the witnesses called upon to give testimony. His report is dated March 26, 1618, from Mexico, and is by far the most substantial of all those we have. The other documents establish various details of the saint's life, and all this information has been infinitely worthwhile to me because through them I have been able to tell the story of St. John. I have leaned, also, on such learned masters of the subject as Father Bruno de Jésus Marie, an outstanding authority whose biography of John, to which Jacques Maritain contributed the preface, is dated 1929, and Father Crisogono de Jesus, from whom I have borrowed many things contained in his text of 1946. Eliseo de la Martires has condensed the teaching of the saint into "seventeen counsels," which will form a fitting conclusion to the present work.

Fray Eliseo wrote down his testimony under oath and in submission to his vow of obedience:

"By virtue of the command which has been given to me, I make the following declaration. . . ."

Hence, we are faced here with a document which gives evidence of long and deep reflection. At the time of its submission, those who were charged with the enquiry were concerned with bringing together all the fragments which made up the sum total of the inquiries needed for the process of beatification of John of the Cross. He had died twenty-six years before, but it is plain that all those who had known him had not forgotten him; their memories had simply been made clearer by time. All the witnesses who speak to us now understood better that they had had the privilege of knowing a saint—a real one—and that there is nothing on this earth more beautiful.

A PORTRAIT OF JOHN OF THE CROSS

Fray Eliseo thus takes up his narrative: "I knew our father, Fray John of the Cross and had to do with him on many and diverse occasions. He was a man of medium height, with a serious and venerable expression, somewhat swarthy and with good features; his demeanor and conversation were tranquil, very spiritual, and of great profit to those who heard him and had to do with him. And in this respect he was so singular and so effective that those who knew him, whether men or women, left his presence with greater spirituality, devotion, and affection for virtue. He had a deep knowledge and a keen perception of prayer and communion with God, and all questions that were put to him concerning these matters he answered with the highest wisdom, leaving those who consulted him about them completely satisfied and greatly advantaged. He was fond of recollection and given to speaking little; he seldom laughed and when he did so it was with great restraint. When he reproved others as their Superior (which happened frequently) he did so with a gracious severity, exhorting them with brotherly love, and acting throughout with a wondrous serenity and gravity."

This is the oldest physical and moral portrait we have of this holy man. Throughout the whole of this book, I have tried to picture him in his gifted character as poet, mystical theologian, director of souls, and faithful friend of God.

Now we shall see all that Fray Eliseo summed up as the most striking of his teaching.

THE FIRST FOUR COUNSELS

"*First Saying*—He greatly objected to imperious commands being given by superiors to their religious, especially in the Reformed Orders, and was wont to say that nothing shows a man to be so unworthy of commanding others as the fact that he commands them imperiously; we should rather endeavour to bring it about that those under us never leave our presence downcast.

"He never spoke with duplicity or artifice, to which he took the strongest objection, for he said:

"*Second Saying*—That artifice violated the sincerity and purity of the Order, and that many did it grievous harm by inculcating methods of prudence of a human kind which caused souls spiritual sickness.

"*Third Saying*—He said concerning the vice of ambition that in reformed communities it is almost incurable, being the most infectious of all vices; it colours and taints the rule and conduct of the Order with appearances of virtue and of the greatest perfection, so that warfare with evil becomes sterner and spiritual sickness more incurable. And he said that this vice is so powerful and pestilent as to make such sinners of those who suffer from it that the devil is able to throw their lives into confusion and entanglement and thus to confound their confessors. He had great perseverance in prayer and in the practice of the presence of God and in anagogical movements and acts and ejaculatory prayers.

"*Fourth Saying*—He said that the entire life of a religious is (or ought to be) a doctrinal sermon, with these words, which should be repeated several times a day, for its text: Die and perish rather than sin. He said that these words, if they spring from the will, cleanse and purify the soul and make it to grow in the love of God, in grief at having offended Him, and in firmness of purpose to offend Him no more."

THE FIFTH COUNSEL

The saint's fifth word of advice is so important that one is inclined to set it apart from the others so that it may stand out. This is, above all else, a practical counsel. It treats of how one is to resist evil leanings and cleave to what is good. This is the great question before all directors of souls; it is the secret fulcrum of their action.

According to St. John of the Cross, two very different methods may be employed to this end.

The first is the most common, although of a lesser degree of perfection. It consists of resisting temptation by acts of virtue which are directly opposed to the temptation in question and the vice in which it is rooted. Thus, after being injured, I can conceive the wish to be avenged and then take refuge against this wish in one of Christ's acts; as Isaias has written, [when he] ". . . was offered because it was his own will, and he opened not His mouth . . ." (53:7). Or again one may reflect upon the fruits of patience, of suffering bravely endured and of victory over selfishness. Or, finally, one may recall the divine precepts on the bearing of injuries, encouraging oneself, within the depths of the soul, to bear with and even to love the affront which one has received, so that God be honored and glorified.

This may be called the classical method. It is an excellent way to resist the spirit of vengeance which one desires to expel from one's heart.

But John of the Cross declared that there is an easier, more advantageous, and more perfect method.

Throughout this volume I have spoken of what John of the Cross called "anagogic motions." I will now explain this term to the best of my ability.

According to the principle of Biblical hermeneutics, the *spiritual sense* of a passage of Scripture is called the *anagogic sense* in order to distinguish it from the *literal sense*. Thus do we pass from some figure in the Bible to the reality of which he is the *type* or *figure,* as, for example, when we see in the persecuted Jeremiah, Christ our Lord, we do so anagogically. Here, according to John of the Cross, we have entered into Mystical Theology. Anagogic motions are therefore synonyms of Godward leaps. The anagogic motion is our *Sursum corda,* by which we lift our hearts up on high.

The motion which we have seen John of the Cross so frequently put into practice is to rise from the banality of earthly conversation in order to go to God by saying to oneself: *Sursum corda.* He made of this the principle of a most efficacious method of dealing with temptations. Let us read what Fray Eliseo tells us on this point, according to the teaching of his venerated master:

> "According to this, by its loving anagogical movements and acts alone, without any other exercises whatsoever, the soul resists and destroys all the temptations of our adversary and attains virtues in the most perfect degree. This, the venerable Father was wont to say, becomes possible after this manner. When we feel the first movement or attack of any vice, such as lust, wrath, impatience, or a revengeful spirit when some wrong has been done to us, we should not resist it by making an act of the contrary virtue, in the way that has been described, but, as soon as we are conscious of

it, we should meet it with an act or movement of anagogical love directed against this vice, and should raise our affection to union with God, for by this means the soul absents itself from its surroundings and is present with its God and becomes united with Him, and then the vice or the temptation and the enemy are defrauded of their intent, and have nowhere to strike; for the soul, being where it loves rather than where it lives, has met the temptation with Divine aid, and the enemy has found nowhere to strike and nothing whereon to lay hold, for the soul is no longer where the temptation or enemy would have struck and wounded it. And then, oh, marvelous thing! the soul, having forgotten this movement of vice, and being united and made one with its Beloved, no longer feels any movement of this vice wherewith the devil desired to tempt it, and was succeeding in doing so; in the first place, because, as has been said, it has escaped, and is no longer present, so that, if it may be put in this way, the devil is as it were tempting a dead body and doing battle with something that is not, feels not, and is for the time being incapable of feeling temptation.

"In this way there is begotten in the soul a wondrous and heroic virtue, which the Angelic Doctor St. Thomas calls the virtue of a soul that is perfectly purged. This virtue, said the holy Father, is possessed by the soul when God brings it to such a state that it feels not the movements of vice, nor its assaults, attacks, or temptations, because of the loftiness of the virtue which dwells in this soul. Hence there arises within it and comes to it a most lofty perfection which takes from it all concern about being praised or exalted or insulted or humbled or about whether men speak well of it or ill. For, as these loving and anagogical movements raise the soul to so high and sublime a state, their truest effect upon the soul is to make it forget all things other than its Beloved, Who is Jesus Christ. Hence, as has been said, when it is united with its God and in converse with Him, it finds that no temptations can wound it, since they cannot rise to that place whither the soul has risen or to which God has raised it: *Non accedet ad te malum . . .* —There shall no evil come to thee . . ." Ps. 90:10).

John of the Cross is aware that this appeal to the "anagogic" upraising of the soul is not within the capacity of beginners. Actually, they are capable of it, but they do not always have sufficient mastery over their own interior activities, still less over a sufficiently strong and assured mystic life for the practice of this wonderful tactic. John of the Cross, therefore, advises beginners in the throes of temptation to do everything possible to cast themselves upon God in a fine outpouring of love. But if they are not immediately and sufficiently successful in this, they should make use of all the spiritual means within their grasp, employing meditation, interior exercises, and fervent prayer.

THE SIXTH TO THE ELEVENTH COUNSELS

VI. The sixth counsel of John of the Cross has as its aim to recall that the love of one's neighbor is most closely linked to the love of God. This is the reason that, according to the Carmelite Rule, the active life is not snuffed out by the contemplative life. Our Lord Jesus Christ has given the example of the perfect life. He actually united the active life most intimately to the life of prayer. Nothing is more in accordance with the love of God than zeal for the salvation of souls.

". . . And it is clearly true that compassion for our neighbour grows the more according as the soul is more closely united with God through love; for the more we love, the more we desire that this same God shall be loved and honoured by all. And the more we desire this, the more we labour for it, both in prayer and in all other possible and necessary exercises." (Spiritual Sayings, No. 6).

VII. John of the Cross teaches that two things help to raise the soul into union with God: affective compassion for Christ's death, and compassion for one's neighbor.

VIII. The eighth counsel is specifically directed to religious who like to visit away from their monasteries or convents. On this point John of the Cross cites the words of Pope Pius II: "A restless prior is worse than a devil." This needs no commentary.

IX. John of the Cross, in commenting on a text from St. Paul (II Cor. 12:12) notes that among the virtues required of an Apostle, he gives higher rank to patience than to miracles. It follows that patience is a surer sign of the truly apostolic man than is the power to resurrect the dead. And in his report, Fray Eliseo thus applies this maxim:

"I can testify that Fray John of the Cross was an apostolic man with respect to that virtue, for he endured with a singular patience and tolerance all the trials that beset him, which were very great and would have brought down the cedars of Mount Lebanon."

X. In the tenth counsel, Fray Eliseo recalls an incident in St. John's life when he was at Granada. He accused himself of having been too indulgent in his spiritual direction of certain female souls, and he said that he had already been punished for this by God in that one such woman, who had deceived him in the past, later caused great scandal in the Order she had wished to enter.

XI. John of the Cross attached great importance to careful maintenance of the forms of civility within the Order. Courtesy was held in honor at Carmel. The brethren never spoke to one another without making use of the most respectful addresses: the expression "Your Paternity" or "Your Reverence" was particularly required. John of the Cross declared that cruelty and ferocity, particularly if practiced by Superiors, is "a vice proper to barbarians." He concluded: "Should cruelty and ferocity in superiors [enter] we should mourn the Order as ruined."

Last Counsels

The final counsels (those from twelve to seventeen inclusive) in Fray Eliseo's report are a development of what we have already read. Superiors who have formed habits of rudeness and harshness in their treatment of their subjects can only train religious who will live in fear and dissimulation, afraid to express their minds clearly in the meetings of the Order so that such superiors no longer have about them anyone who can warn or contradict them when they fall into error. We have seen John of the Cross standing alone in several Chapter Meetings of his Order when he criticized certain plans and projects because others among his brethren thought it would cause trouble to declare their feelings. Nothing struck more at his heart than this passive cooperation of his brethren when faced by authoritarian superiors. He called this abuse of authority by the superiors ambition, and in it he saw the most pernicious of all vices because it destroys the virtues of justice and charity by which a religious order should be dominated.

Such is the deposition made by Fray Eliseo de la Martires. Into his text he has poured all the veneration which filled his heart for the spiritual master to whom he owed the lessons he had received in his youth.

The Glorification of John

But if Fray Eliseo was one of the most outspoken of John's admirers in respect and veneration, he is far from being the only one. As the years have rolled by, the master has come to be more and more appreciated and honored in his own Order for the true greatness that marked him.

And what is the current estimation of this man?

He was beatified January 25, 1675, and canonized December 27, 1726. But it required another two centuries to measure his doctrinal significance. It was not until August 24, 1926 that St. John of the Cross was proclaimed a Doctor of the Church by that learned Pope, Pius XI. It cannot be denied that in our own day greater interest than ever has been shown in him. As evidence that we are always trying to penetrate more deeply into the mind of the great Prince of Mystical Theology, there stand the celebrated dissertation of 1924 by Baruzi, the book *Quatre Saints* by Louis Lavelle (1951), the learned biographies I have already mentioned, more recent works like those by Pierre Gageac (*Saint Jean de la Croix dans son Voyage au bout de la Nuit,* Paris: Gabalda, 1958), Gilles Mauger (*Saint Jean de la Croix,* Paris: Apostolat de la Presse, 1959), Dom Chevallier (*Saint Jean de la Croix, Docteur des Ames,* Paris: Aubier, 1959), and others. Pierre Gageac has not hesitated to call him "the saint of our own time," seeing in him a force of counteraction to contemporary materialism.

Once one has sat at his feet, one cannot leave John. The contemporary soul is gravely ill. It needs to learn again that great truth which John of the Cross can so well teach: *The health of the soul is the love of God.*

If it be true, as Bergson thought, that the world is "a machine whose purpose is to hammer out gods," then it is clear that we can become gods only by God and in God, and it is mysticism alone which can lead us to this end in the full meaning of history and in the full meaning of life.

Like John of the Cross, each one of us may aspire to say in truth:

> "I remained, lost in oblivion;
> My face I reclined on the Beloved.
> All ceased and I abandoned myself,
> Leaving my cares forgotten among the lilies."

DEO GRATIAS ET MARIAE DEIPARAE

67. Soul walking in His company – nothing can upset it, nothing deprive it 3 peace.

23. Cross was the central point the the life & deeds of Chr

CARMELITE MONASTERY
Beckley Hill
Barre, Vt., 05641

DATE BORROWED